Lost Christianities: Christian Scriptures and the Battles over Authentication
Part II

Professor Bart D. Ehrman

THE TEACHING COMPANY ®

PUBLISHED BY:

THE TEACHING COMPANY
4840 Westfields Boulevard, Suite 500
Chantilly, Virginia 20151-2299
1-800-TEACH-12
Fax—703-378-3819
www.teach12.com

ISBN 1-56585-691-0

Bart D. Ehrman, Ph.D.

Professor and Chair of the Department of Religious Studies
The University of North Carolina at Chapel Hill

Bart Ehrman is The James A. Gray Professor and Chair of the Department of Religious Studies at the University of North Carolina at Chapel Hill. With degrees from Wheaton College (B.A.) and Princeton Theological Seminary (M.Div. and Ph.D., *magna cum laude*), he taught at Rutgers for four years before moving to UNC in 1988. During his tenure at UNC, he has garnered numerous awards and prizes, including the Students' Undergraduate Teaching Award (1993), the Ruth and Philip Hettleman Prize for Artistic and Scholarly Achievement (1994), the Bowman and Gordon Gray Award for excellence in teaching (1998), and the James A. Gray Chair in Biblical Studies (2003).

With a focus on early Christianity in its Greco-Roman environment and a special expertise in the textual criticism of the New Testament, Professor Ehrman has published dozens of book reviews and more than 20 scholarly articles for academic journals. He has authored or edited 12 books, including *The Apostolic Fathers* (Loeb Classical Library; Cambridge, Mass: Harvard University Press, 2003); *Lost Christianities: The Battles for Scripture and the Faiths We Never Knew* (New York: Oxford University Press, 2003); *Jesus: Apocalyptic Prophet of the New Millennium* (Oxford University Press, 1999); *The New Testament: A Historical Introduction to the Early Christian Writings* (Oxford, 1997; 3rd ed. 2004); *After the New Testament: A Reader in Early Christianity* (Oxford, 1999); *The New Testament and Other Early Christian Writings: A Reader* (Oxford, 2nd ed. 2004); and *The Orthodox Corruption of Scripture* (Oxford, 1993). He is currently at work on a new commentary on several non-canonical Gospels for the *Hermeneia Commentary* series, published by Fortress Press.

Professor Ehrman is a popular lecturer, giving numerous talks each year for such groups as the Carolina Speakers Bureau, the UNC Program for the Humanities, the Biblical Archaeology Society, and select universities across the nation. He has served as the President of the Society of Biblical Literature, SE Region; book review editor of the *Journal of Biblical Literature*; editor of the Scholar's Press Monograph Series *The New Testament in the Greek Fathers*; and co-editor of the E.J. Brill series *New Testament Tools and Studies*. Among his administrative responsibilities, he has served on the executive committee of the Southeast Council for the Study of Religion and has chaired the New Testament textual criticism section of the Society of Biblical Religion, as well as serving as Director of Graduate Studies and Chair of the Department of Religious Studies at UNC.

Table of Contents

Lost Christianities: Christian Scriptures and the Battles over Authentication
Part II

Lost Christianities: Christian Scriptures and the Battles over Authentication

Scope:

Christians of the second and third centuries held a remarkably wide range of beliefs. Although some of these beliefs may sound ludicrous today, at the time, they seemed not only sensible but *right*. Some Christians maintained that there were two Gods, or twelve, or thirty, or more. Some Christians claimed that Jesus was not really a human being, or that he was not really divine, or that he was two different beings, one human and one divine. Some Christians believed that this world was not created by the true God but by a malicious deity as a place for punishment for human souls, which had become entrapped here in human bodies. Some Christians believed that Jesus' death and resurrection had no bearing on salvation, and some Christians believed that Jesus had never actually died.

Lost Christianities is a course that considers the varieties of belief and practice in the early days of Christianity, before the church had decided what was theologically acceptable and determined which books should be included in its canon of Scripture. Part of the struggle over belief and practice in the early church was over what could be legitimately accepted as "Christian" and what should be condemned as "heresy." This course considers the struggle for *orthodoxy* (that is, right belief) and the attempt to label, spurn, and overthrow *heresy* (that is, false belief). In particular, it tries to understand Christians who were later deemed heretical on their own terms and to explore the writings that were available and could be appealed to in support of their views.

Christians today, of course, typically think of the New Testament as the basis for a correct understanding of the faith. But what was Christianity like *before* there was a New Testament? It is striking that all the ancient Christian groups, with their distinctive views about God, Christ, salvation, and the world, had books that—like those that eventually came into the New Testament—claimed to be written by Jesus' own apostles. Some of these *pseudepigraphical* (that is, falsely ascribed) books have been discovered by archaeologists and rummaging bedouin in Egypt and the Middle East in modern times, gospels, for example, that claim to be written by Jesus' disciples Peter, Thomas, and Philip. These pseudepigrapha portray a different understanding of Christianity from the one that became dominant in the history of the religion and is familiar to most people today. In this course, we will study these non-canonical books and the forms of Christian belief they represent, from the second and third centuries—that is, from the time soon after the death of Jesus' apostles up to the time when most of these earlier understandings of Christianity had been weeded out of the church, leaving the one form of "orthodoxy" that became triumphant in the early fourth century with the conversion of the Roman emperor Constantine.

The course is divided into several components. After an introductory lecture that deals with the wide diversity of Christianity in the modern and ancient worlds, we will launch into a discussion of three forms of Christianity that were highly influential during the second and third Christian centuries: the Ebionites, a group of Christians who insisted on maintaining their Jewish identity while believing in Jesus; the Marcionites, a group that rejected everything Jewish from its understanding of Jesus; and the Gnostics, a wide-ranging group that understood this world to be an evil place of imprisonment from which one could escape by learning the truth of one's identity through the secret teachings of Jesus.

We will then begin to consider, in separate lectures, important books read and revered by each of these groups and by the group that represented the forebears of the kind of Christianity that eventually became dominant in the Empire, a group that we will label "proto-orthodox" (because they held to the views that *eventually* came to be declared orthodox). Many of these books are pseudonymous, forged in the name of one or another of the apostles. Included in our consideration will be "Gnostic Gospels," such as the Gospel of Thomas; "Infancy Gospels," which narrate fictional events from Jesus' life as an infant and young boy; Apocryphal Acts, which describe the entertaining escapades of several of Jesus' apostles (including the woman, Thecla) after his death; apocryphal epistles allegedly written by the apostle Paul and others; and one apocryphal apocalypse, a description of a guided tour of heaven and hell given to the apostle Peter by Jesus himself.

After considering these fascinating documents, many of which have come to our knowledge only during the twentieth century, we will turn to consider the conflicts among the various forms of Christianity in the early centuries, to see how it is that one understanding of the faith came to be dominant and to squelch all its opposition. In this final section of the course, we will consider how the proto-orthodox party invested ecclesiastical power in its clergy (forming the structure and hierarchy that became a mainstay of the church through the Middle Ages); developed its canon of Scripture (the New Testament, which was not finalized as a canon until the end of the fourth century); and formulated standard creeds (e.g., the Apostles' Creed and the Nicene Creed) as statements of faith to be adhered to by all believers, thereby eliminating the possibility of alternative understandings of what it might mean to be a follower of Jesus.

Lecture Thirteen
The Acts of John

Scope:

In this lecture, we move from non-canonical gospels to non-canonical Acts of the Apostles. To some extent, the five major surviving accounts of the apostles are modeled on the Book of Acts in the New Testament, but they differ in that each is concerned principally about just one of the major apostles in early Christendom: John, Peter, Paul, Andrew, and Thomas. Moreover, all of them are filled with highly legendary, but entertaining, narratives. The Acts of John presents the exploits of John, the son of Zebedee, who takes the gospel of Christ to Asia Minor, overcoming numerous obstacles to his mission, showing his supernatural powers as the agent of Christ by his many miracles (including spectacular resurrections of the dead), and proclaiming his message of sexual abstinence and avoidance of the pleasures of this world. The book contains, as well, some intriguing, possibly even heretical, reflections on the nature of Christ.

Outline

I. In the past several lectures, we have considered several of the non-canonical gospels that were forged by early Christian writers.

   A. We have seen that there are different kinds of apocryphal gospels: collections of Jesus' sayings, accounts of his ministry and passion, narratives of his birth and childhood.

   B. These apocryphal gospels derive from a variety of groups of early Christians: Jewish-Christian, Gnostic, and proto-orthodox.

   C. But all of them are late and legendary, and most are forged in the name of an apostolic authority.

   D. We now move to a different genre of early Christian apocrypha, the Apocryphal Acts of the Apostles. These, too, are late and legendary, but they are not forged: They are written *about* the apostles, not allegedly *by* them.

II. Accounts of the lives of Jesus' apostles were common in early Christianity.

    A. The first is in the New Testament, the Acts of the Apostles.

        1. This is an account of what happened to the followers of Jesus after his death and resurrection as they spread the gospel of Jesus throughout the Roman world.

        2. The two main characters of the account are Peter, the original head of the early church, and Paul, the greatest missionary of the early church.

        3. These two and other apostles are empowered by God to spread the church to different parts of the Roman world, eventually to Rome itself, and among different peoples, both Jew and Gentile.

        4. The account narrates miracles performed by the apostles and conversions to the faith (including the conversion of the apostle Paul).

        5. The account also details the internal conflicts in Christianity, particularly the conflict over whether Christians must become Jewish before they can convert to faith in Christ.

        6. The theme is that the spread of the gospel comes from God and that nothing can stop this mission.

        7. This early account was written by the same author as the Gospel of Luke, sometime in the latter part of the first century.

    B. In the second and third centuries, other accounts of the lives of the apostles were written by anonymous authors.

        1. Unlike the Book of Acts, these accounts focused on the lives and exploits of individual apostles—legendary, imaginative, and entertaining accounts of the wondrous activities of Jesus' closest followers.

        2. Along with lots of smaller fragmentary accounts, we have five fairly complete Apocryphal Acts: the Acts of John, Peter, Paul, Andrew, and Thomas.

        3. We will not be able to examine all these apocryphal accounts in this course, but we will look at three of the most interesting ones.

III. The Acts of John concerns the adventures of John, the son of Zebedee.

A. John was one of Jesus' closest disciples in the gospels of the New Testament.

B. He is an important figure in the history of the early church, according to the Book of Acts in the New Testament, but he drops out of sight early on in that narrative.

C. Our late-second-century Acts of John gives a fuller account of his activities. Unfortunately, this text has not survived intact but only in fragments that scholars have had to piece together from various manuscripts.

IV. In this account, we learn of many of John's exploits.

A. His activities are principally in Asia Minor, in and around Ephesus.

B. There, he engages in numerous miraculous activities as he spreads the gospel of Christ, as narrated in entertaining stories.

C. He is portrayed as having a unique ability to raise the dead.

1. This is seen in an account involving Lycomedes, the commander-in-chief of the Ephesians, and his beautiful young wife, Cleopatra, who has died prematurely, but whom John raises to the joy and wonder of the entire city.

2. Later in the account is the even more bizarre narrative of the raising of Drusiana, the chaste and beautiful wife of Andronicus—a narrative that involves almost unheard-of chastity and crass immorality, a tale of attempted necrophilia, supernatural intervention, miraculous resurrection, and conversion to the life of purity.

3. These stories show commitment to Christ as being more important than love or sex.

D. John's supernatural powers are portrayed in other stories, as well.

1. He is shown to be a superman whose powers can dispel and overthrow all pagan forms of worship, for example, in his powerful destruction of the temple of Artemis in Ephesus.

2. He is shown to be superior to all nature, for example, in an amusing anecdote in which he orders the bedbugs to leave him peace for a good night's sleep.

E. This portrayal of John as superhuman is used to show the superiority of his gospel proclamation.

   1. It is important to remember that the Acts were being produced in a world where the population was largely pagan. Christians in the second and third centuries were a small, persecuted minority (only 2 to 3 percent of the population).

   2. The author's description of Christ, however, appears to be somewhat suspect in terms of its orthodoxy.

   3. In one of the most intriguing passages of the book, he describes Christ as one who did not have a real flesh-and-blood body, who could changes appearances at will, who did not leave footprints when he walked, and who was not actually physically present on the cross at the crucifixion.

   4. It is difficult to tell whether this lengthy passage was originally part of the book or if it came from a different writing altogether.

   5. Its connections are more with gnostic than proto-orthodox writings, whereas the rest of the book, while entertaining and imaginative, appears entirely orthodox.

V. Most scholars date the Acts of John to some time in the second century. This would make sense of its overarching themes.

A. Christianity is portrayed as superior to all opposition, both pagan (pagans are said to worship demons) and Jewish (the Jews are said to have been misled by evil angels).

B. The apostles are thought of as superhumans, whose miracles seem even greater than those of Jesus recounted in the New Testament.

C. There is a strong emphasis on the need for purity and, especially, sexual chastity, an ascetic view that became increasingly popular in the second century.

D. Overall, there is a stress on "otherworldliness," on rejecting the lure of the material things of this world in exchange for the treasures of heaven.

E. We will see these themes as well in the other Apocryphal Acts in the lectures to come.

Essential Reading:

J. K. Elliott, *Apocryphal New Testament*, pp. 303–345.

Edgar Hennecke and Wilhelm Schneemelcher, eds., *New Testament Apocrypha*, vol. 2, pp. 152–212.

Supplementary Reading:

Jan N. Bremmer, ed., *The Apocryphal Acts of John*.

Questions to Consider:

1. What are the different ways that a book such as the Acts of John may have functioned in early Christianity? In other words, why was this account written?

2. Why would an entertaining account of one of the apostles that seems otherwise entirely orthodox contain passages that could easily be given a heretical interpretation?

Lecture Thirteen—Transcript
The Acts of John

In the past several lectures, we've considered some of the non-canonical gospels that were produced by early Christian writers—the Gospel of Truth, the Gospel of Peter, the Gospel of Thomas, the Infancy Gospel of Thomas. We've seen that there are different kinds of apocryphal gospels. Some of them are collections of Jesus' sayings; others are accounts of his ministry and passion; others are narratives of his birth and childhood. These apocryphal gospels derive from a variety of groups of early Christians, Jewish Christians, Ebionites, Gnostics, proto-orthodox Christians. But all of these non-canonical gospels are relatively late, starting with the second century—they date up actually through the eighth century—and all of them are highly legendary; all of them except, perhaps, the Coptic Gospel of Thomas.

Most of these non-canonical gospels are forged, in the name of an apostolic authority. In this lecture, we'll move to a different genre of early Christian apocrypha—the Apocryphal Acts of the Apostles. These, too, are late and legendary. But they are not forged. They are written about the apostles, not allegedly by them. Accounts of the lives of Jesus' apostles were common in early Christianity. The first account we have is actually in the New Testament itself—the New Testament book of Acts of the Apostles. The Acts of the Apostles is an account of what happened to the followers of Jesus after his death and Resurrection, as they spread the gospel of Jesus throughout the Roman world.

The account begins with Jesus appearing to his disciples after his Resurrection and then ascending into heaven. Prior to his ascension, he has a brief discussion with them, in which they want to know whether the kingdom of God is now to arrive on earth. Jesus tells them that it's not really up to them to know when the time of the end is to come; instead, they are to be his witnesses throughout the world. As he says in Acts Chapter 1, verse 8: "You will be my witnesses first in Jerusalem, then in all of Judea and Samaria and then unto the ends of the earth."

The Book of Acts, in fact, describes the spread of Jesus' gospel in Jerusalem, then into the areas of Judea and Samaria, and then, finally, throughout the Western Roman Empire, into the city of Rome, with anticipation that it will go, in fact, even further to the

West. The two main characters in the account of the Book of Acts are Peter, the closest disciple of Jesus, who was the original head of the early church, and Paul, who became the greatest missionary of the church, who becomes the main figure for most of the Book of Acts. Peter and Paul and the other apostles are empowered by God to spread the gospel to different parts of the Roman world—eventually to Rome itself. And they spread it among different kinds of people; first to Jews, then to Samaritans, then to Gentiles.

The account of the Book of Acts narrates numerous events that happened to the apostles—numerous miracles that they themselves performed, as these apostles, like Jesus before them, could heal the sick, cast out demons, and even raise the dead. It describes numerous conversions to the faith. Early on, thousands of people convert to become followers of Jesus in Jerusalem, at the preaching of the apostle Peter. The biggest conversion of all is of the apostle Paul, narrated in Acts Chapter 9—Paul, who becomes a follower of Christ after being a persecutor of Christ. And then once Paul converts, he becomes a great missionary. Lots of the Book of Acts narrates his own missionary journeys.

It also details the internal conflicts that occur within Christianity—especially the conflict of whether Christians have to become Jewish, over whether people who are not Jewish need to become Jewish before they can convert to the faith in Christ. These are all readily resolved, as the Holy Spirit comes to direct the Christian mission, according to this book. Persecutions come against this early church, but they too are readily overcome. The theme of the Book of Acts is that the Christian mission, the spread of the gospel, comes from God as the apostles are empowered by the Holy Spirit and nothing can stop this mission. This Book of Acts does not provide a straight historical account of what transpired in the early days of Christianity. It obviously contains a theological understanding of the early Christian mission, written from a particular religious point of view of the author, the same author who wrote the Gospel of Luke in the New Testament. This account, the Book of Acts, was written sometime in the latter part of the first century, soon after Luke wrote his Gospel, probably around 80 or 85 of the Common Era, 80 or 85 A.D.

In the second and third centuries, other accounts of the lives of the apostles were written by anonymous authors. Unlike the Book of

Acts in the New Testament, these other accounts focused on the lives and exploits of individual apostles. These are legendary, imaginative, and entertaining accounts of the wondrous activities of Jesus' closest followers. Among the Apocryphal Acts we have a large number of fragmentary accounts, but five that are fairly complete books. The five are the Acts of John, Peter, Paul, Andrew, and Thomas.

These are individual books on these five different apostles. Even many of these books are found in fragments. But in most of these fragments are extensive, they can be put together into one long narrative for these five apostles. We won't be able to examine all of these five accounts in this course. But we will be looking at three of the most interesting ones. Today, we will be looking at the Acts of John. In the next lecture, we will be looking at the Acts of Thomas, and then finally we will look at the Acts of Paul, especially the section of the Acts of Paul called the Acts of Paul and (his female disciple) Thecla.

In this lecture we deal with the Acts of John, which concern the adventures and the missionary activities of John, the son of Zebedee. John the son of Zebedee was one of Jesus' closest disciples in the New Testament. In the New Testament Gospels, Jesus has an inner circle among the Twelve. He has these twelve disciples, but there's this inner circle that's comprised of Simon Peter, James, and John. James and John are brothers who were fisherman before converting to follow Jesus, sons of a man named Zebedee. Traditionally, John the son of Zebedee was thought to be the "Beloved Disciple," who's described in the Gospel of John and who is thought, traditionally, to have been the author of the Gospel of John. He was quite an important figure in the history of the early church. According to the Book of Acts, he was a prominent figure in the spread of Christianity in its early stages. But then he soon dropped out of sight in that narrative.

Our late second century Acts of John gives a fuller account of his activity. Unfortunately, this is one of the texts that has not survived completely intact, but in fragments. Scholars, though, have been able to piece together these fragments from various manuscripts to construct a running narrative. The narrative is very interesting. In it we learn many of John's exploits while engaged in his missionary activities in Asia Minor, which is modern-day Turkey—especially in and around Ephesus, a major city of Asia Minor. During his missionary activities, John engages in a number of miraculous acts which help him spread the gospel of Christ, as narrated in a number of entertaining stories. In this lecture, I'll talk about some of these stories, to show how John is being portrayed as a miraculous figure, and then, hopefully, through these stories we'll be able to see something of the overriding emphases of this particular Apocryphal Acts, The Acts of John.

John is portrayed in this account as having a unique ability to raise the dead. One of the early accounts that shows his miraculous powers is an interesting story with a man named Lycomedes and his beautiful young wife named Cleopatra. As it turns out, Cleopatra has died prematurely, but John is able to raise her from the dead, to the joy and wonder of the entire city of Ephesus. I'll summarize the story and read you sections of it, so you get a sense for how these Apocryphal Acts actually worked. We're told in the account that John had hastened to Ephesus prompted by a vision. "When he came near the city, Lycomedes, the commander-in-chief of these Ephesians, who was a wealthy man, met us," we're told, so this is being written in the first person by somebody other than John. We're not told who the author actually is.

As it turns out, this leader of the Ephesians, Lycomedes, has found out from a vision that John was coming to visit the Ephesians, and he asks John to come and help him, because his wife has been paralyzed for seven days, and he asks John to show compassion on her by raising her up. "When Lycomedes and John came to the house in which the woman was lying," we're told, "he grasps his feet again"—Lycomedes grabs John's feet:

> See, Lord, the lost beauty. See the youth, see the much talked of bloom of my unhappy wife, the admiration of all Ephesus. Woe to me, unhappy man. I was envied, humbled, and the enemy's eye was fixed on me.

He goes on to bemoan his fate, because now, it turns out, Cleopatra is not just paralyzed, Cleopatra has died. "Lycomedes spoke to Cleopatra, went up to her couch"—she's lying there dead on the couch—"and he cried bitterly. But John drew him away and said, 'Abandon these tears and unbecoming words.' But Lycomedes fell to the ground and wept dejectedly."

And it turns out, from grief for his fallen wife, Lycomedes now himself has died. "The man lies here lifeless," we're told. "And I know that I shall not leave this house alive," says John. John is afraid that since Lycomedes has died while he was there, that the Ephesians were going to rise on him and kill him. John cries out, "'Why do you delay, O Lord, from raising her from the dead?' While he was crying, the entire city of Ephesus had run to the house of Lycomedes." You can get a sense of some of the hyperbole, with the entire population, of many thousands of people living in Ephesus, running to Lycomedes's house.

> The entire city of Ephesus ran to the house of Lycomedes, supposing him to be dead. When John saw the multitude, he prayed to the Lord. "Now is the time of refreshing and confidence has come with you O Christ." And he went over to Cleopatra.

He touches her face and he says to her:

> Cleopatra, he whom every ruler fears and every creature, power, abyss and darkness and unsmiling death and the heights of heaven and the caverns of the lower world and the resurrection of the dead and the sights of the blind, etc....

He is talking about God, Who is all-powerful. He says:

> In His name, rise; and become not a pretext for many who will not believe and an affliction for souls that hope to be saved. And Cleopatra immediately rises up and says, "I will rise, Master. Save your handmaiden." When she had risen after the seven days, the whole city of Ephesus was stirred by the miraculous sight.

But then there's still a problem, because Lycomedes is dead; and Cleopatra then follows John into the room, and sees her husband dead in front of her. And then John gives her the power, Cleopatra, to raise her husband from the dead.

> She went and spoke to her husband as she was told, and immediately she raised him. Having risen she fell down and kissed the feet of John. He lifted him up and said, "Man, kiss not my feet, but God's, by Whose power both of you have risen."

Here's an account, then, of the power of the apostle who is able to raise people from the dead through the power of Christ. This is typical of the Acts of the apostles, showing that these apostles were not mere mortals. They were men who were inspired by the power of God, who were able, then, even to raise the dead.

There is another account of John raising the dead in the Acts of John. It's an account that's somewhat more bizarre than the one we've just examined. This bizarre account is actually quite famous, and made quite an impact on Christian imagination through the Middle Ages. It's the story of the raising of Drusiana, the chaste and beautiful wife of a man named Andronicus. This is an account that involves almost unheard-of chastity and crass immorality—a tale of attempted necrophilia, supernatural intervention, miraculous resurrection, and conversion to the life of purity.

It's a long and somewhat involved story. Rather than read it, I'll summarize the main parts of the narrative, just to give you a sense of how entertaining some of these early Christian fictions can be. According to this account, Drusiana is the beautiful wife of a man named Andronicus. They, too, live in the city of Ephesus. According to the account, both of them have converted to Christianity through the missionary preaching of the apostle John. And as part of their commitment to Christ, they decide to remain celibate, even with one another.

But there's another man, who is a prominent citizen of Ephesus named Callimachus, who enters into the picture, who falls in love with Drusiana. Even though she's married and committed to chastity, Callimachus wants to commit adultery with her. She feels incredible guilt in stirring up such a wicked desire in Callimachus. And as a result of her feeling so guilty, she becomes ill and she dies. They buried Drusiana in her family tomb. Callimachus continues to feel passion for her, so much so that he bribes the family steward to let him into the crypt, so that he can have sex with her even though she's dead. So he bribes the steward, and he's let into the crypt. But before he can perform the wicked deed, a serpent appears that bites the steward that had let him in, killing him. And then the serpent entwined itself around Callimachus.

As it turns out, the apostle John and Andronicus come to the crypt. They find the doors open. Entering in, they find an angel who warns them of what happened. They then see the dead steward and they see

Callimachus lying underneath the serpent. And, of course, they see the dead Drusiana. After that, there's a scene of repeated resuscitation. First, John raises Callimachus, who has been planning this act of necrophilia. He raises him up from the dead. Callimachus confesses to everything that he had done and everything that he had wanted to do. Then John raises Drusiana from the dead. Drusiana wants the steward to be raised from the dead, and she does so herself. Callimachus, after rising from the dead, converts to faith in Christ, and becomes a pure and chaste Christian. The steward that is raised from the dead does not convert to Christ as a result of his resurrection. Instead, he curses them all, wishes himself still to be dead and runs from the tomb. As it turns out, they find him later, dead, felled by a poisonous serpent bite. And so the story ends.

This, then, is the kind of entertaining romance one can find in the Apocryphal Acts of the apostles. These stories often involve sex and love and adventure and death and miracles; but in particular, they involve commitment to Christ as being more important than either love or sex. Sex, in fact, according to these accounts—and we will see more extensively in subsequent ones that we read—sex in these accounts is to be spurned for the sake of one's commitment to God through Christ.

This account shows, then, John's ability to raise people from the dead. It shows his supernatural powers in other ways as well. John, in these accounts, is shown to be a superman whose powers can dispel and overthrow all pagan forms of worship. We need to remember that these Apocryphal Acts, written in the second century, the third century, are being produced in a time when the world was principally, and almost exclusively, pagan. It's hard to know the demographics of the ancient world. In the Roman Empire, it's usually thought that the population at this time, second and third century, was around 60 million people. Moreover, it's normally thought that among the 60 million people, something like seven percent of the population was probably Jewish, maybe four million Jews in the world at that time.

But Christianity, in the second and third century, is a very small minority. Starting at the beginning of the second century, we're talking maybe hundreds of thousands of Christians, not millions yet. Second and third centuries, the numbers start increasing. Not until the beginning of the fourth century can Christianity claim anything like five percent of the population. So in the second and third century we're talking about maybe two percent, three percent.

Christians, as we've seen already to some extent, and as we'll see more extensively later, were a persecuted minority in the Roman empire, in part because they refused to worship the state gods. They refused to participate in state religion. The Jews did, as well; but they had ancient traditions that they could fall back upon. The Christians did not. The Christians saw themselves as a beleaguered minority. So it's no surprise that these Christians tell stories of the superiority of their faith to everything that the pagans can offer.

This can be seen in the interesting story of the Acts of John, of John overcoming the goddess Artemis, who was the city goddess of Ephesus. Artemis has a huge temple in Ephesus. During the birthday of this temple, they have a huge celebration, we're told. Everyone from the city comes to worship Artemis in her home there, where her idols are kept. John, himself, goes to this temple, not to worship Artemis, but in order to show the superiority of his God to the gods of the pagans. Everyone appears in this temple dressed in white, but we're told that John appears dressed in black.

People are afraid when they see John present among them, because they know his supernatural powers, they know the tales of him raising people from the dead. They know, in fact, that his God is more powerful than the gods of the city, especially than Artemis. They ask John not to harm them. But John utters a prayer to the one true God and as a result of his prayer, the foundations of the temple begin to quake. An earthquake happens. The altar is split in half and many of the idols are shattered, simply on the basis of John's prayer.

This is a story that's attempting to show that the God of John—who is the God of Jesus—is superior to anything you can find in the world. These Christians are telling stories like this in order to justify their own faith and in order to show that people need to convert to faith in this God, because this God is more powerful than any other.

In the ancient world, people worshipped the gods principally because the gods would be able to provide them with the things that were necessary for life. Pagan religions were centered around the present life; what one can acquire from the gods now when living is dangerous, when people don't have enough to eat, when people are worried about the crops, people are worried about their health—the gods can provide the things that they need. If the God of Jesus can be shown to be more powerful than the other gods, then surely people will convert to faith in the God of Jesus. In this account, when John destroys the temple of Artemis, in fact, everybody converts and says that the God of John is all-powerful. So it includes kind of a conversion story to faith in this God.

John is shown to be powerful in a number of other stories as well, some of them rather amusing. Probably the best-known anecdote from these Apocryphal Acts of John involves John's power over the forces of nature, in the presence of bedbugs in an inn in which he is staying. John is staying in an inn during his endeavors; he's got a group of people who are following along with him, other Christians also engaged in his missionary activities. He decides to spend the night at an inn and crawls into the bed that's available, but it's filled with bedbugs. He's irritated, because it's been a long day and he wants to sleep. He commands the bedbugs to leave the bed so that he can rest in peace. His fellows laugh at him for doing this, but then in the next morning they wake up and see that, in fact, hundreds of bugs are gathered underneath the door. John then wakes up refreshed from an evening's sleep, and he tells the bedbugs they can now return to their home. He gets up, they return to the bed, and he goes on his missionary endeavors.

This portrayal of John as superhuman—who has power over death, power over gods and power over the bedbugs—this portrayal of John as superhuman is designed, of course, to show the superiority of his own gospel proclamation. One of the most interesting features of the Apocryphal Acts of John, however, is that the description of Christ in this gospel proclamation appears somewhat suspect in terms of its orthodoxy. The portrayal of Christ is suspected as being somewhat unorthodox, in this account.

In one of the most intriguing passages of the book, John describes Christ as one who did not have a real flesh and blood body, who could change his appearances at will, and who was not actually present, physically, at the cross during the Crucifixion. The account otherwise sounds completely proto-orthodox. But is it, in fact, influenced by Gnostic or docetic understandings of Christ?

Let me read for you some of the passages involved. This is from one of the fragments of the account of John's activities. John says that:

When Jesus had chosen Peter and Andrew, who were brothers, he came also to me and my brother James saying, "I have need of you, come to me." My brother said, "John, this child on the shore who called us, what does he want?" And I said, "What child?" He replied, "The one that's beckoning to us." And I answered, "Because of our long watch that we kept at sea, you're not seeing straight, brother James. Don't you see the man that stands there, fair and comely and of a cheerful countenance?" But he said to me, "Him I don't see, brother. But let's go and we shall see what this means."

So James sees a young child on the shore, but John sees a grown man. Well, as it turns out, Jesus changes appearances, and he appears to different people in different guises at the same time.

Yet to me there appears a still more wonderful sight for I tried to see Jesus as he was and I never at any time saw his eyes closing, only open.

So Jesus doesn't blink.

And sometimes, he appears to me as a small man and unattractive, and again as one that's reaching up to heavens. Sometimes his breast felt to me smooth and tender, and sometimes hard, like a stone. So I was perplexed in myself and said, Well, what does this mean?

He goes on to say:

Another glory I'll tell you, brothers; sometimes when I meant to touch him, I met a material unsolid body and at other times, when I felt him, the substance was immaterial and bodiless as if it were not existing at all. And often when I was walking with him, I wished to see whether the print of his foot appeared upon the earth, for I saw himself raising himself from the earth, but I never saw the footprint.

So Jesus doesn't blink, his body sometimes is immaterial, he doesn't leave footprints. What kind of understanding of Jesus is this? Well, it sounds very much like an understanding that we've seen in non-orthodox circles in Gnostic and docetic understandings of Jesus, where he doesn't have a real body.

This becomes particularly clear when John is describing what happens at the Crucifixion, where, in fact, Jesus is talking to John, and he says:

> As for seeing me as I am in reality, I've told you, this is impossible, unless you are able to see me as my kinsman, you hear that I suffered, yet I suffered not. That I suffered not, yet I did suffer. You heard that I was pierced, yet was I not wounded? Hanged and was I not hanged?

In other words, you saw me hanged, yet I was not hanged.

> The blood flowed from me, yet it did not flow. In a word, those things that you say of me, I did not endure, and those things that they do not say, those I suffered.

This is one of those complete paradoxes; that Jesus suffers, yet he doesn't really suffer. He feels pain, yet he doesn't really feel pain. He looks to be mortal, he looks to be human, but in fact, he's not really human.

It's difficult to know whether this lengthy passage describing Christ was originally part of the book, or if it was instead taken from a different writing. But it's quite clear that these passages, at least, look more Gnostic than proto-orthodox, whereas the rest of the book, entertaining as it is, appears entirely orthodox.

As I've indicated, most scholars date the Acts of John sometime in the second century. This would make sense of its overarching themes. Let me summarize them for you now, in conclusion. Christianity is portrayed here as superior to all opposition, both pagan and Jewish; the apostles are thought of as superhumans, whose miracles seem greater than those even of Jesus himself, as recounted in the New Testament; there's a strong stress on the need for purity, especially sexual chastity—this is an ascetic view that had become increasingly popular in the second century; and overall there's a stress on otherworldliness, on rejecting the lure of the material things of things of this world in exchange for the treasures of heaven. These, then, are the themes that we will see, as well, in the other Apocryphal Acts, in the two lectures to come.

Lecture Fourteen
The Acts of Thomas

Scope:

This lecture situates the Apocryphal Acts in their own cultural and literary context, as books resembling the ancient *romances* (or *novels*), another entertaining kind of ancient fiction but popular chiefly among pagan audiences. The romances describe the exploits of tragically separated lovers who fight the odds (and pirates, shipwrecks, natural disasters, and everything else fate can throw at them) to be restored to each other and consummate their love, thereby maintaining harmony in the social order. The Christian "Acts" use many of the conventions of this romance genre (shipwrecks, disasters, near-death experiences, and the like), but do so to counteract the views they embrace. This can be seen in the apocryphal exploits of Thomas, the twin brother of Jesus and missionary to India, whose message of sexual abstinence and rejection of this world directly undermines the assumptions and world view of the pagan romances.

Outline

I. In our last lecture, we examined one of the most interesting of our surviving non-canonical accounts of the lives of the apostles, the Acts of John.

    A. This account of the legendary exploits of an apostle is typical of the genre, Apocryphal Acts, in which we find travels, dangers, controversies, deliverances, thwarted sexual trysts, and miraculous demonstrations of the power of God, all in a single episodic narrative.

    B. But this genre is not unrelated to other kinds of literature popular from about the same time, the ancient equivalent of the modern novel, sometimes called *romances*.

II. We have five complete examples of Greek romances that survive from antiquity and two examples of romances in Latin.

    A. These are often named after their leading characters, two star-crossed lovers, such as Chaereas and Callirhoe, Daphnis and Chloe.

B. The plots and narrative structures of these works are remarkably consistent: They are generally about two lovers who are tragically separated before they can consummate their love. The plots involve the lovers' desperate attempts to return to each other's arms, frustrated by pirate abductions, kidnappings, war, shipwreck, and evident death. The books typically climax when the lovers find a way through their suffering to reunite and consummate their love.

C. In one sense, the books are all about overcoming the tragic fate of this world to consummate the greatest of gifts, the sexual love of a man and a woman. It is a strong feature of these works that this socially sanctified act of love provides the basis for social peace and prosperity, that civilizing forces in the world depend on strong family life embodied in the sexual ties of the rich and beautiful leaders of the city-state.

D. The Apocryphal Acts use many of the same characteristics and concerns of the romance genre—travels, disasters, wealth, beauty, sexual relations, social life—but completely turn them around.

    1. In these books, the wealth and beauty are to be despised for the rewards of heaven.

    2. Social life, here, is to be spurned for the life of heaven.

    3. Sexual love is to be renounced for the greater love of God, reserved for those who maintain their continent purity.

III. Nowhere can this paradoxical twisting of the genre be seen more clearly than in possibly the most famous of the Apocryphal Acts of the Apostles, the Acts of Thomas. This narrative is well known because it is the first account of the familiar legend that the apostle Thomas became a missionary who spread the gospel of Christ in far-off India. The Acts of Thomas tells the tale of how it happened.

A. The book was originally written in Syria, probably in the third century.

B. There is considerable doubt about the historical accuracy of its tales, even the basic theme that Thomas took the gospel to India.

C. There is little doubt, though, about the entertaining nature of the narrative or its overarching intent to cast aspersions on values of contemporary society: wealth, power, sexual love.

IV. The plot itself is basic: Thomas is portrayed as Jesus' twin brother, who is sold into slavery by his "master" (= Lord), after Jesus' death, to an Indian merchant so that he will be forced to go abroad to spread the gospel among the people and royal family of India (chs. 1–2).

A. The overarching themes of the book can be seen in the series of tales that takes place in the course of its narrative.

    1. Some have to do with showing the supernatural nature of the main character, Jesus' twin brother, who has prophetic power (ch. 6, 9).

    2. This book stands in direct opposition to the celebration in the Greek romances of marital love as the glue that holds together society. Here, sex of any kind, even within marriage, is seen as foul and to be avoided at all costs (chs. 11–16).

    3. Also opposed are other values that seemed so commonsensically good to many ancients: for example, the accumulation of wealth (thus, ch.17, the palace of Gundaphorus).

    4. Stressed is the power of God, especially in his sacraments (ch. 51) and in the life to come, where those who commit sins—especially sexual sins—are punished forever (chs. 55–57).

B. Many of these themes are celebrated in the Hymn of the Pearl, one of the most moving pieces of poetry to come down to us from the ancient world, which is embedded in the Acts of Thomas, perhaps as an illustration of many of its themes (chs. 108–113).

    1. The story is of a lad who is sent by his royal family to retrieve a pearl from a great serpent in Egypt, but who, after arriving in Egypt, forgets who he is and why he has come. His royal parents send him a letter, reminding him of who he is and why he has gone, after which he fulfills his mission and returns to great fanfare and reward.

    2. Of the many interpretations of this moving poem, probably the most sensible for its immediate context, is that humans, too, have a heavenly origin and need to recall who they really are and why they have come, rather than be caught up in the trappings of this world, its beauty, riches, and sensual pleasures.

V. This is, in fact, the teaching of many of these Apocryphal Acts, that there is a greater world that cannot be seen, far superior to this one that can be, and that life in this world should be directed entirely toward that other one, lest we become entrapped in the bodily desires of this world and suffer dire consequences in the world to come.

Essential Reading:

Harold W. Attridge, "Thomas, Acts of," *Anchor Bible Dictionary*, vol. VI, pp. 531–534.

J. K. Elliott, *Apocryphal New Testament*, pp. 439–511.

Edgar Hennecke and Wilhelm Schneemelcher, eds., *New Testament Apocrypha*, vol. 2, pp. 322–411.

Supplementary Reading:

Bentley Layton, *The Gnostic Scriptures*, pp. 366–370 (on the "Hymn of the Pearl").

Questions to Consider:

1. In view of the values embraced by the Acts of Thomas, explain why Christianity may have been seen as socially dangerous in the ancient world. In what ways does a tale like this appear to work against "family values" in the modern context?

2. How could the Hymn of the Pearl be explained as a gnostic composition?

Lecture Fourteen—Transcript
The Acts of Thomas

In our last lecture, we examined one of the most interesting of our surviving non-canonical accounts of the lives of the apostles, the Acts of John. This account of the legendary exploits of the apostle is characteristic of the Apocryphal Acts, in which there are typically travels, dangers, controversies, deliverances, thwarted sexual trists, miraculous demonstrations of the power of God, all within a single episodic narrative. The genre, though, is not unrelated to other kinds of literature, popular from about the same period and in about the same parts of the world—the ancient equivalent of the modern novel. This ancient genre, comparable to the modern novel, is sometimes called "romances."

We don't have a large number of romances that survive from the ancient world, although they appear to have been popular literature at the time. These romances were, probably, books not for the high-flowing literary elite, but for the masses. Generally they involve love stories; hence their name, romances. We have five complete romances that have survived from antiquity in Greek, and we have two examples of romances in Latin. The Latin ones are probably more familiar to readers today. The two Latin romances that survived—one of them is complete, one is in fragments—the complete one is *The Golden Ass*, sometimes called *The Metamorphoses* of Apuleius. The other one is Petronius's *Satyricon*.

The Golden Ass is a particularly interesting story. It's the account, well known from the ancient world, of a man who is entranced by magic, who wants to learn more about magic; and he watches a woman, who is a witch, who is able to apply certain ointment to her body and she becomes an owl. Wanting to do the same thing for himself, he seduces the maid of the woman to get him the ointment. But unfortunately she gives him the wrong ointment; and he spreads it over his body, and rather then becoming an owl, he becomes an ass.

As it turns out, he's unable then to turn himself back because, before anything can be done to get the antidote, robbers break into the house and they steal all the goods, including him—the ass—and they lead him off and put him to work. And then there are a series of tales involving his exploits—some of them are, oddly enough, involving sexual exploits of him as an ass—until, at the very end of the narrative, he is turned back into a human.

That's an interesting account. The Latin tends to be a little bit more episodic, and they tend to be a little more bawdy, than the Greek versions that we have. The Greek versions are less known, probably, to people today. They typically involve star-crossed lovers, after whom the books are usually named. For example, there's a book named Chaereas and Callirhoe, who are two star-crossed lovers; or one that's probably more familiar to people, the account of Daphnis and Chloe.

The plots and narratives of these Greek novels, these Greek romances, are remarkably consistent. They are generally about two lovers who are tragically separated before they can consummate their love. Usually the way it happens is that either they become engaged, or else they actually get married, but before they can enjoy sexual love with one another, they become separated by some sort of tragedy. One of them gets kidnapped; one of them grows ill and appears to die; there are various ways to get these two loves separated before they can consummate their love. The plots of these accounts involve their desperate attempts to return to each other's arms. But they are always frustrated in their attempts, by pirate abductions, kidnappings, war, shipwreck, evident death. The books typically climax by the lovers finding a way through their suffering, to reunite and to consummate their love.

In one sense, these ancient romances are all about overcoming the tragic fate of the world, to consummate the greatest of gifts, the sexual love of a man and a woman. It's a strong feature of these works that this socially sanctified act of love provides the basis for social peace and prosperity. That's one of the themes behind these books, that the love between a man and a woman is one that provides the integrity for society, the glue that holds society together. The civilizing forces in the world depend on strong family life, as embodied in the sexual ties of the rich and beautiful leaders of the city state. These two people who fall in love are always members of the upper classes, the high-ranking aristocracy.

The Apocryphal Acts, a Christian genre written not about two star-crossed lovers but about the exploits of the apostles, utilize many of the same characteristics of the romance genre and many of the same concerns. In these books, there are travels and disasters; there's wealth and beauty; there are sexual relations and social life. But these characteristics and concerns of the romance genre are completely turned on their head in the Christian Apocryphal Acts.

In these books, as we've seen already in the Apocryphal Acts of John, the wealth and beauty of this world are to be despised for the rewards of heaven. Social life here is to be spurned for the life of heaven. And sexual love is to be completely renounced for the greater love of God, reserved for those who maintain their continent purity. Sexual love of every kind is to be spurned; not just extra-marital love, even within the confines of marriage. Married couples are not to engage in sexual activities, so as to maintain their purity before God. So we have, in these Apocryphal Acts, a kind of paradoxical twisting of the genre of the ancient romances. Nowhere can this paradoxical twisting of the genre be seen more clearly than in the possibly most famous of the Apocryphal Acts from the ancient world, the Acts of Thomas.

The Acts of Thomas are probably best known because they provide us with the first account of the well-known legend that the apostle Thomas became a missionary who spread the gospel of Christ to far-off India. The Acts of Thomas tell the tale of how this happened. Today, Christians in India believe their church was founded by the missionary activities of Thomas—Thomas of the New Testament. Well, this is the first account that we have of the missionary activities of Thomas to India. The book was probably written, not in India, but in ancient Syria, probably in the third century. People typically understand this to be a representative of Syriac Christianity. As you know from the earlier lecture on the Coptic Gospel of Thomas, in Syria it was thought that Thomas was, in fact, Judas Thomas, sometimes called Didymus Judas Thomas. He was understood to be Jesus' twin brother; Didymus meaning twin, Thomas meaning twin, Jude or Judas being his name.

This is, then, the story of Jesus' twin brother. The idea that he is an identical twin gets played out in this particular book, the Acts of Thomas. There's considerable doubt about the historical accuracy of the tales found in this account, including the basic theme that Thomas is the one who took the gospel to India. Scholars find little historical evidence that the gospel was actually taken to India by Thomas. There's little doubt, though, about the entertaining nature of this narrative, or its overarching intent, to cast aspersions on the values of contemporary society—contemporary to its time: wealth, power, and sexual love.

The plot of the narrative is itself fairly basic. Thomas is portrayed as Jesus' twin brother, who is sold into slavery by his master, that is his lord, Jesus, after Jesus' death. He's sold to an Indian merchant so that he'll be forced to spread his gospel abroad, among the people and royal family of India. The tale of his being sold into slavery so that he has to go to India is rather interesting, and it's how the account actually begins.

We're told at the beginning of this account that, "We apostles were all in Jerusalem, Simon, Paul, Peter, Andrew, his brother James son of Zebedee, John, his brother Bartholomew, etc...." They list the twelve apostles. "And we portioned out the regions of the world in order that each of us might go into the region that fell to him by lot." So they drew lots to decide who would be a missionary where. By lot, India fell to Judas Thomas, who was also called Didymus. "But he did not wish to go, saying that he was not able to travel on the account of the weakness of his body." So he doesn't want to go to India. He refuses to take the task.

> While he was considering this and speaking, the Savior, Jesus, appeared to him during the night and said, "Don't be afraid, Thomas, go away to India and preach the word there, for my grace is with you." But Thomas would not obey, saying, "Wherever you want to send me, send me—but elsewhere. For I'm not going to the Indians."

So he refuses to go; well, so Jesus arranges that he has to go. The way it happens is it turns out that there's a merchant named Abban, who has come from India, who's sent from the king of India, named Gundaphorus. Gundaphorus wants to find somebody who's a carpenter, who can build him a palace. Well, of course Jesus was a son of a carpenter, and Thomas was his twin brother, so he apparently was apprenticed to be a carpenter as well; and so he would be a prime suspect if you're looking for a carpenter somewhere. Here happens to be one.

Jesus, who by now is dead and ascended to heaven, comes back and makes a special appearance, Abban, who is looking for a carpenter. He meets Abban in the marketplace around noon, and Jesus, come back from heaven, says to Abban, "Do you want to buy a carpenter?"

And he says to him, "Yes." Jesus says, "ell, I have a slave who's a carpenter and I want to sell him." So they work out a deal and Jesus actually writes out the bill of sale saying, "I, Jesus, son of the carpenter Joseph, declare that I have sold my slave, Judas by name, to you, Abban, a merchant of Gundaphorus, the king of the Indians."

And so there's a bill of sale, it's an official deal. And so Abban then goes up to Jude—who doesn't know what's going on; he just knows he doesn't want to go to India—Abban goes up, and he points to Jesus in the crowd, and says, "Is this your master?" Well, the word "master" is the same word for "lord." He says, "Is this your lord?" Jude replies; he says, "Yes, he is my Lord." So Abban says to him, "I have bought you from him." And so the apostle held his peace and now he becomes a slave who's sold to Abban, who's going to take him back to India to build a palace for Gundaphorus. This is how Jesus arranges for his brother Thomas to head off and spread the gospel in India.

So he goes off. Then we get into the narrative, a rather episodic narrative in which we have the exploits of the apostle Thomas laid out for us. The overarching themes of this narrative can be seen in the adventures of these tales that take place in the course of his adventures on the way, and then in India. Some of these tales have to do with the supernatural nature of the main character, of Jesus' twin brother. So there are a number of stories that are designed to show that he, like his brother, has supernatural powers.

On the road to India, they arrive at a city named Andropolis. In Andropolis, there's a city-wide wedding feast going on when they arrive. The king of Andropolis has an only child, who's a daughter. She's getting married that day, so there's a wedding feast for the entire city, and everybody comes out to this wedding feast. Well, Abban decides that they are going to go to this wedding feast. Thomas isn't interested; but he's the slave, so he has to go along.

At this wedding feast, we have the first instance of Thomas being shown to have supernatural powers. In this case, it has to do with his prophetic abilities. He can tell the future, and maybe even influence the future by what he says. There's a girl there who's a flute player, who plays the flute, and everybody is taken with her flute-playing. But Thomas refuses to look at her, because she's quite attractive. Throughout this account, there's going to be downplay on anything that has to do with sexual attraction.

So he looks at the ground while she's playing the flute. And there's a servant nearby who's one of the cupbearers for the king, who is upset with him for not playing the flute. So this cupbearer strikes him on the head. The apostle, raising his eyes, looks at the man who struck and says, "My God will forgive you for this wrong in the world to come. But in this world he shall show you his wonders. And I shall soon see that the hand that struck me is being dragged along by dogs."

That's not a very nice prophecy, but as it turns out, she finishes playing her song and this cupbearer goes outside to the fountain to draw some water. There happened to be a lion there, which killed him and left him in the place, after tearing his limbs asunder, we're told. And dogs immediately seized his limbs, among them a black dog, which grasped his right hand in his mouth and brought it to the banquet. So this prophecy that he would see the hand that struck him brought in carried by dogs, in fact, then becomes true.

There are a number of these minor miraculous instances throughout the account. The book, though, is far more interested in opposing sexual activity, than it is in simply showing the power of the apostle. This is a book that has an agenda. The agenda involves direct opposition to the Greek romances celebration of marital love as the glue that holds together society. In this text, unlike the romances, sex of any kind, even within marriage, is foul and to be avoided at all costs. When this event with the cupbearer's hand passes, there's a continued celebration of the bride and the bridegroom. Then at the end of the celebration, Thomas, who's a special guest apparently, utters a prayer over the now-married couple in which he beseeches Jesus, his Savior, that he does to these people what helps, benefits, and is profitable to them. Then he lays his hands on them and says, "Let the Lord be with you." He gives a benediction to them. Then he leaves, and the whole crowd leaves, because now it's time for the bride and the bridegroom to enter into the bridal chamber.

Well, as it turns out, what happens is the bridegroom raises the curtain of the bridal chamber, so that he can take the bride to himself, but we're told that he saw the Lord Jesus talking with the bride. But the Lord Jesus had the appearance of Judas Thomas, the apostle who had shortly before blessed and departed. So the bridegroom was confused—"I thought we left you outside"—because it's Thomas's twin brother now, Jesus, talking to the bride. And Jesus explains,

"The one you left behind is Judas Thomas, my brother." The Lord said, "Why don't you sit here on these couches?" He has the bride and the bridegroom sit on the couches, and he sits on the bed, and he starts talking to them. He tells them:

> Remember, my children, what my brother said to you, and to whom he commended you. And know that if you refrain from this filthy intercourse, you will become temples holy and pure. You will be released from afflictions and troubles, known and unknown, and you will not be involved in the cares of life and children, whose end is destruction.

They're saying, avoid getting involved in sex tonight. I know it's your wedding night. You need to avoid sex at all costs, because then you will be pure. Sex involves filthy intercourse. And if you have sex, you're going to have babies, and babies are a problem. He goes on to explain why babies are problem.

> If you get many children, for their sakes you become grasping and avaricious. Most children become unprofitable, being possessed by demons, some openly and some secretly. And though they'll be healthy, they'll be again good for nothing, doing unprofitable and abominable works, for they'll be detected either in adultery or in murder or in theft or inchastity, and by all these you will be afflicted.

So in other words, if you have children, they are going to be demon-possessed, they're going to be good for nothing. Even if they're okay kids, they're still going to be involved in sin, so they're going to bring more sin into the world. So simply avoid having sex. You'll be pure. You'll avoid bringing more sin into the world, and things will be much better.

Well, this little talk of Jesus' proves remarkably successful. The bridegroom and the bride decide they're not going to have sex. They're going to commit themselves, and lead a life of chastity. And so we're told that "they believed the Lord and they gave themselves over to him and refrained from filthy lust, and they remained that night in that place."

Well, the morning arrives and the king comes in with his queen, expecting that now they've had a consummated marriage and they can expect a descendant for the throne. But as it turns out, the bride and the bridegroom have not made love, and they try to explain this to their father. She explains to the father that, "I have set at not this husband and these nuptials which have passed away from before my eyes, because I have been joined in a different marriage," she says. "I had no conjugal intercourse with a temporary husband whose end is repentance and bitterness of soul, because I've been united to my true husband."

So now she is married, in some sense, to Jesus, not to this man. This is one of the earliest references to people who are chaste being actually married to Jesus, and this tradition had continued down through the Middle Ages to today, among Christians, to commit themselves to lives of chastity. Well, when the king heard this, he was not pleased at all. We're told that he rent his garments and he said to those standing near him, "Go out quickly and search the whole city and seize and bring that man, the sorcerer, who has come by evil chance into this city." So they go and fetch Thomas who has caused all this problem. But, in fact, they can't find him, because he set sail and is on his way already to India.

So this account has a very strong sense that sexual love is wrong altogether, even within marriage, and should be avoided. There are other values that are attacked in this account—other values that seem so common-sensically good to many ancient people and to modern people as well; for example, the accumulation of wealth. A major polemic against wealth in this account, especially found in the account of the building of the palace of Gundaphorus, which is why Thomas went to India in the first place—he goes there to build this palace.

Well, he arrives in India, we're told. He meets with Gundaphorus, who asks him, "How will you build this palace?" Thomas explained how he would set it up, and he measures out the palace with a reed. He shows him where the doors will be facing. He explains the layout he has in mind. Gundaphorus is quite excited by this and decides, yes, this will be great. So he gives Thomas a ton of money to pull it off. Then he goes back to his capital city and periodically writes letters to Thomas to find out how it's coming. Thomas writes back and says, "Oh, it's going great. We're doing great stuff. You're going to be really pleased."

But, in fact, he's not building the palace at all. He takes the money that Gundaphorus has given to him and he distributes it to the poor. He gives it away as alms. Finally, Gundaphorus writes and says,

"Are you nearly done?" And Thomas says, "Yes, it's all done except for the roof. We need more money for the roof." So he sends Thomas more money. He gives the money away to the poor. Finally, Gundaphorus comes to see his palace, and there's nothing. He's obviously quite upset. He decides that Abban, his merchant who he sent to get Thomas, and Thomas himself have deceived him. So he throws them in jail. He's going to execute them.

But that night, as it turns out, Gundaphorus's brother takes ill and dies. He goes to heaven and the angels takes him around heaven and say, "You've got all these places here you can live. Where would you like to live?" He sees this unbelievably exquisite palace and he says, "I want to live there." They say, "Sorry, you can't live there. That's the palace that the apostle Thomas has built for your brother Gundaphorus." He says, "Ay, ay, ay, just let me go back. Let me go back and get Gundaphorus to give it to me." So the angels agree, and let his brother come back into his body.

Just as they're preparing him to bury him, he wakes up. He calls in his brother, and he says, "Brother, I know that you'll give me anything I ask because you love me." His brother says, "Certainly; you're back from the dead, I'm grateful, I'll give you anything." He says, "I want you to sell me the palace." "What palace? The palace was never built." He says, "No, you've got a palace. It's fantastic. I want to buy it." He says, "Well, what palace do you mean?" "There's a palace waiting in heaven that Thomas has built for you, and it's the most exquisite building up there, and I really like it." Gundaphorus realizes what has happened and says, "No, I'm sorry. I can sell you other things, but I can't sell you that." So the story ends that Gundaphorus, then, ends up converting to faith in Jesus, and releases, of course, Thomas—and thus begin Thomas's missionary activities in India.

So this is still some very interesting stories of sex, love, death, resurrection, wealth—the abandonment of wealth—and so on. Many of these themes are celebrated in one of the most interesting passages in the entire book—a passage that was probably written separately than the rest of the book, but was probably incorporated into it, into the Acts of Thomas at a later time. The passage is called the Hymn of the Pearl.

It's actually a song that's sung in prison by one of the prisoners that Thomas happens to hear, but it looks like this is an independent account that was incorporated in. It's a fascinating and moving story, though—the Hymn of the Pearl is kind of a story within the story, that's been embedded there. It's a story of a lad who has been sent by the royal family to retrieve a pearl from a great serpent who is in Egypt. But when the lad arrives in Egypt in order to retrieve the pearl, he forgets who he is and he forgets why he's come, until his parents send him a letter to remind him who he is. And then he remembers and he retrieves the pearl and returns home. Let me read portions of this Hymn of the Pearl, this story within a story in the Acts of Thomas, because I think it embodies a number of the themes, and I think it's quite a terrific piece. It's told in the first person.

> When I was a lad, a little child in my father's palace and I enjoyed the luxury of those who nurtured me, my parents equipped me with provisions and sent me out from the East our homeland.

He goes on to say that they take away the garment that he had been wearing which had been studded with gems and spangled with gold.

> They made an agreement with me and wrote it in my mind that I might not forget. The agreement was, "If you go down to Egypt and bring the one pearl that is in the land of the devouring serpent, you shall put on again that garment, set with stones, and the robe which lies over it. And your brother, our next in command, shall be a herald for our kingdom with you." So I departed from the East, on a difficult and frightening road, led by two guides.

So he goes from the East to Egypt, with his companions. When he arrives in Egypt his companions leave, and he goes straight to the serpent and stays near the serpent's den, "until he should slumber and sleep, that I might take the pearl from him." He's waiting so he can grab the pearl. But then he sees one of his kinsmen there, a freeborn man from the East, who's a young, fair, and beautiful young man. "He came to me and kept me company and I made him my intimate friend."

He decided to hang out with this fellow that he met. He clothed himself in garments, like the Egyptian garments, so he wouldn't appear to be a stranger and as one who had come from abroad to take the pearl, lest the Egyptians might arouse the serpent against me. But then I no longer recognized that I was the king's son, that I had served the king and I forgot the pearl for which my parents had sent me. I fell into a deep sleep because of the heaviness of their food. While I was suffering these things, my parents were aware of it, and they grieved over me.

The parents find out what's happened. They send him a letter. The courtiers bring him the letter. The letter says:

> To our son in Egypt, greetings. Awake! Rise from your sleep. Listen to the words in this letter. Remember, you are the son of kings. Recall the pearl for which you were sent to Egypt. Your name has been called for the book of life.

So he remembers why he has come to Egypt. He goes and he fetches the pearl. He returns to his parents in the East, and then his parents reward him by giving him, once again, the great garment that he had worn before; and he lives now as the son of kings, as a great member of this kingdom in the East.

This Hymn of the Pearl is a very interesting story, a moving poem. Probably it makes most sense in its immediate context. It's referring to humans who have a heavenly origin, who need to be recalled to who they really are and why they have come here, rather then being caught up in the trappings of this world. Like the rest of the Acts of Thomas, the idea here is that people are to give up the trappings of this world, because they have a heavenly origin; and by giving into their desires and giving into their pleasures here, and being concerned for sexual pleasure, and for wealth, and for beauty, they become trapped here in this world that isn't really their world. Their world is from heaven. People have a heavenly origin, and it's to heaven to which they should return.

That has a kind of Gnostic ring to it, which has led some people to suspect that if the Acts of Thomas is not actually itself Gnostic, perhaps it was influenced by Gnostic ideas of why we're here and why we need to reject this world. But in fact this teaching is the teaching of many of the Apocryphal Acts. There's a greater world above us that cannot be seen, that's far superior to the one that we live in. Life in this world should not be directed towards this world, but toward that other world, lest we become entrapped in our bodily desires and suffer dire consequences in the world to come.

Lecture Fifteen
The Acts of Paul and Thecla

Scope:

One of the most popular apocryphal accounts from Christian antiquity involved the conversion and exploits of Thecla, an aristocratic woman of Asia Minor who converted to the Christian faith through the preaching of Paul. The account survives as part of the Acts of Paul, a narrative that was evidently forged by a well-meaning Christian in Asia Minor, who later confessed to the deed. The narrative indicates that Thecla is principally drawn to Paul's proclamation of sexual abstinence. This leads to difficulties, because Thecla's fiancé and mother take offense at her decision not to marry and arrange for her to be executed by the state for her Christian beliefs. Through a series of miraculous interventions, though, Thecla is eventually set free and allowed to follow Paul, then go forth on her own to proclaim the gospel of ascetic living.

Outline

I. To this point, we have looked at two of our non-canonical Acts, those of John and of Thomas. In this lecture, we exam a third, one that was possibly the most popular in antiquity and is almost certainly the most popular among scholars of antiquity, the Acts of Paul and Thecla.

A. This is a legendary narrative about the exploits of one of Paul's early converts to Christianity, the aristocratic young woman Thecla, who abandons her home, her family, and her fiancé to follow Paul's teachings of strict sexual renunciation.

B. The account forms a portion of the larger narrative known as the Acts of Paul, a collection of tales already attested to by the late second century.

　1. The proto-orthodox church father Tertullian condemned the account for its lax attitude toward the role of women in the Christian church.

　2. According to Tertullian, the entire account was, in fact, fabricated by a presbyter in Asia Minor, who was caught red-handed in the act and later confessed to making the forgery.

C. Why and how did people forge documents?

  1. Sometimes, people forged documents as a way to make money.

  2. People also forged documents as an act of humility.

  3. More commonly, documents were forged in the ancient world because, by claiming to be someone famous, the writer could get a hearing for his views. This appears to be the principal reason that Christians forged documents in antiquity, writing their views in the name of an apostle.

  4. Such forgers attempted to inject aspects of verisimilitude into their forgeries, for instance, adding offhand comments presumably made by the author.

  5. Forgeries could be recognized by comparing the writing style, vocabulary, and views to those of the author under whose name the forger was writing.

D. This account contains numerous earlier traditions about Paul and his converts, none of which is more riveting than the narrative known as the Acts of Paul and Thecla, which may have originally circulated independently of the Acts of Paul.

II. As with the other Apocryphal Acts, this book can be seen as a kind of Christianized version of the popular literature known as romances or novels.

  A. It shares many of the generic characteristics and concerns of ancient novels. These books are all about love, magic, danger, escape, and restoration.

  B. But the Christian versions of the novels stand against the pagan versions in central and striking ways.

   1. The pagan romances are all driven by a concern to set forth the sanctity of marriage and marital love in the context of religion and in relation to an overarching concern for the integrity of the social fabric (strong families and marital institutions work to preserve the good of society).

   2. The Apocryphal Acts are concerned to promote strict sexual renunciation and illustrate how the gospel of Christ destroys the social fabric of family and community, all for the sake of the greater truth of heaven and the world above.

C. These similarities and differences can be neatly seen in the gripping tale of the Acts of Paul and Thecla.

III. The narrative can be divided into four scenes of action.

    A. First scene: Thecla's dramatic and socially disruptive conversion to Paul's message of sexual renunciation.

        1. The main characters: a wealthy aristocratic young woman, Thecla; Thecla's mother, Theoclia; Thecla's fiancé, Thamyris; and the apostle Paul.

        2. The action: Paul arrives in Thecla's city of Iconium to preach his gospel that eternal life will come to those who abstain from sexual activity, even within marriage. Thecla listens to Paul for three days on end from the window of her home and converts to his message, to the severe consternation of her mother and fiancé.

    B. Second scene: Trial by fire in Iconium.

        1. The main characters: Thecla, Paul, Thamyris, the governor of Iconium.

        2. The action: Thamyris and other men of the city, outraged that Paul's message has taken their wives and fiancées from them, have him arrested. Thecla shows her absolute devotion to Paul by bribing the guards to let her in to see him. Out of frustration, Thamyris and Theoclia hand her over for punishment. The governor condemns her to death by burning. But God miraculously intervenes at the last moment, dousing the fire with a thunderstorm, and Thecla is set free.

    C. Third scene: Thrown to the wild beasts in Antioch.

        1. The main characters: Paul, Thecla, Alexander (an influential citizen of Antioch), the governor of Antioch, and the Queen Tryphaena.

        2. The action: Paul and Thecla travel to Antioch, where she is accosted by Alexander, who desires her. She publicly humiliates him and, in response, he arranges to have her condemned to the wild beasts. Before her execution, the governor hands her over for safekeeping to an aristocratic woman, Tryphaena, relative of the emperor, who befriends her. When taken to the arena, Thecla is again miraculously protected from the wild beasts by God and eventually throws herself into a vat of wild, ravenous seals and baptizes herself there. When no beast will molest her, she is again set free.

D. Final scene: Resolution and restoration.
    1. The main characters: Thecla and Paul.
    2. The action: Thecla longs for Paul, seeks after him and finds him, and receives his blessing to teach the word of God. She finds her mother, Theoclia, is restored to her, and moves to Seleucia, where she lives long and happy as a celibate preacher of the gospel.

IV. Some of the overarching themes of this fascinating account can be taken as representative of all the Apocryphal Acts.

    A. Passion and desire are not eliminated here but redirected; their proper objects are not sexual partners but God, Christ, and their earthly representatives.

    B. Those who reject this world and its pleasures and trappings are those who have found the truth of the world above and are in a right standing with God, both now and for eternity.

    C. Those who accept the gospel of Christ and renounce the pleasures of this world, including sexual love, will be socially disruptive and hated by the rest of the world.

    D. But God will protect them and miraculously vindicate the truthfulness of their message.

    E. No wonder that, looking at it from the outside, Christianity was seen to be such a dangerous religion by some pagans in the Roman Empire. It struck at the very heart of what most pagans held dear: social structure, family life, marital love, and the enjoyment of the simple pleasures of this life.

    F. Why were these accounts—and the idea of asceticism—so popular among Christian women?
        1. Scholars believe that the social structure in the Roman Empire, where women were forced to be subservient to men, played a role in leading women to this new ideology that denied marriage.
        2. Without sex or marriage, women were liberated from a male-dominated society.
        3. A cult surrounding Thecla continued into the Middle Ages, and women saw her as a model to be followed in their daily lives.

Essential Reading:

J. K. Elliott, *The Apocryphal New Testament*, pp. 364–372.

Edgar Hennecke and Wilhelm Schneemelcher, eds., *New Testament Apocrypha*, vol. 2, pp. 220-223.

Supplementary Reading:

Jan Bremmer, *The Apocryphal Acts of Paul and Thecla*.

Stephen Davies, *The Revolt of the Widows: The Social World of the Apocryphal Acts*.

Dennis McDonald, *The Legend and the Apostle: The Battle for Paul in Story and Canon*.

Questions to Consider:

1. Some scholars have maintained that the Acts of Thecla may well have been authored by a woman. What arguments can you think of both for and against this theory?

2. Explain why the example of Thecla may have seemed "liberating" to Christian women in the patriarchal societies of the ancient world.

Lecture Fifteen—Transcript
The Acts of Paul and Thecla

To this point, we've looked at two of our non-canonical Acts of the Apostles, the Acts of John and the Acts of Thomas. In this lecture, we examine a third—one which was possibly the most popular in antiquity and is almost certainly the most popular among scholars of antiquity today, the Acts of Paul and Thecla.

The Acts of Paul and Thecla is part of the larger Acts of Paul, which we have in a number of fragments. This particular portion of the Acts of Paul is a legendary narrative about the exploits of one of Paul's early converts to Christianity, the aristocratic young woman, Thecla, who abandoned her home, her family, and her fiancé in order to follow Paul's teachings of strict sexual renunciation. As you can tell already, this will be playing out some of the themes we've seen in the earlier acts. The collection called the Acts of Paul was probably already written by the end of the second century. It may be based, though, on stories that were in an oral circulation at a much earlier date. There's some speculation that, in particular, the Acts of Paul and Thecla were floating around for decades prior to then being written down and put into this Acts of Paul.

We know about the Acts of Paul and Thecla from a late second/early third-century source. The proto-orthodox church father, Tertullian, who we've already met in conjunction with Marcion, condemns the account of Thecla for its lax attitude toward the role of women in the Christian church. In particular, Tertullian was upset because he knew that this account of Thecla was being used in order to justify the practice of women performing baptizisms. Tertullian was one of these church fathers who took a very strict, rigorous, ethical stand on most issues and is known for being one of the most highly misogynist authors from early Christianity. His idea is that women should not be involved at all or in any leadership roles in the churches. They should not be participating in giving out the sacraments in any way; they should not be baptizing. Tertullian thought that women should be silent and that women should be subservient to men. He knew that this account of Paul and Thecla was being used by people to justify the practice of women baptizing because of a scene that we'll see once we start looking at the account; and so he condemned it. But Tertullian actually tells us that, in fact, this account was fabricated, forged by a presbyter living in

Asia Minor, who was caught red-handed in the act, and later confessed to making the forgery. This is a very interesting comment of Tertullian, because we have a lot of people in the ancient world who talk about forgery, but rarely do we have anybody who mentions the circumstances of somebody being caught committing the forgery.

I would like to take a few minutes to talk more broadly about forgery in the ancient world, and attitudes towards it, as a way of setting up this business with Paul and Thecla, and because this relates to the wider themes of our course. As I pointed out previously, there were a number of forgeries that were done in the ancient world. We've seen a number of them in our course. We haven't asked the broader questions—why people forged documents, and how they managed to pull it off. In some instances, of course, they didn't pull it off; and we have one at hand here, where somebody forged something and was caught.

Why did people forge documents in the ancient world? Well, there are several reasons. One of them, which doesn't pertain to our particular subject, but does pertain to other matters of antiquity, has to do with economic motive. Sometimes people forged documents because they could make money out of doing so. This was especially the case when an ancient library wanted to get copies of a book or, in fact, would pay good gold for original copies of, say, the classical authors. If a library, say in Alexandria or in Rome, were paying gold on the head for an original version of Plato's writings, then you'd be surprised how many original versions of Plato's writings would show up. Sometimes people would forge documents for money.

Sometimes people forged documents out of humility, as odd as this might seem. We know of one philosophical school in the ancient world, the Pythagorean philosophical school, or more accurately, the Neo-Pythagorean philosophical school, in which it was taught that forging a document in Pythagoras's name is not only the right thing to do, it is an act of humility. The logic was that people who were later followers of Pythagoras felt that they had acquired all of the insights into the world from their master, and so, if they wrote a tractate in which they spelt out their understanding of a particular philosophical notion, they would sign it "Pythagoras," because otherwise they'd be claiming for themselves something that they didn't really have, namely, this kind of insight. So, as an act of humility, they would sign off as Pythagoras.

More commonly, documents were forged in the ancient world because people wanted to get a hearing for their views, and they knew that by claiming to be someone famous, they'd be more likely to get their views heard. Imagine, for example, that you're a philosopher living in Alexandria and nobody has heard of you—your name's Marcus, or Aristiades, or something, and you want people to read your philosophy. Well, if you sign your philosophical tractate Marcus Aristiades, nobody is going to read it. But if you sign it Aristotle, then people probably will read it. And so, if you want your views more broadly known, then you sign off pretending to be somebody that you're not.

That appears to be the principal reason that Christians forged documents in antiquity. They wanted their views heard, and they wanted their views to be accepted as authoritative, and so they wrote down their views in the names of apostles. And so they would write a gospel and sign off "Peter," or they'd write a gospel and sign off "Thomas," or they'd write an epistle and they'd sign off "Paul," so that their writings would be heard.

How did they pull it off? Well, the best way to pull off a forgery is to make it sound like the author whom you are trying to imitate. You inject aspects of verisimilitude into your account. You have off-the-hand comments that you think, well, nobody would say that unless it's the actual author. And so you write a letter and you say, "Oh, by the way, bring me my cloak that I left behind in Ephesus," pretending to be Paul. You say, well, why would a forger say that? It's verisimilitude. It's a way of making someone think it's the actual author.

Forgery was talked about a lot in ancient antiquity. When it was talked about, people who mentioned it condemned it. Sometimes it's stated, by people who don't seem to know any better, that forgery was widely practiced, but everybody could see through it and nobody was fooled and nobody really much cared in the ancient world. That, in fact, is not true. People did care in the ancient world, and people didn't appreciate it when they were duped.

We have one instance of a second-century Roman author, a famous physician named Galen, in which—he tells this account in the first hand—he was walking the street in Rome and he passed by a bookseller's shop and he saw a book on display in the window written by Galen. In fact, it was a book he hadn't written. He got rather upset by this. So Galen wrote a book that he entitled, How to Recognize Books Written by Galen, so people would buy his books and not somebody else claiming to be him.

People didn't appreciate it when others forged books in their name. How did people recognize forgery so well? Pretty much the way we recognize forgery. If the writing style does not coincide with an author's writing style otherwise; if vocabulary is used that is not typical of this author; if ideas are put forth that the author, in fact, opposes; then those are clues that these books are not written by the person they claim to have been written by. There are scholars in antiquity who prided themselves on being able to detect forgeries. They didn't have the data-retrieval systems that we have today, and so it was much more difficult. But occasionally they could detect forgery.

The Acts of Paul was allegedly forged by a presbyter, a proto-orthodox church leader in Asia Minor, who was caught red-handed in the act. He said, according to Tertullian, that he had written this account out of his love for Paul. I think probably what that means is that he wrote something that Paul himself would have been proud of, because he wanted to celebrate the exploits of the apostle. Nonetheless, he fabricated the account. He made it up; it was a work of fiction, not a work of fact.

Nonetheless, it's an interesting work of fiction and it deserves our attention. This account contains numerous earlier traditions about Paul and his converts. The person who wrote these down didn't just make these up; he heard stories and he wrote down a number of the stories. None of the accounts is more riveting than the narrative that's known as the Acts of Paul and Thecla, which I believe probably circulated independently of the other Acts of Paul.

As with the other Apocryphal Acts, this Acts, the Acts of Paul and Thecla, can be seen as a Christianized version of the popular literature known as romances, or ancient novels. It shares the many generic characteristics and concerns of ancient romantic novels. These books are all about love, magic, danger, escape, restoration. The Christian versions of these novels stand over against the pagan versions in some striking ways, as we saw in our previous lecture.

The pagan romances are all driven by a concern to set forth the sanctity of marriage and marital love, in the context of religion and in relation to an overarching concern for the integrity of the social fabric—strong families and marital institutions. These work together to ensure the good of society, according to the ancient romances.

The Apocryphal Acts, on the other hand, are concerned to promote strict sexual renunciation, and to illustrate how the gospel of Christ destroys the social fabric of family and community. They are not interested in preserving society; they are interested in disrupting society. Why? Because those invested in society don't have their minds in heaven, they have their minds on earth. The point of these novels, these Christian novels—these Christian Apocryphal Acts—is to show that there is a greater truth in heaven, and that people should live in the world above.

The similarities and differences between the pagan romances—the Greek romances—and the Christian Apocryphal Acts can be neatly seen in this ripping tale of the Acts of Paul and Thecla. The narrative of the story is divided into four scenes of action. The way I'll proceed, in the rest of this lecture, we'll go scene by scene. I'll summarize who the main character is in each scene, and what the plot is, and how the narrative actually flows. Then I'll read selections from each one.

So, the first scene. This is a scene of Thecla, a woman disciple of Paul—Thecla's dramatic and socially disruptive conversion to Paul's message of sexual renunciation. As we'll see, Paul, in this book, doesn't teach the gospel that the historical Paul himself actually preached, which is that one needs to believe in the death and Resurrection of Jesus. In this account, Paul's teaching is that one needs to be sexually pure. He manages to convert Thecla to this belief. The main characters of this first scene are Thecla, who is a wealthy, aristocratic young woman; Thecla's mother, named Theoclia; Thecla's fiancé, named Thamyris; and the apostle Paul. So, four main characters in this opening scene.

The action in this opening scene is, Paul arrives in Thecla's home city of Iconium. Iconium is in Asia Minor, modern-day Turkey. Paul arrives there to preach his gospel, that eternal life will come to those who abstain from sexual activities, even within marriage. Thecla listens to Paul for three days on end, from the window of her home, overlooking where he was preaching. She ends up converting to his message of sexual renunciation, to the severe consternation of her fiancé and her own mother, who's looking forward to a good marriage for her own welfare in the future. So let me read some of the selection. "After Paul had come to the house of Onesiphorus," he's the guy that Paul is staying with:

> There is great joy and bowing of knees and breaking of bread and the word of God about abstinence and the Resurrection. Paul said, "Blessed are the pure at heart, for they shall see God. Blessed are those who have kept the flesh chaste, for they shall become a temple of God and blessed are the continent for God shall speak with them."

So his message is all about sexual renunciation and sexual chastity.

> While Paul was speaking in the midst of a church in the house of Onesiphorus, a certain virgin named Thecla, the daughter of Theoclia, betrothed to a man named Thamyris, was sitting at the window close by and listened day and night to the discourse of virginity, as proclaimed by Paul.

So she's riveted by this preacher from out of town and she stays at the window listening to him, three days solid. "She did not move from the window. And so her mother said to Thamyris, her fiancé," the mother said to Thamyris:

> "I have a strange story to tell you, Thamyris. For three days and three nights Thecla does not rise from the window, either to eat or to drink, looking earnestly, as if upon a pleasant sight, she is devoted to a foreigner teaching deceitful and artful discourses. Thamyris, this man will overturn the city of the Iconians and your Thecla too, for all the young women and young men go to him to be taught by him."

So everybody is flocking to hear Paul about how they don't have to have sex anymore.

> "He says that one must fear only one God and live in chastity. Moreover, my daughter, clinging to the window like a spider, takes hold of what is said by him with a strange eagerness and fearful emotion."

This upsets Thamyris, of course, because he is espoused to Thecla and is looking forward to a happy marriage, with some sexual love, and, well, now she's clinging to this message of renunciation.

So he comes to her and he says, "Thecla, my betrothed, why do you sit thus? What sort of feeling holds you distracted?" And he makes no headway with her, because it turns out, she says, "I'm going to break off the engagement, and I'm going to follow the message of this apostle."

> Those who were in the house wept bitterly. Thamyris for the loss of a wife, Theoclia for that of a daughter, and the maidservants for that of a mistress.

So that's the end of the first scene, when Thecla converts to the preaching of Paul, who she hasn't even met yet. She simply hears him preaching from the window.

Second scene: Trial by fire in Iconium; but there'll be a miraculous intervention that prevents it. The main characters in this scene, again, are Thecla, the apostle Paul, Thamyris—again, Thecla's fiancé—and the governor of Iconium, who plays in this second scene. The action is that Thamyris, the fiancé of Thecla, and other men of the city become outraged that Paul's message has taken their wives and fiancés away from them. And so they arrange to have them arrested. Thecla shows her absolute devotion to Paul, though, by bribing the guards to let her in to see him. So she bribes the guards and goes in to see Paul in the prison. There are some interesting scenes in which they go to meet each other, and she kisses his bonds that he's chained with.

Out of frustration, when Thamyris and Theoclia realize that she's really committed to Paul, they hand her over for punishment. The governor condemns her to death by burning. But then God miraculously intervenes. So some of the extracts that I'll read from this:

> Thamyris goes into the house of Onesiphorus along with the rulers and officers and a great crowd with batons and they say to Paul, "You've deceived the city of the Iconians, and especially my betrothed bride, that she will not have me." The whole crowd says, "Away with the sorcerer, for he has misled our wives." The multitude was also incited.

So Thamyris stands before the tribunal and he says with a great shout,

> "Oh proconsul, this man—we don't know where he comes from—makes virgins averse to marriage." But the governor kept his resolve, and he called Paul and said, "Who are you and what do you teach, for they bring no small accusation against him?" Paul lifts up his voice and he says, "God has sent me that I may rescue them from corruption and uncleanness and from all pleasure and from death that they may sin no more."

The governor, then, orders Paul to be sent into prison. Thecla bribes the guards, comes in, kisses his bonds. They break into the jail-cell; they find her there, so to say, chained to Paul by affection. They end up taking Paul away, and Thecla starts rolling around in the ground where Paul had sat. As should be becoming clear, this account about sexual renunciation, in fact, is laden with all sorts of sexual innuendo. But it's not physical sexuality so much as being completely being taken over with passion for this apostle who preaches the sexual renunciation.

They order her to go off and be burned, because of her involvement with this man who is causing such trouble. The governor is greatly moved. He scourges Paul and casts him out of the city, since he's not a citizen. But he orders Thecla to be burned at the stake. She goes to the stake and everyone's amazed at her. They strip her naked, tie her to the stake. As it turns out, though, God performs a great miracle. They light the fire; the fire doesn't touch her body; suddenly there's a huge thunderstorm that puts out the fire from above, and so Thecla's life is saved. She, in fact, then is released, leading to scene three.

In scene three, we have another account of an attempted execution, in which Thecla is thrown to wild beasts in Antioch. In this case, the main characters are Paul and Thecla and an influential citizen of Antioch whose name is Alexander, along with the governor of Antioch and a figure who is a queen, related to the emperor—Queen Tryphaena.

In this scene, what happens is Paul and Thecla reunite. They go to Antioch. Thecla, though, is accosted by this citizen Alexander, who is very wealthy, who desires her sexually. She, of course, has renounced sex, won't have sex with her fiancé, let alone with this guy Alexander. She, in fact, publicly humiliates Alexander. He responds by raging to have her condemned to the wild beasts. The governor of Antioch condemns her to the wild beasts; but prior to her execution, the governor hands her over for safekeeping to this aristocratic woman—the queen, Tryphaena, relative of the emperor, who befriends Thecla.

Thecla is finally taken to the arena, where once again she is protected miraculously from the wild beasts by God. Eventually, then she'll be set free. Let me read you, then, some of the excerpts from this third scene. In particular, I am interested in the scene where she's being thrown to the wild beasts. As it turns out, she's thrown first to a lion. "They bind her to a fierce lioness. And the lioness," I guess seeing a kindred soul in Thecla, "instead of attacking her, sits at her feet and licks her feet while all the multitude stands astonished."

They next decide to throw her to other beasts. They take her out; it didn't work that day. They bring her back the next day. They strip Thecla. They put a girdle on her. They throw her into the arena. The lions and bears are set loose on her. But then a fierce lioness—I wonder if it's the same one or not—ran up and lay down at her feet. The multitude of the women cried aloud. A bear came up to attack her, and the lioness went out and tore it to pieces. Then a lion, who had been trained to fight against men, who belonged to Alexander, ran up against her. The lioness encountered the lion and killed the lion, but the lioness was also killed.

Thecla now didn't have a lioness to protect her, and so she decides to take matters into her own hands. There's a large vat that is sitting there, a vat of water, in which are found a large number of man-eating seals—I don't know what man-eating seals are like—but there they are, in this vat of water, waiting for her. Thecla, though, is thinking about the water, not the seals. And she decides that she hasn't been baptized yet, she's not a full Christian, and so she takes matters into her own hands.

Seeing the large vat of water, she says, "Now it is time to baptize myself." She throws herself in and says, "In the name of Jesus Christ, I baptize myself on my last day." So she threw herself into the water in the name of Jesus Christ. The women in the multitude are crying out, 'Don't do it, there are man-eating seals in there.' She does it anyway. She jumps in. The seals, though, are immediately

©2002 The Teaching Company.

killed because there's a flash of lightening that comes down and strikes the water. They all float dead on the surface. There's a cloud about the vat, but then she hops out, unscathed.

They end up tying her to a bunch of wild beasts, bulls. They tie her between these bulls and they put red-hot irons under the bulls' genitals so that they will pull her apart. These red-hot irons, though, end up, in fact, burning the ropes that were tying her to it. So once again, she miraculously escapes. The governor realizes that all of these miraculous escapes must come from God, and he decides that he better release her or else he himself might get in trouble with the divinity. And so he sets her free, ending the third scene.

The final scene is a scene of resolution and restoration. In scene four, the main characters are just Thecla and Paul. Here I'll just summarize the account. Thecla longs for Paul, and seeks after him, and finally finds him. She receives his blessing to go about on missionary activities, missionary journeys, teaching the word of God. So Paul is authorizing this woman to teach as an apostle. She finds her mother, Theoclia, and is restored to her. Then she moves to Seleucia, where she lives long and happy, as a celibate preacher of the gospel. That, then, ends the story of Paul and Thecla.

Some of the overarching themes of this fascinating account can be taken as representative of all of the Apocryphal Acts. It's interesting, as I intimated earlier, that passion and desire are not eliminated here. Instead, they're redirected. Their proper object, passion and desire, are not sexual partners. Their proper objects are God, Christ, and their earthly representatives. So that there is passion and desire here, but in God and Christ.

Secondly, those who reject this world, and its pleasures and trappings, are those who have found the truth of the world above— who are in a right standing with God, both now and for eternity. Rejecting the world means acquiring the world from above. Third, those who accept the gospel of Christ and renounce the pleasures of this world, including sexual love, will be socially disruptive and hated by the rest of the world. But God will protect them and miraculously vindicate the truthfulness of their message.

These are major themes of the Apocryphal Acts. It's no wonder that, looking at it from the outside, Christianity was seen to be such a dangerous religion by pagans in the Roman empire. It struck at the very heart of what most pagans held most dear—social structure, family life, marital love, and the enjoyment of the simple pleasures of life.

At the same time, it's not surprising that these accounts proved to be so popular among Christians and especially, as it turns out, Christian women. Some of the pagan attackers of Christianity—some of the opposers of Christianity that we know about from pagan authors of the second and third century—charged that Christianity was largely made up of women. Moreover—this was a charge because women were thought to have a secondary status among people in that world—we have reason to believe that stories like Paul and Thecla were especially popular among women, and the ascetic movement in early Christianity took hold especially among women. Why would that be? Why would these accounts be so popular, specifically with women? Why would asceticism appeal particularly to women in the ancient world?

Scholars have come to think that one of the reasons that asceticism proved so popular among women had to do with the social structure of the ancient world. Women in the Roman Empire, by and large, were forced to be subservient to men. They were either under the control of their father or, when they were married, under the control of their husband. What happens, though, if a new ideology emerges which denies marriage, and insists on a life of chastity with no sex? What happens if women buy into an ideology in which they don't have to be married but, in fact, can be on their own, accepting the life of the world above, rather than accepting the life here?

What happens is they escape the patriarchal confines of that world. Without sex, without marriage, women experience an ancient equivalent of liberation—liberation from a male-dominated society. If this is right, if that is what is attractive to women in Christianity, or part of what is attractive to women in Christianity, then it's no wonder that tales like the tale of Paul and Thecla would have been so popular among women, as we know in fact that it was. Thecla, in fact, became a patron saint for many women. There was a cult surrounding Thecla that went on to the Middle Ages, as women saw her as a model to be followed in their own lives.

Lecture Sixteen
Forgeries in the Name of Paul

Scope:

A number of letters survive from Christian antiquity that claim to be written by the apostle Paul but that were, in fact, clearly fabricated at a later time. This lecture considers two sets of pseudonymous Pauline correspondence. The first is, like the exploits of Thecla, part of the Acts of Paul. It consists of a letter from the Corinthians asking for Paul's help with some heretical teachers who advocate a docetic Christology (maintaining that Christ was not really a flesh-and-blood human and that there would not be a resurrection of the flesh) and Paul's response, in a letter traditionally called "3 Corinthians." The second is an exchange of fourteen letters between Paul and the famous first-century philosopher Seneca. Although evidently forged in the fourth century, these letters were meant to show that Paul was equal to the greatest minds of his day.

Outline

I. To this point, we have examined two genres of early Christian pseudepigrapha: gospels and acts.

    A. These are two of the four genres of writings found in the New Testament and account for most of the surviving early Christian forgeries.

    B. The third genre, however, is the most common in the New Testament: epistles (twenty-one of twenty-seven books). Epistles are not widely found among the early Christian pseudepigrapha (even though they are the most common form of pseudepigrapha *within* the New Testament).

II. A large number of epistles in the New Testament are pseudepigrapha or anonymous.

    A. Of the twenty-one epistles in the New Testament, thirteen were allegedly written by Paul. Six of those thirteen are heavily disputed by scholars.

        1. There are debates over whether Paul wrote the letters to Ephesians, Colossians, and Thessalonians, now labeled the Deutero-Pauline Epistles.

2. Three other letters—the Pastoral Epistles (letters of 1 and 2 Timothy and Titus)—are regarded by scholars as not having been written by Paul.

B. The Book of Hebrews is included in the New Testament but is considered to be anonymous.

C. The Book of James was accepted into the canon because people thought it was written by Jesus' brother, even though the author does not claim to be *that* James.

D. The Books 1 and 2 Peter claim to be written by Simon Peter, but most scholars agreed that 2 Peter was not written by him.

E. The Book of Jude claims to be written by someone named Jude and was brought into the canon because it was thought that Jesus' brother wrote it.

F. The Books 1, 2, and 3 John were included because they were thought to be written by John, the son of Zebedee, even though no such claims had been made.

III. In this lecture, we will consider several of the most interesting letters, allegedly written to and by the apostle Paul. These are conveniently called 3 Corinthians and the correspondence of Paul and Seneca.

A. Readers of the New Testament are familiar with 1 and 2 Corinthians but have, by and large, never heard of 3 Corinthians.

B. The book is nonetheless found in a number of ancient manuscripts and was part of the New Testament canon accepted by the churches of Syria and Armenia. It is now found in the manuscripts of the "Acts of Paul" (cf. Paul and Thecla).

C. The letters to the Corinthians in the New Testament are themselves a series of letters that Paul sent (2 Corinthians may represent five different letters sent at different times, later cut and pasted together).

1. These letters show numerous problems in the church in the city of Corinth that Paul tries to deal with, including, prominently, the disunity of the church and the problem of other "apostles" who arrived after Paul, teaching doctrines that he disagreed with, especially that it is the soul, not the body, that is saved.

2. Some of these same problems are evident in the later correspondence of 3 Corinthians, as well.

D. In the Acts of Paul, the letter is introduced by a letter from the Corinthians to Paul.

1. The Corinthians write that they have been disturbed by the teachings of two teachers, Simon and Cleobius, who maintain that the Old Testament prophets are not valid; that the God of this world is not the true God; that he did not create humans; that there is no future resurrection of the flesh; that Jesus was not really flesh and blood and was not really born of Mary.

2. In other words, the opponents are some kind of docetists, like Marcion, whom we discussed earlier, or possibly, some kind of Gnostic.

3. But for early proto-orthodox Christians (including the forger of 3 Corinthians), it was important to think not only that God created this material world, but also that he would redeem this world, including the human body, which would be raised from the dead, not left to corrupt.

E. The letter of 3 Corinthians is a response that takes on all these points one by one.

1. "Paul" (that is, the forger writing in Paul's name to address these second-century heretical views) claims that Jesus really was born of Mary (something the real Paul never mentions); that he was true flesh; and that God was the creator of all there is, who sent the Jewish prophets and Jesus to overcome the Devil, who had corrupted the flesh.

2. He ends the letter with an attempt to demonstrate that the flesh is actually raised from the dead by pointing to three analogies: the sowing of wheat (which goes into the ground naked but emerges as a new plant); Jonah (who appeared again in the flesh after disappearing into the great fish); and an apocryphal tale of the prophet Elisha (whose dead bones could bring bodies back to life).

F. The letter of 3 Corinthians is, then, a mid-second-century forgery in Paul's name in which a proto-orthodox Christian appealed to the apostle's authority to counteract doctrinal problems caused by heretical teachers of his own day.

IV. The dispute against heresy was not the only reason to pen letters in Paul's name, however, as can be seen in the correspondence between Paul and the famous Roman philosopher Seneca.

A. Seneca was probably the most well known and most influential philosopher of Paul's day: tutor and later political advisor to the Emperor Nero and highly prolific author of moral essays, philosophical tractates, poetical works, and scientific treatises.

B. At a later time (fourth century), Christians were puzzled that the important figures in their religion, especially Jesus and Paul, were completely unknown to major political and intellectual leaders of their day (neither of them, in fact, is ever mentioned by any Roman author of the first century).

C. The pseudepigraphic correspondence between Paul and Seneca works to redress this situation.

    1. There are some fourteen letters that survive, eight allegedly from Seneca to Paul and six from Paul to Seneca.

    2. In them, Seneca and Paul are portrayed as close companions, with Seneca expressing admiration and astonishment at Paul's brilliance and learning, and Paul acting as a teacher who has convinced Seneca of the truth of the Christian message.

    3. More than that, in these letters, Seneca indicates that he has read Paul's writings to the Emperor Nero, who is amazed and moved by Paul's learning.

    4. Several references in these forged letters attempt to provide verisimilitude for their claims to authenticity, especially letter 11, which mentions the fire in Rome that Nero blamed on the Christians.

    5. The point of the letters, then, is to show that Paul was known and acknowledged by one of the greatest and most influential thinkers of his day, that his views were superior to the pagan philosophical traditions, and that his influence reached to the very upper echelons of Roman power and authority.

    6. The letters, though, were clearly forged, evidently sometime in the fourth century.

V. In sum, 3 Corinthians and the correspondence between Paul and Seneca are two sets of forged epistles that meet two major items on the proto-orthodox agenda: showing that their points of view are grounded in apostolic authority and that the founders of their faith were recognized for their brilliance and authority by the greatest minds of their day.

Essential Reading:

Bart Ehrman, *After the New Testament*, readings 46–47.

Bruce Metzger, "Literary Forgeries and Canonical Pseudepigrapha," *Journal of Biblical Literature* 91 (1972): 3–24.

Supplementary Reading:

Dennis McDonald, *The Legend and the Apostle: The Battle for Paul in Story and Canon*.

Questions to Consider:

1. We have seen a number of forgeries in this course to this point, and some of the forged documents urge their recipients to engage in ethical behavior, but is forgery ethical? How do you explain the irony that authors who were trying to deceive readers about their own identities were also trying to have them behave in morally upright ways?

2. Given the extensive forgeries from early Christianity that are *outside* the New Testament, is there any reason to think that there could not be forgeries *within* the New Testament?

Lecture Sixteen—Transcript
Forgeries in the Name of Paul

To this point, we've examined two genres of early Christian pseudepigrapha—the apocryphal gospels and the Apocryphal Acts. These are two of the four genres found in the New Testament. As I've already indicated, within the New Testament, the four genres are the four Gospels that begin the New Testament; the Book of Acts, which is an account of the spread of Christianity, followed then by Epistles, which are letters written by Christian leaders to other Christians in the communities; followed finally, then, by the Apocalypse of John. These four genres are found also among the apocrypha. This lecture will be moving beyond the apocryphal gospels and Acts to consider apocryphal epistles.

The Acts and the gospels that we've already considered account for most of the surviving Christian forgeries from the ancient world. It's interesting, though, that within the New Testament, it's epistles that make up most of the books. Of the 27 books in the New Testament, 21 of them are actual or alleged epistles. I say "actual or alleged," because some of these books are actual letters written by Christian leaders to other Christians, and some of them take the form of letters written. So they might be a persuasive essay, for example, written in the form of an epistle. The word "epistle" and the word "letter" are synonymous in this context.

What's striking—though 21 of our 27 books found in the New Testament are epistles, so that the most popular form of writing that survives from the first century of Christianity is the epistle, among our apocrypha, our pseudepigraphic works, there are very few epistles. Within the New Testament, though, even though we have these 21 out of 27 books that are epistles, what is striking is that most of these books themselves have questions asked to authorship. In other words, even though there weren't very much epistolary pseudepigrapha in the second century, there appear to have been many epistolary pseudepigrapha in the first century, some of which appear to have made it within the New Testament.

That's one way of saying that some of the epistles in the New Testament appear to be forgeries. This is not a new discovery; this is something that scholars have known for a very long time. Since the Enlightenment, scholars have examined the books of the New Testament to decide whether the books allegedly written by the people who claim to be their authors, actually were. Let me give you some of the details, just to set up what I want to do in this particular lecture.

Of the epistles in the New Testament, thirteen go under the name of Paul. Thirteen of the 21 letters, allegedly, are written by Paul. But, as it turns out, six of those thirteen are heavily disputed by scholars. The Letters of Ephesians, Colossians, and Thessalonians are frequently labeled the "Deutero-Pauline" Epistles, because it's that they have a secondary standing—*deutero*—within the Pauline corpus, because there are debates about whether Paul actually wrote these letters. There are themes, vocabulary, writing styles that differ in these letters from the letters Paul wrote. So there's a question about it.

Three other letters, the so-called Pastoral Epistles—First and Second Timothy and Titus—are widely regarded by critical scholars as not having been written by Paul, so that about three of the letters scholars are fairly sure are pastoral epistles, three others there are debates about. Six of the thirteen are thought possibly, or certainly, not to have been written by Paul. In addition, included among the Epistles of the New Testament is the Book of Hebrews, which was included in the canon by Church Fathers in the first and fourth centuries because they thought Paul had written it, even though the book doesn't claim to be written by Paul. In that case, though, we should say that the book is not forged, it's not pseudonymous, in fact, it's anonymous. The Book of James in the New Testament was accepted into the canon because people thought it was written by James, Jesus' brother, even though the author doesn't claim to be that James.

First and Second Peter do claim to be written by Simon Peter. In the case of Second Peter, virtually everybody agrees that Peter could not have written it. It was probably written in the early second century, long after Peter had died. There are disputes about First Peter, whether Peter wrote it. The Book of Jude is a book that, again, claims to be written by somebody, by Jude or Judas. It doesn't claim to be Jesus' brother. But it was brought into the canon because people thought Jesus' brother, Jude, had written it. First and Second and Third John were included because they thought John the son of Zebedee wrote them. Again, those books don't claim to be written by John the son of Zebedee.

A large number of our Epistles in the New Testament, then, are either pseudepigrapha, or are anonymous, or are written by people who had the same name as an important person and were included in the canon, because they thought that important person was the one who wrote the book. We have more pseudepigrapha, then, among our epistles in the New Testament than in any of the other genres. Oddly enough, though, we do not have any pseudepigraphic epistles from the second and third centuries.

In this lecture, we will be looking at two of the most interesting of the pseudepigraphic epistles from the early times, allegedly written to and by the apostle Paul. The two books, or the group of books we'll be looking at, are conveniently called Third Corinthians and the Correspondence between Paul and Seneca. We begin with Third Corinthians.

Readers of the New Testament are, of course, familiar with First and Second Corinthians but, by and large, have never heard of Third Corinthians. Nevertheless, a Third Corinthians does exist. This book of Third Corinthians is found in a large number of ancient manuscripts. It was accepted as part of the canon of the New Testament by churches located in Syria and Armenia; so it was a popular book, and was accepted as canonical in some parts of Christianity. Now, this Third Corinthians is included in manuscripts of the Acts of Paul; just as the Acts of Paul and Thecla were included in the Acts of Paul, so too were Third Corinthians.

Let me give you a bit of a background to set up what I want to say about Third Corinthians. The Letters to the Corinthians in the New Testament are, themselves, probably a series of letters that Paul sent. The book that we call Second Corinthians appears to be a collection of letters that have been put together by scissors and paste. It appears that Paul sent a number of letters to this church located in Corinth, and that at a later time somebody took several of those letters—some scholars think two, some think three, I happen to think five—five letters that were cut and pasted together to form one large letter; so that there were a series of letters between Paul and the Corinthians.

We know of other correspondence between Paul and the Corinthians that didn't survive at all. In First Corinthians Chapter 5, Paul mentions an earlier letter that he had written. That letter doesn't survive. This means that there was a constant flow of letters going on between Paul and the Christians in Corinth. Why were there so many letters? Paul was the founder of the church in Corinth—I'm talking now about the historical Paul—Paul himself actually founded the church in Corinth during his missionary endeavors. Once he left that city, though, a number of problems emerged, and the letters back and forth are dealing with a variety of these problems that emerged in Corinth. Especially, what emerged were problems involving disunity in the church, and problems with other apostles arriving after Paul teaching doctrines that he disagreed with. In particular, these other apostles taught that it would be the soul, not the body, that is saved on the last day.

Paul writes First and Second Corinthians to deal with these various problems. The problems are especially evident in the book of First Corinthians, which is loaded with problems that Paul deals with one after the other. There's disunity in the church. Paul says that there are factions in the church, some claiming to follow Paul, some claiming to follow Apollos, some claiming to follow Peter, some claiming to follow Jesus. These are different groups of people claiming authority, with one or another Christian leader. Even Jesus himself, one group claims to be their ultimate authority.

Some of the disputes in the church had gotten completely out of hand. Paul indicates, then, in fact, there are people within the church, up front, who are taking each other to court, suing each other over we're not sure what, rather than dealing with their problems internally. Disruption within this community is evident in its worship services. Paul indicates that the worship services in the Corinthian church have gotten completely chaotic, as people are trying to usurp one another's authority and to show that each one is more spiritual than the other.

So, particularly in this church, it's become popular for spiritual leaders to speak in tongues, where they speak a language that they're not familiar with, inspired by the spirit. When they speak in this language they're not familiar with, it shows they've got a special endowment of the spirit. So to show that they've got a special endowment of the spirit, different leaders are speaking in tongues during the worship services, and everything has gotten completely out of hand. Nobody knows what's going on. It's complete chaos. When somebody visits the congregation they think that the place is an uproar.

The disunity is extended to the meals that the community has together. The Lord's Supper was celebrated, not as it is today in many churches where, at the end of worship service, there's a cup of wine, or little glasses of grape juice passed around, with wafers. In the early church, in fact, the Lord's Supper was celebrated as a meal, as a supper. The problem in Corinth is, they would have one of these suppers on a weekly basis. The people who were rich would come early, and they would eat all the food and get drunk. Then the people who had to work late, including the slaves who would come—there would be nothing left to eat or drink, once again showing disunity within the church.

And there was some fairly flagrant immorality going on in the church. There were people in the church in Corinth, Christian men, who were visiting prostitutes and coming into church to brag about it afterwards. One guy in the church was shacking up with his stepmother. This church, by the way, is addressed by Paul. He begins by saying that he's writing this letter to the saints who are in Corinth. One wonders, if these were the saints, what the sinners looked like.

Well, there were other problems. Some of the Corinthians had genuine questions about how to conduct themselves. Some of them wondered about what to do about eating meat that had been offered to pagan gods; whether this meat, which was sold at a discount, could be eaten by Christians or not. Some of them had questions that involved—we've looked at in our Apocryphal Acts–sex. Is it appropriate to have sex, even if married?

Paul writes to deal with all of these problems, and he deals with them one by one. He saves the big problem until the very end. In First Corinthians 15, he deals with the largest problem that he has to deal with—a problem that, in fact, covers all of the other problems; the Christians in Corinth don't understand the nature of the future resurrection. Paul, in First Corinthians 15, explains that there's going to be a future resurrection of the body. People will live their eternal lives in the flesh. For Paul, that has serious social implications. If the future afterlife is a fleshly, bodily existence, if what happens is that Christ returns and their bodies are reanimated, they become flesh again to live eternally in the body, that means that the body is important to God, that the body has to be treated in certain ways. The body cannot be neglected. People need to be careful with what they do with their body, because the body matters to God. So all of these other problems are bodily problems, that need to be dealt with. That's First Corinthians.

Similar set of themes in Second Corinthians. And, as it turns out, similar problems are evident in the later correspondence known as Third Corinthians. Now there is no dispute at all about whether Paul wrote First and Second Corinthians—he did, these are among the undisputed letters of Paul. Third Corinthians is a letter, though, that he did not write, even though it deals with some of the same problems that you find in the earlier correspondence.

In the Acts of Paul, the letter of Third Corinthians is introduced by a letter from the Corinthians to Paul. So the Corinthians write a letter to Paul, in which they indicate that they are having problems, and they ask him to help them. The Corinthians write that they've been disturbed by the teachings of two teachers who have come into town, two guys named Simon and Cleobius. This Simon and Cleobius have maintained that the Old Testament prophets are not valid, that the God of this world is not the true God, that he did not actually create humans. They teach that there's no future resurrection of the flesh. And they maintain that Jesus himself was not really flesh and blood, that he was not really born to Mary. That's the letter of the Corinthians that is sent to Paul, and they ask Paul to help them deal with these problems.

It sounds, reading through this letter, sent from the Corinthians to Paul that the opponents are some kind of Gnostics, or some kind of docetists. If you remember, docetists like Marcion maintained that Jesus didn't have a real flesh and blood existence, and that people themselves need to recognize that the afterlife would be a spiritual afterlife, that the one true God came to redeem people from the God of this world, who wasn't the true God. And remember the Gnostics, who thought that this world was a kind of evil joke, a catastrophe that occurred that, in fact, needs to be escaped and overcome; that people will live eternally in their spirits, but not in their flesh, as this evil material world will pass away.

It may be that this is the problem being dealt with in the letter of the Corinthians to Paul, that he's being asked to address. I don't mean by this that there actually was a problem like this in Corinth in the second century, and that there really were two guys named Simon and Cleobius. I think that this whole thing is forged by somebody, though, who's concerned about Gnostic problems, or docetic problems, in his own community. Paul then, or pseudo-Paul, writes a letter in response. His letter deals with these problems one by one, and emphasizes the importance of the flesh for salvation. So let me read you some excerpts from Paul's Third Letter to the Corinthians:

> Paul, the prisoner of Jesus Christ to the brethren at Corinth. Greetings. Being in many afflictions, I marvel not the teachings of the Evil One had such rapid success among you. My Lord, Jesus Christ will quickly come since he is rejected by those who falsify his teaching.

Okay, that's just his introduction to what he wants to say. Now he's going to deal some of the issues they've raised.

For I deliver to you, first of all, what I received from the apostles before me who were all with Jesus Christ, that Our Lord Jesus Christ was born of Mary.

Jesus was really born. It's interesting that you have that as an emphasis in the Third Corinthians, because Paul himself never mentions Jesus' birth to Mary. He doesn't Mary's name in his writings. But here Jesus really was born of Mary, "that he might come into this world and save all flesh by his flesh, that he might raise us from the dead."

Okay, so Jesus saves our flesh by his flesh. This is emphasizing the flesh in the nature of salvation. "Also, from the spirit of Christ he poured out upon the prophets who proclaimed the true worship of God for a long period of time." So that the prophets found in the Old Testament, in fact, had the spirit of Christ. This is emphasizing— against Marcion probably, or somebody like him—trying to emphasize that the Old Testament scriptures are, in fact, given by God.

> By his own body Jesus Christ saved our flesh. They who follow them are not children of righteousness but his wrath [so following these false teachers is not a righteous activity] who despise the wisdom of God and, in their disbelief, assert that heaven and earth and all that is in them is not the work of God. They have the accursed belief of the serpent. Those who say there is no resurrection of the flesh shall have no resurrection, for they do not believe him who has been risen.

This letter, then, is emphasizing that there is a future resurrection and that those who believe in it will participate in it. The author concludes by giving three analogies to show there must be a resurrection of the flesh. As with most analogies, these will be convincing, probably, to people who already accept the idea.

First, he points out, when wheat is sown in the ground, well, it doesn't just die there. What happens is plants emerge. So too the human body. When it goes into the ground plants emerge, the human body emerges, there's going to be a human resurrection because what's fleshly gets sown, what's fleshly gets raised. A second example he gives; Jonah. Jonah was swallowed by a great fish and disappeared for three days, and then reappeared. But he reappeared as a human being, in the flesh. So too, humans who are buried appear actually in the flesh at the resurrection. Finally, he gives the analogy from the apocryphal tale of the prophet Elijah. There's an apocryphal story that Elijah's dead body could bring others back to life. There's a tale of some children who take a corpse and they throw it on Elijah's dead bones, and this corpse then is reanimated, comes back to life. This is a demonstration of what the resurrection will be like, when bodies return into their fleshly state.

Third Corinthians, then, is a mid-second century forgery, written in Paul's name, which advances a proto-orthodox agenda. It was evidently written by a proto-orthodox Christian claiming to be Paul, appealing to the apostle's authority in order to counteract doctrinal problems that had been caused by heretical teachers of his own day; possibly Gnostics, or those influenced by a docetism similar to Marcion's.

We move now to the second piece of epistolary pseudepigrapha. We want to consider the famous correspondence between Paul and the Roman philosopher, Seneca. This correspondence is interesting, in part, because it shows that the dispute against heresy was not the only reason to pen letters in Paul's name.

Seneca was probably the best known and most influential philosopher of Paul's own day, in the second half of the first century. Seneca was the tutor and the political advisor, later in life, to the emperor Nero. He was actually Nero's teacher and his political advisor. He was a highly prolific author who wrote moral essays, philosophical tractates, poetical works, and scientific treatises, and we still have a large number of Seneca's writings.

At a later time, in the fourth century or so, Christians had become puzzled that such an important figure as Seneca and other important figures of his day actually appeared to be ignorant of Jesus and Paul, the two most important figures in Christianity. How is it that Jesus and Paul were completely unknown to the major political and intellectual leaders of their own time? That's a question that plagued Christians, possibly in the third, and certainly by the fourth century. How could that be?

Well, we know, in fact, that Paul and Jesus were probably unknown to such important people. It's striking when we first get references to Christianity in pagan authors. We have a lot of authors from the first century, from the Roman Empire. We have people who were historians, who were philosophers, who were poets, who were natural scientists. We have people who wrote personal correspondence—hundreds of letters that we have from this time period. We have people who wrote inscriptions on buildings. We have hundreds and hundreds of documents from the first century, from important literary people to *hoi polloi* who were simply writing to their friends. In all of these hundreds of documents, from many different authors in the first century, neither Jesus nor Paul nor any other Christian nor Christianity itself is every mentioned at all, in any writing from the first Christian century. If Jesus died in the year 30, as most people think, and you take a hundred-year gap from the time of his death, so say between the year 30 and the year 130—there are only three references to Christianity in any surviving authors.

Pliny the younger, who was a governor of a province in the Roman Empire, mentions Christians as those who are illegally gathering together, in a letter that he wrote to the emperor Trajan, in the year 112. That's the first reference to a Christian or Christianity from any pagan source; year 112—80 years after Jesus died. A few years later, the Roman historian Tacitus refers to Christians briefly as being held responsible for the burning of the city of Rome under Nero, and he gives a short account why Nero held Christians accountable and then persecuted them for burning Rome, even though he himself had burned Rome.

About that time, the Roman historian Suetonius mentions Christians possibly in a reference in which he mentions Jews had been excluded from Rome under the reign of Claudius because of the instigation of riots by a person that he calls Chrestus—some people think this might be a reference to a Christian. Those are the only three references to Christianity within a hundred years after the death of Jesus. Christians later were puzzled why is it that such important figures as Paul and Jesus weren't known to the intellectual leaders of the empire. Well, the pseudepigraphic correspondence between Paul and Seneca works to redress that situation.

These are fourteen letters that were written by a Christian—fourteen, at least, that survived. Eight of them allegedly were written from Seneca, the Roman philosopher, to Paul and six of them are written from Paul to Seneca. In these letters, Seneca and Paul are portrayed as close companions, with Seneca expressing admiration and astonishment at Paul's brilliance and learning, and Paul acting as a teacher who has convinced Seneca of the truth of the Christian message. So I'll just read you an excerpt or two from the first letter. Seneca writes to Paul and says:

> We've read your book and we're completely refreshed. These thoughts, I believe, were expressed, not by you, but through you. They are so lofty and so brilliant with noble sentiments that, in my opinion, generations of men could hardly be enough to become established and perfected in them.

He goes on to say in the second letter, "I count myself fortunate in the approval of man who is so great." So here the greatest philosopher of the first century is saying that, in fact, Paul is the greatest mind ever to exist.

More than that, Seneca goes on to indicate that he has read Paul's writings to the emperor Nero, who is amazed and moved by Paul's learning. And so, in Letter Seven:

> For the holy spirit that is in you and high above you expresses such lofty speech, thoughts worthy of reverence. And in order that I may not keep anything secret from you, brother, and burden my conscience, I confess that Augustus was moved by your sentiments. When your treatise on the power that is in you was read to him, this was his reply; he was amazed that one whose education has not been normal could have such ideas.

So even the Roman emperor is completely taken with Paul's writings.

Several references in these forged letters attempt to provide verisimilitude for their claims to authenticity, especially Letter 11, which mentions the fire in Rome that Nero blamed on the Christians. In this letter, Seneca writes to Paul and he says that he's been "saddened and grieved because you innocent people are being repeatedly punished." He points out that the populace knows that the Christians aren't at fault. They know very well who is at fault. The source of the frequent fires with which the city of Rome suffers is plain. "That rotten whoever he is, whose pleasure is murdering and whose refuge is lying, is destined for his time of reckoning. And just as the best is sacrificed as one life for many, so he shall be sacrificed for all and burned by fire." He goes on to point out that 136 private homes and 4,000 apartment buildings were burned in six days.

This appears to be based on the report of Tacitus who, as I indicated, specifies that Nero burnt the city; he did it to implement his own architectural designs on the city. But when people suspected that he had done it, he blamed the Christians and used them as scapegoats. That's the first instance we have of an emperor persecuting. But Nero persecuted Christians not because they were Christians, but simply because he needed a scapegoat for the fires that he set.

The point of these letters, then, between Paul and Seneca is to show that Paul was known and acknowledged by one of the greatest and most influential thinkers of his day—that his views, in fact, were superior to the pagan philosophical traditions, and that his influence reached to the very upper echelons of Roman power and authority. The letters though were clearly forged, evidently some time in the fourth century.

In sum, Third Corinthians and the Correspondence between Paul and Seneca are two sets of forged epistles that meet two major items on the proto-orthodox agenda; showing that their points of view are grounded on apostolic authority, and showing that the founders of their faith were recognized for their brilliance and authority by the greatest minds of their day.

Lecture Seventeen
The Epistle of Barnabas

Scope:

Unlike the letters we already considered, the Epistle of Barnabas was not forged; although later attributed to Paul's traveling companion Barnabas, it is actually anonymous. Some early Christians thought so highly of it, though, that they included it in the canon. The history of Jewish-Christian relations would have changed drastically had they succeeded, because this is one of the most virulently anti-Jewish treatises of Christian antiquity, designed to show that the Jewish people have always misunderstood their own law. According to this author, the Mosaic laws concerning kosher food, circumcision, the sabbath, and so on were meant figuratively, not literally; the Jews, misled by an evil angel, misunderstood them. The Jewish people, he avers, had broken God's covenant as soon as it was given to them through Moses. Therefore, they, unlike the followers of Jesus, have never been the people of God.

Outline

I.   In our previous lecture, we considered non-canonical epistles allegedly written by the apostle Paul.

   A. These books of 3 Corinthians and the letters to Seneca were forged by proto-orthodox Christians to promote their own perspectives.

   B. This is true of all the early Christian pseudepigrapha, including the one we will examine in this lecture, allegedly written not by the apostle Paul but by his trusted companion, Barnabas.

   C. The Epistle of Barnabas was widely considered to be Scripture in some circles of early Christianity and nearly made it into the New Testament (it is still found in one of our earliest Greek manuscripts of the New Testament).

      1. The manuscript, the Codex Sinaiticus, was discovered in the nineteenth century by Constantine von Tischendorff in St. Catherine's Monastery on Mount Sinai.

2. It is the earliest complete manuscript of the New Testament, but it also contains two other books, one of which is the Epistle of Barnabas.

3. The history of Western civilization may have been drastically changed had the Epistle of Barnabas been included in the canon. It is a virulent attack on historical Judaism, which may well have fanned even further the flames of anti-Semitism.

II. We must first consider some background to the Epistle of Barnabas.

A. This particular book, written about 130–135 A.D., is not actually forged; the author is anonymous.

B. Only later was the book attributed to Barnabas, a well-known figure from the early church as a traveling companion of Paul.

C. The historical context of the epistle involves the developing relationship of Jews and Christians in the early decades of the second century.

D. It is important to bear in mind a few features of early Jewish-Christian relations.

1. Jesus and his followers were all Jews; Jesus appears to have wanted to give the right *interpretation* of Judaism, not to set up a new religion in *opposition* to Judaism.

2. His follower Paul advocated the view that even though Jesus was the Messiah of the Jews, he could be accepted by non-Jews for salvation, *without* their having to become Jewish first.

3. By the end of the first century, most people converting into the Christian church were non-Jewish.

4. This led to natural tensions between Christians, whether Jewish or Gentile, and non-Christian Jews, because both claimed to be the true heirs of the Jewish Scriptures given by God to the Jewish people.

5. That set of arguments is reflected in the Epistle of Barnabas.

III. According to Barnabas, Jews rejected God and, thus, God rejected them. It is the Christians who are the true heirs of salvation promised to the people of Israel; the Old Testament is *their* book, not the book of the Jews.

A. Barnabas argues that God's promises in the Old Testament are meant for Christians, not Jews.

B. He maintains that Jews were led astray by an evil angel into taking Moses' laws literally. But they were meant figuratively, as indications of how people were to behave.

    1. The kosher food laws were not about foods to eat and avoid; they indicate how people should behave toward God and one another.

    2. The law of observing sabbath was meant to show that God was soon to bring the entire creation to a period of rest and enjoyment.

    3. The law of circumcision was not meant to require Jews to mutilate their baby boys but was a prediction of the coming crucifixion of Jesus. Barnabas explains this point by applying the numerological method of interpretation called *gematria*, by which the letters of a word are given numerical equivalence and interpreted accordingly.

C. For Barnabas, Jews are not God's covenantal people and never have been. They violated the covenant they had with God, already on Mount Sinai while Moses was still receiving the law. And it was never restored.

D. God has now created a new people to replace the disobedient Jews.

IV. This, then, is one of the earliest and most virulent Christian writings in opposition to Jews and Judaism.

A. The opposition makes historical sense, even if it violates our modern moral sense. In order for non-Jewish Christians to claim to stand in a special relationship with the God who created the world and chose Israel to be his people, they had to show that the Jews were *not* his people.

B. This point of view became increasingly prominent in the second century.

    1. The Christian philosopher Justin Martyr, writing around 150 A.D., claimed that God had given the Jews circumcision so they could easily be recognized by those wanting to persecute them.

    2. The Christian apologist Tertullian, writing around 200 A.D., claimed that Jerusalem had been destroyed by the Romans as punishment for the Jewish rejection of Jesus.

3. The Christian preacher of the late second century Melito of Sardis claimed that by killing Jesus, Jews were guilty of killing their own God. This is the first instance of any Christian charging Jews with the sin of deicide.

C. It is important to place these various accusations against the Jews in their own historical context, without excusing them.

    1. Christians making these claims were a tiny minority that felt defenseless against larger Roman society.

    2. They wanted to maintain that, in fact, they were not a new and suspect religious sect. They were as old as the law of Moses and the ancient traditions of Judaism.

    3. In making these claims, though, they necessarily had to attack Jews, who could rightfully claim these religious traditions for themselves.

    4. These attacks may have been simply defensive posturings by Christians in the early years. Problems arose when Christianity acquired more converts and more power and, eventually, complete power, religious and secular.

    5. After the conversion of the Emperor Constantine in the early fourth century, when Christians could exercise real social, economic, and military force, they took the anti-Jewish claims that had developed much earlier in such writers as Barnabas and applied them literally, maintaining that Jews were the enemies of their own God and, therefore, had to be punished and destroyed.

    6. The ugly, painful, and notorious history of Christian anti-Semitism is in some ways a direct result of writings such as these.

    7. One can only imagine how much worse it would have been had the epistle of Barnabas actually succeeded in making it into the canon.

Essential Reading:

Bart Ehrman, *After the New Testament*, reading 15.

Jay Treat, "Barnabas, Epistle of," *Anchor Bible Dictionary*, vol. I, pp. 611–614.

Supplementary Reading:

John Gager, *The Origins of Anti-Semitism: Attitudes toward Judaism in Pagan and Christian Antiquity.*

Rosemary Ruether, *Faith and Fratricide: The Theological Roots of Anti-Semitism.*

Marcel Simon, *Verus Israel: A Study of the Relations between Christians and Jews in the Roman Empire (135–425).*

Questions to Consider:

1. How are Barnabas's attitudes toward Jews and the Jewish Scriptures still evident among Christians today?

2. To what extent can the horrific acts of anti-Semitism of the twentieth century be traced back to the kind of anti-Jewish polemic that we find in early Christian authors?

Lecture Seventeen—Transcript
The Epistle of Barnabas

In our previous lecture, we considered non-canonical epistles, allegedly written by the apostle Paul. These books, Third Corinthians and the Letters to Seneca, were forged by proto-orthodox Christians to promote their own perspectives. This is true of all the early Christian pseudepigrapha, including the one we'll examine in this lecture, allegedly written not by the apostle Paul, but by his trusted companion Barnabus.

The Epistle of Barnabas was widely considered to be Scripture in some circles of early Christianity, and it nearly made its way into the New Testament. In one of our oldest surviving manuscripts of the New Testament, in fact, the Epistle of Barnabas is included as part of Scripture. This is a famous manuscript, discovered in the nineteenth century, by a textual scholar named Constantine von Tischendorff, who went on a number of journeys throughout the Middle East in order to find manuscripts in libraries and monasteries. On Mount Sinai, at Saint Catherine's monastery, Tischendorff discovered a manuscript that is now known as "Codex Siniaticus," named after its place of discovery, Sinai.

Codex Siniaticus is our only early complete manuscript of the New Testament from the fourth century. It's the earliest complete manuscript that has all the books of the New Testament. But in addition to the New Testament books, it has two other books which appear to be have included by a scribe in the mid to late fourth century, as Scripture. One of these two is The Epistle of Barnabas. The history of Western civilization might have been drastically changed if the scribe of Siniaticus had had his way, and this book had been included in the sacred Scriptures of the Christian church. Western civilization might have been drastically changed, because this book is a virulent attack on historical Judaism. Had it been included in the Scriptures, it might well have fanned even further the flames of anti-Semitism that arose in late antiquity through the Middle Ages, and have come down to us today in modern times.

In this lecture, then, we'll look at this attack on Judaism in the Epistle of Barnabas. First, some words of background to the epistle. Unlike the letters that we looked at in the previous lecture, this one is not actually forged. The book is assigned to Barnabas, or was assigned to Barnabas, by later Christians, but the author doesn't

©2002 The Teaching Company.

claim to be Barnabas. So this would be a case of false attribution, rather than a case of somebody claiming to be somebody he wasn't. This is not a forgery.

This book was probably written somewhere about the year 130 or 135 A.D. We know that, because in the book there's a reference to a political situation, where it is clear from what the author says that the temple in Jerusalem is in ruins. Well, the temple was destroyed in the year 70 by the Roman armies. This author indicates, though, that there is some expectation that the temple is going to be rebuilt. This was the case, in fact, that there were people anticipating the rebuilding of the temple, in the early second century. They thought that the Romans would allow the Jews to rebuild the temple. But all of that ended in the years 132 to 135, when the Romans built their own temple in Jerusalem on the site of the old Jewish temple, ending any speculation that the temple of the Jews would be rebuilt.

Barnabus indicates that there is some expectation that the Jewish temple will be rebuilt, and so he must have, then, been writing sometime between the years 70 and the year 135. And most people think that it is closer to the year 135. So it is probably written sometime around the year 130. That means, though, that the historical Barnabas, who was a figure known to the apostle Paul in the 60s and 50s of the Common Era—A.D.—could not have been the author of this book. He would have been long dead. And so this book is not forged; it's simply misattributed to Barnabas, a well-known figure from the early church as a traveling companion of the apostle Paul. Barnabas is mentioned in both Paul's own writings, in the Book of Galatians, and in the Book of Acts, which is an account of Paul's missionary journeys. So Barnabas is known as being a missionary who traveled with Paul from these contexts.

The historical context of this epistle that was falsely attributed to Barnabas involves the developing relationships of Jews and Christians in the early decades of the second century. To begin our discussion of the epistle of Barnabas, it's important for us to bear in mind a few features of early Jewish-Christian relations. As we've seen in previous lectures, Jesus and his followers were all Jews. Jesus appears to have wanted to give the right interpretation of Judaism to his followers. Jesus appears not to have had any intention of starting a new religion, but intended to give proper understanding of Judaism. He was understood to be a teacher of the Jewish law, a rabbi, one who could give the correct understanding of what God had commanded to Moses. Jesus himself tried to urge his fellow Jews to repent their sins and to prepare for the coming judgment that was soon to come, sent by the God of the Jews, to destroy their enemies and destroy anybody who opposed him.

Jesus' trying to get people to repent, trying to urge the people of Israel to turn around, offended some of the leaders of Israel. When he went to Jerusalem in order to celebrate a Passover, they arranged to have him taken out of the way. And as we know from the Gospels, then they handed him over to Pontius Pilate, who had him crucified. Throughout the entire ministry, though, Jesus was not about trying to start a new religion. He was trying to reform Judaism as he saw it.

Soon after his death, his disciples claimed he had been raised from the dead; and this completely changed how they understood the significance of Jesus. Jesus came to be understood as the Messiah, whose death could bring salvation. His death must have been important, they concluded, because God had raised him from the dead. That shows that God put His stamp of approval on Jesus' message. Jesus, then, must actually be the one who brings salvation through his own death. And so missionaries, like the apostle Paul, began to preach the importance of Jesus' death and Resurrection for salvation.

Very soon though, Paul and others like him maintained that Jesus' salvation came, not just to the Jews, but to all people, to Jew and Gentile. One of the earliest issues in Christian history, as we've seen, is the question about whether Gentiles had to become Jews before becoming Christian. Paul insisted that, no, they did not. Gentiles could be saved by believing in Christ's death without first becoming Jewish. By the end of the first century, most people converting into the Christian faith were, in fact, non-Jewish. This led to natural tensions between Christians, whether Jewish or Gentile, and non-Christian Jews. Both groups, both the Christians and Jews, claimed to be the true heirs of the Jewish Scriptures as given by God to His people. So this is one of the ironies of early Christianity, that people who were Gentile are claiming to be heirs of the promises given to Jews, claiming that the Jews have rejected their own promises, because they have rejected Jesus, their own Messiah who was sent by the Jewish God.

The Jewish people responded that this was a claim of hubris, to claim that you Gentiles are heirs to promises made to our forefathers. You're not even Jews; you don't even keep the Jewish law; and you claim to be heirs to our promises and traditions? This caused, obviously, a good bit of tension between Jews and Christians in the early centuries. These tensions are reflected in the Epistle of Barnabas—the epistle that's designed to show that Christianity is, in fact, the heir to the promises of God made to the Jewish people. According to this author, whom I'll continue to call Barnabas, Jews rejected God, so that God rejected them. According to this author, it is Christians who are the true heirs to the salvation promised to the people of Israel. And most strikingly of all, for this author, the Old Testament is a Christian book, not a Jewish book.

How does this author go about trying to establish that the Old Testament is a Christian rather than a Jewish book? It was a difficult claim to sustain for most Christians, because Jews could point out that Christians don't keep the laws found in the Old Testament. If Christians are claiming that this is their book, why don't they keep the laws? Why don't keep the kosher food laws? Why don't they observe the Sabbath? Why don't they circumcise their baby boys? Why don't they keep the Jewish festivals? You claim this is your book, and yet you don't even follow this book.

Barnabas wants to maintain, though, that in fact the Old Testament is intended for Christians, and has a Christian interpretation, and that the Jews have misunderstood their Scriptures and have always misunderstood their Scriptures, from the very beginning. Barnabas maintains, in fact, that Jews were led astray by an evil angel into misinterpreting their Scriptures. More specifically, he maintained that this evil angel led Jews to think that the laws given to Moses were to be taken literally. In fact, for this author, the laws of Moses are not to be taken literally; they were meant figuratively as indications of how people were to behave.

A good proportion of this book goes into the laws of the Old Testament, showing that these laws were meant to be taken figuratively rather than literally. This includes the kosher food laws, the laws given to the Jewish people of what foods they could eat and what foods they should avoid. According to Barnabas, these laws are not actually about what you should eat; these laws are about how people should behave towards God and towards one another.

Let me read you a few examples in which Barnabas actually quotes the Jewish law and then shows his own symbolic, figurative interpretation of these laws. I'm quoting from Barnabas, Chapter 10. Barnabas says: "Now when Moses indicated that one should eat neither pig, nor eagle, nor hawk, nor crow, nor any fish which is without scales, he received in his understanding three doctrines." He's going to go on and explain why, according to the kosher food laws of the Jews, they're not supposed to eat pig, eagle, hawk, crow, or fish without scales.

For this reason, he says, Moses mentions the pig. Do not associate, he is saying, with such people—people who are like pigs; that is, people who forget their Lord when they are well-off, but when they are in need they acknowledge the Lord, just as when pigs are eating they ignore their master because they are content, but it's when they are hungry that they make a din, because they want to have food given to them. He is saying, don't be like that. Don't behave like a pig, where you pay attention to God only when you need something. You should be paying attention to God all the time, and that is what Moses meant. When he said don't eat the pig he meant, don't be like a pig.

He goes on, "Neither shall you eat the eagle, nor the hawk, nor the kite, nor the crow." What does that law mean? Again, it meant something figurative. Do not, he is saying, associate with nor be like such people—people who do not know how to procure their own food by honest labor and sweat, but in their lawlessness they plunder the possessions of others. These birds, in other words, are scavengers. You are not to be a scavenger. You are to work for your own food, with the sweat of your own brow. So this isn't meant to be taken literally. It's meant to be taken figuratively.

He goes on against other examples of food that are forbidden for Jews to eat, and he shows it again. These are meant to show how you're supposed to behave, not what you're supposed to eat. Verse 6: "Neither shall you eat the hairy-footed animal," which is probably a reference to not eating rabbit. Why not? "Do not, he is saying, be one who corrupts children, nor be like such people." What does rabbit have to do with corrupting children? "Because," he says, "the hare has an anus every year, and thus as many holes as it is old." Well, this in reference to the tradition that rabbits multiply quickly. Why do they multiply so quickly? Well, it's because they grow holes every year, and you're not supposed to be like that; which means you're not meant to be engaged in wild licentious activities and corrupting children.

Verse 7: "Neither shall you eat the hyena. Do not, he is saying, be an adulterer, nor a corruptor, nor like such people. Because," he says, "this animal, the hyena, changes its nature, each year. One year it is a male. The other year it is female." So the hyena is transsexual from one year to the next. You're not supposed to be like that, which means you're not supposed to be somebody who is sexually licentious, an adulterer, nor a corrupter.

Finally, Verse 8. "He also"—Moses also—"hated the weasel fittingly. Do not, he is saying, be such a person, like a weasel." Not, you can't eat the weasel; don't be like the weasel. "We hear of such people, who perform the lawless deed uncleanly with the mouth. Neither associate with these unclean women who perform the lawless deed with the mouth, for this animal conceives with the mouth." In other words, Moses' commandment not to eat the weasel means people should not engage in oral sex.

But Barnabas has a number of interesting interpretations of the kosher food laws. His point is that these laws are not meant to be taken literally; they are symbolic laws about what one should and should not do. So, too, with other laws found in Scripture. For example, Jews are commanded on every seventh day to take a rest, a Sabbath day. Jews took this, of course, quite literally. On Saturday, Jews are not allowed to work or engage in other activities that they would be involved with during the week. Barnabas thought that, in fact, this law was not about taking a vacation once a week. I should point out, Jews were somewhat unusual in the ancient world for doing this. Ancient people did not have weekends the way that we have. It used to be that people in the Western world would take one day of the week off. When Christianity came on the scene, rather than taking Saturdays off, Christians took Sundays off from work. But then, eventually, that developed into having a weekend where Saturdays and Sundays were off every week. Well, that wasn't the case throughout the ancient world, in which people didn't get one day of the week off, or more. So Jews were commonly maligned for being lazy, since they took the day off every week. Jews, of course, looked on this as a great good, having one day off out of seven.

Barnabas, in any event, doesn't think that God's commandment to have a Sabbath day holy refers to taking a seventh day off at all. As he says, Moses mentions the Sabbath at the beginning of creation in the words, "God made the works of his hand in six days and he finished on the seventh day, and he rested on it and kept it holy." "Pay attention, children," says Barnabas, "to what he says. He finished in six days. Moses is saying this, that in six thousand years the Lord will finish everything, for with him the day signifies a thousand years. And he bears me witness on this point saying, 'Behold, a day of the Lord shall be as a thousand years.'"

In other words, Barnabas interprets the idea that the Sabbath day be holy, the seventh day is a day of rest, not in reference to one day of the week when a Jew is to take off from labor. Instead, Barnabas refers to the Scripture that says with the Lord a day is as a thousand years and a thousand years is a day. God created the world in six days, and then took a seventh day of rest. Jews then take a seventh day of rest. But, in fact, it's not talking about days; it's talking about thousand-year period.

Barnabas is the first author we know about who thinks the world is going to last for six thousand years and then end. This has been an important teaching throughout the history of Western civilization, the logic being that God's creation is six days—or six thousand years—after which there's a millennium, or another thousand years of rest. This has been an important teaching, even in modern times. Since the seventeenth century, there have been Christians who believed the world was created in the year 4,000 B.C. This was based on calculations made by seventeenth-century scholars, who read the Bible and read ancient Babylonian and Greek records, and decided that the world must have been created sometimes around the year 4000.

The most famous person to come up with this calculation was, in fact, a very erudite, learned scholar in Ireland named James Ussher who calculated that the world was created in the year 4004 B.C.—in fact, on October 23, 4000 B.C. Now if the world is to exist for 6,000 years after that, well, if you take 4004 and add 6,000 years to it then, as it turns out, the world was supposed to end—this is the twenty-first century—the world was supposed to end some years ago.

Back in the late 1990s, in fact, there was some furor among some fundamentalists who thought that the world would last 6,000 years, and that it had been created in the year 4004. Some people thought, in fact, the world was soon to reach its end. That kind of teaching goes all the way to Barnabas. He thought that the command about Sabbath was not a commandment about taking a day off. It was an indication about how long the world would last before it ended.

So, kosher food laws, the Sabbath law, are meant symbolically; so too the law of circumcision. Barnabas insists that the law of circumcision, in which Jews are required to cut off the foreskin of the penis of their baby boys, was, in fact, not a requirement of mutilation; that instead, according to Barnabas, the law of circumcision was a prediction of the coming crucifixion of Jesus. How does he get to that? Well, it's a very interesting explanation that he has.

Barnabus maintains that the father of the Jews, Abraham, was the first to receive the law of circumcision, and he notes how, in fact, he receives this law of circumcision in the Book of Genesis, when Abraham was going out to rescue his nephew Lot, who had been taken captive by some other kings, and he's taking an army of his own servants with him. We're told that he took 318 servants with him. These 318 servants were circumcised by Abraham in preparation for their battle. Three-hundred and eighteen is an interesting number for Barnabas. He applies a symbolic way of interpreting numbers from the Bible. This is a method of interpretation that is called *gematria*.

Gematria is a system of interpretation whereby one understands words and numbers in the Scripture. In the ancient Hebrew writings, as in ancient Greek and in most ancient languages, there was not a separate system used to indicate numerals from the alphabet. In fact, the alphabet and numerals used the same signs. The letters of the alphabet substituted for numerals. So, for example, in Greek alpha is 1, beta is 2, gamma is 3, until you get up to the tenth letter, iota. And after iota the eleventh letter is kappa, that becomes 20. Lamda then is 30, 40, 50, until you get up to 90. Then they go on by hundreds. That means any word in Greek has letters, which can also function as numbers, which means every word has a numerical value to it. Likewise, every number can be a group of letters.

Barnabas is struck that at the first instance of circumcision, Abraham circumcises 318 servants. He notes that when one spells out the number 318 in Greek, the way it is spelt out is, first, with the letter tau, which looks like our T, which in fact looks like a cross. That's the number for 300. The number for 18 is an iota eta, which would be put into English as a J, E—which happened to be the first letters of the name, Jesus.

In other words, the circumcision of these servants, these 318, is not a demonstration of what literally happened, it's a foreshadowing of the cross, the *tau*, of Jesus, *iota-eta*. By *gematria*, Barnabas tries to demonstrate that circumcision is a prediction of the coming crucifixion of the savior of the world, Jesus. He ends this discussion, in which he lays out this interpretation, by saying he has never taught a better lesson to anyone in his life. That may well be true.

For Barnabas, Jews are not God's covenantal people, by circumcising their babies, keeping Sabbath, keeping ksher. In fact, Jews have never been God's covenantal people. Why? Because of what happened when they were given God's covenant, God's agreement. When God gave the Law to Moses, how did it work? God gave the Law to Moses on Mount Sinai, according to Barnabas, quoting the Old Testament.Moses, though, learns that the people at the foot of the mountain are engaged in wild and lawless activities. They built idols for themselves, which they are worshipping. He goes down and he sees that it's true, and he throws the tablets of stone from his hands, smashing them into smithereens.

According to Barnabas, this shows that the Jews violated the covenant when it was given, and that the covenant was broken, literally broken, from the hands of Moses. Jews never were the covenantal people, because they broke the covenant the second they received it. According to Barnabas, the covenant was never restored to the Jewish people. They were misled into thinking that these laws that were given to Moses were to be taken literally. Instead they were to be taken figuratively, and the Jews never realized it. God, according to Barnabas, has now created a new people to replace the disobedient people of the Jews. In other words, the Christians are the fulfillment of the Scriptures. The Scriptures are the Christian books. This then, this Letter of Barnabas, is one of the earliest and most virulent Christian writings in opposition to Jews and Judaism.

The opposition that Barnabas evidences makes historical sense, even if it violates our modern moral sense. In order for non-Jewish Christians in his day to claim that they stood in a special relationship with the God Who created the world and Who chose Israel to be His people, these Christians had to show that the Jews were not God's people, because if the Jews were God's people, then who were the Christians? Christians had to show that the Jews were not God's people. This point of view became increasingly prominent in the second century.

For example, there was a second-century Christian philosopher named Justin, who is known to history as Justin Martyr because he eventually suffered martyrdom for his faith. Justin Martyr proclaimed, around the year 150, that God had given the Jews circumcision so that Jews could be easily recognized and set apart for persecution. That's why God gave circumcision. The Christian apologist Tertullian, whom we've met before, writing around the year 200, claimed that Jerusalem had been destroyed by the Romans as a punishment for the Jewish rejection of Jesus. Some of the same kind of polemic.

Most vitriolic of all was a Christian preacher of the late second century named Melito. Melito lived in the city of Sardis; he was a bishop there, who wrote a sermon that claimed that by killing Jesus, Jews were guilty of killing their own God. Melito understood that Jews were responsible for killing Jesus, so that Jews are responsible for killing God. This is the first instance we know about of any Christian charging Jews with the sin of deicide, the sin of murdering God. These are not very pleasant teachings of polemic, by these early Christian proto-orthodox authors. But it's important for us to place these accusations against the Jews in their own historical context, not in order to excuse this polemic at all, because this polemic led to horrendous acts of anti-Semitism. But in their day, these accusations were being made by a tiny, oppressed minority that felt defenseless against a larger Roman society.

Again, I'm not trying to justify this polemic, but I am trying to explain it. These Christians making these claims about Jews were a very small persecuted sect who felt defenseless. They wanted to maintain, in fact, that they, the Christians, were not a new and suspect religious sect. They wanted to claim they were old, they had antiquity. Their traditions were ancient, as ancient, in fact, as the Law of Moses. To claim the Law of Moses for themselves, though, they had to reject the claim of Jews to have the Law of Moses, which meant that these Christians necessarily had to attack Jews.

These attacks may have been simply defensive posturing by Christians, in the early years. Problems, though, arose when Christians acquired more converts and more power and eventually complete power, religious and secular. After the conversion of the Roman emperor Constantine in the fourth century, Christians could exercise real social, economic, and military force. They took the anti-Jewish claims of their predecessors such as Barnabas quite literally, and they maintained that Jews were the enemies of their own God, and therefore had to be punished and destroyed. The ugly painful and notorious history of Christian anti-Semitism is, in some ways, a direct result of writings such as these.

Lecture Eighteen
The Apocalypse of Peter

Scope:

We have already seen one Apocalypse of Peter, a gnostic document discovered at Nag Hammadi. In this lecture, we consider one other, which is completely unrelated, a proto-orthodox composition that represents the first surviving narrative of a guided tour of heaven and hell, a forerunner of Dante's *Divine Comedy*. In the account, Jesus shows the apostle Peter the eternal blessings of the saved and, in somewhat more graphic detail, the eternal torments of the damned, who are condemned to suffer fates commensurate with the sins they committed in life. In the end, the account is meant not only to evoke ethical behavior from its readers through some rather lurid scare tactics, but also to show that, appearances notwithstanding, it is God who is sovereign over this world and who will have the final say.

Outline

I. To this point in the course, we have considered early Christian pseudonymous gospels, acts, and epistles.

    A. These are three of the four genres that are also represented in the New Testament. The fourth is the apocalypse genre, represented in the New Testament by only one book, the Revelation of John.

    B. There are non-canonical apocalypses, as well, the earliest of which is an apocalypse allegedly written by Jesus' closest disciple, Simon Peter.

    C. This is the first surviving Christian account of a guided tour of heaven and hell, a precursor of Dante's *Divine Comedy*.

II. To understand the text, we need to set it in a broader literary and historical context.

    A. The *apocalypse* genre originally emerged in Jewish circles and is closely connected with a Jewish worldview (*apocalypticism*) that arose about 200 years before the ministry of Jesus.

        1. Many Jews had long held to a theology that indicated that God blessed here on earth those who did his will but punished those who did evil. According to this older view (found throughout much of the Hebrew Bible), people suffer when they oppose God.

2. But incidents arose in which foreign powers oppressed Jews precisely for trying to be Jewish. It was difficult to believe that God caused cruel suffering on Jews for trying to keep his law.

3. Some Jews began to believe, then, that this suffering came not from God but from God's cosmic enemies (especially the Devil), who had been temporarily granted charge of this world and were determined to harm anyone who sided with God.

B. This new worldview of apocalypticism was dualistic (there are two forces in the world: good and evil, God and the Devil) and pessimistic (things are going to get worse in this world until, literally, all hell breaks out), yet it affirmed the ultimate sovereignty of God (he would soon enter into judgment with the forces of evil to bring in his good kingdom on earth).

C. One of the ways apocalyptic thinkers expressed their views was through a kind of writing called an "apocalypse."

1. In general, this genre consisted of pseudonymous writings that narrated a revelation given by God through a heavenly mediator (e.g., an angel), in which the mundane realities of earth (e.g., current sufferings and future vindication) were explained in light of the ultimate truths of heaven.

2. In some of these apocalypses, a prophet is shown a symbolic vision that mysteriously describes the future fate of the earth, when the forces of evil will be overthrown and God's kingdom will come (such as in the Book of Daniel in the Hebrew Bible).

3. In others, a prophet is taken up into heaven to see the heavenly realities that foreshadowed the ultimate triumph of God on earth (such as in the Book of Revelation).

D. Originally, these apocalypses were concerned with the fate of the earth and of people on it. God had created this world, and he would redeem it. These books, in other words, were theodicies, attempts to explain how evil and suffering could exist in a world created and maintained by an all-powerful and loving God.

E. But Christians who later adopted this apocalyptic worldview became, over time, less concerned with the salvation of this world and more concerned with the salvation of each person's soul.

    1. This is a shift away from the teachings of Jesus, who appears to have thought that there was to be a real physical overturn of the forces of evil here on earth when God brought in a good kingdom for his people.

    2. When this never happened, Christians began to transmute the original apocalyptic message of a future kingdom on earth into a spiritual kingdom in heaven.

    3. In other words, when the original expectation of the overthrow of forces of evil here in this world never occurred, Christians began to emphasize, instead, the salvation of the soul in the world beyond. Heaven and hell then became centrally important categories.

III. This transformation of emphases can be seen in the Apocalypse of Peter.

    A. The book was unknown until it was discovered in a monk's tomb in 1886.

    B. But it was mentioned by authors of the late second century; thus, it was written possibly within fifty years of the Revelation of John.

    C. The account begins with Jesus teaching his disciples on the Mount of Olives, and the disciples asking when the end will come.

    D. Jesus then describes the future—his return as judge of the earth and the torments and ecstasies awaiting people at his judgment—in such a way that gives one the sense that he is actually taking his followers on a tour of the places of the damned and blessed.

        1. The torments are particularly lurid and show that the punishments of the damned match their crimes (blasphemers are hanged by their tongues over eternal fire; adulterers, by other bodily parts; and so on).

2. The blessings are less graphic but are clearly meant to convey the sense of eternal bliss for those who experience them.

IV. The author of this firsthand narrative (allegedly Peter himself) had several major points to make with his account.

A. Anyone who sides with God will reap a reward; anyone who opposes God will pay an eternal and horrific price.

B. Ultimately—appearances notwithstanding—God is in control of all that happens in this world.

C. In other words, this account, like other early Christian apocalypses, is not meant merely to scare people into avoiding certain kinds of behavior—lying, committing adultery, blaspheming, relying on wealth, and so on—but also to explain that the evil and suffering of this age will be resolved in the next; that what happens here will be overturned there; that those who succeed by being wicked now will pay an eternal price later. In contrast, those who suffer for doing what is right now will be vindicated forever, as God shows once and for all that he and he alone is sovereign over this world.

Essential Reading:

J. K. Elliott, *Apocryphal New Testament*, pp.593–612.

Martha Himmelfarb, *Tours of Hell: An Apocryphal Form in Jewish and Christian Literature*.

Supplementary Reading:

Edgar Hennecke and Wilhelm Schneemelcher, eds., *New Testament Apocrypha*, vol. 2, pp. 620–638.

Questions to Consider:

1. What other kinds of theodicies (explanations of how there can be evil in a world controlled by an all-powerful and all-loving God) have been put forth to make sense of suffering? How does the apocalyptic mode of theodicy compare and contrast with other kinds?

2. Why do you suppose apocalyptic thinking survives in some Christian circles still today but appears, for the most part, to be absent from the "mainstream" churches?

Lecture Eighteen—Transcript
The Apocalypse of Peter

To this point in our course, we've considered early Christian, pseudonymous gospels, acts, and epistles. These are three of the four genres represented, also, in the New Testament. The fourth genre in the New Testament is the apocalypse, represented in the canon of the New Testament by only one book, the Revelation of John.

There are non-canonical apocalypses as well, though, the earliest of which is an apocalypse allegedly written by Jesus' closest disciple, Simon Peter. This book is different from the Coptic Apocalypse of Peter discovered at Nag Hammadi, that we discussed in an earlier lecture. The one we'll be considering now is the first surviving Christian account of a guided tour of heaven and hell, a precursor of Dante's *Divine Comedy*.

To understand this very interesting text from the ancient Christian church, we need to set it in its own broader literary and historical context. The apocalypse genre originally emerged in Jewish circles, and is closely connected with the Jewish world view known as apocalypticism. I've described apocalypticism in a previous lecture. But I need to review some of the historical background at this point in order to make sense of this genre, the apocalypse. So, some historical background to apocalypticism.

Many Jews, for centuries before Jesus, had held to a theological point of view that indicated that God blessed, here on earth, those who did his will, but punished those who did evil. This, of course, is a view that continues to be held by Christians and Jews and many others today—that when something wrong happens it's because it's a punishment for something you've done, and if you prosper it's because God, or the gods or the fates, are looking out for you.

Within the Jewish tradition, the older view of God rewarding those who do his will and punishing those who don't is found, especially in the prophets, throughout the Hebrew Bible. According to the Hebrew prophets, people suffer when they oppose God. But, as we saw in an earlier lecture, incidents arose in the history of Israel in which foreign powers oppressed the Israelites, and later oppressed Jews, precisely for trying to be Jewish. It was difficult for many people Jewish people to believe that God was causing cruel suffering on Jews for trying to keep his law. And so some Jewish thinkers began to understand that suffering came, not from God, but from God's cosmic enemies, especially the Devil, who had been temporarily granted charge of this world and were determined to harm anyone who sided with God.

This new point of view, this apocalyptic point of view, is not found in most of the Hebrew Bible, the Old Testament. In most of the Hebrew Bible, you don't find a single word about the Devil as God's personal enemy. You do find this talk, though, in apocalyptic texts that were written after the Bible. I should point out that Satan does appear in the Book of Job. But Satan in the Book of Job is the adversary of humans, but he's not the evil Devil, God's cosmic enemy. In fact, he's a member of God's counsel, up in the heavenly places. The word Satan, *HaSatan* in Hebrew, simply means "the adversary". At a later time, when apocalyptic thought developed, about 200 years before Jesus' ministry, this Satan figure had become God's cosmic enemy, the Devil.

This new apocalyptic worldview that emerged after most of the Hebrew Bible was written, but prior to the advent of Christianity, about 200 years before Jesus ministry, consisted of four major tenets to the apocalyptic world view. First, dualism. Apocalyptic Jews were dualistic, maintaining that there were two forces in the world; there were the forces of God and the forces of the Devil. There's good and evil—God and the Devil. God has His angels, the Devil has his demons. God has the power of life, the Devil has the power of death. God has the power of righteousness, the Devil has the power of sin. These are cosmic powers that are in the world, and people are obedient to one set of powers or the other. Everybody lines up either with good or evil.

Moreover, it was understood that history as we know it divides into two ages, corresponding to the two powers. The present age that we live in is an age of evil, controlled by evil forces. But there is an age that's coming that will be good, controlled by God. God is going to intervene in this evil age and overthrow the powers of evil, and bring in His good kingdom here on earth. Two ages of this world: this age controlled by evil; the future age, the coming age, controlled by God. The first characteristic of apocalypticism, then, is that it was dualistic.

Second, apocalypticists were pessimistic. Apocalypticists that things were going to get worse in this age. We were not going to be able to improve our lot by throwing more money into the welfare system, improving our national defenses, by fighting terrorists abroad and at home. We weren't going to be able to make our lives better by putting more cops on the beat or more teachers in the classroom. Nothing that we do is going to improve things in this age, because things are going to get worse. The powers of evil are in control of this age, and they are going to continue to assert their powers till the end when, literally, all hell breaks out.

Third characteristic of these systems—they believed in vindication. Ultimately God was going to have the last word. God was going to vindicate His name and creation, by overthrowing the forces of evil and bringing His good kingdom here on earth. When He did so, there would be a judgment for all who sided with the forces of evil, and there would be a resurrection of dead people. People would be raised from the dead to face judgment. A person should not think that they can side with the forces of evil and prosper by it, become rich, become powerful, and then die and get away with it. For apocalypticists, you can't get away with it, because God's going to raise you from the dead, you're going to face judgment, and there's nothing you can do to stop it. Third characteristic, then, vindication.

Fourth characteristic—imminence. This end of the age was going to come very soon. It was right around the corner. Things had gotten about as bad as they possibly could get, God was soon going to intervene and bring in His good kingdom. When is it going to happen? "Truly, I tell you, some of you standing here will not taste death, before they see that the kingdom of God has come in power." The words of Jesus—Mark, Chapter 9, Verse 1. "Truly, I tell you, this generation will not pass away before all these things take place," says Jesus, Mark Chapter 13, Verse 30.

Jesus and his followers were apocalyptic Jews, expecting the imminent end of the age, expecting that God would soon intervene in the course of history and bring in His good kingdom here on earth, in which there would be no more evil, no more suffering, no more hatred, no more war, no more disease, no more drought, no more famine, no more death. It would be a perfect utopian kingdom, in which love and God would reign supreme.

One of the ways apocalyptic thinkers, from around the time of Jesus and afterwards, expressed their views was from a kind of writing, a genre of writing, scholars have called apocalypse. There were a lot of apocalypses written in the ancient world. It was a common genre among Jewish and Christian apocalyptic thinkers. When people today read the Book of Revelation, it seems very odd, very peculiar, unlike anything else they ever read. For many Christians, this is, serves as, an indication or a sign of its inspiration. There's nothing like it that exists anywhere in our experience. But in the ancient world, in fact, there were a lot of books like this that existed. In fact, it was an entire genre of literature.

We have a number of ancient writings from both Jews and Christians that are of this genre, the apocalypse. In general, the characteristics of the genre are as follows. First, most apocalypses are pseudonymous writings. They are written in the name of somebody who is famous, and so they are forged in the sense that whoever is writing them claims to be a famous person that they are not. Second, the genre of usually pseudonymous writings consist of a narrated revelation given by God. God has revealed something to the person writing it, who is portraying himself as a prophet. That's why the genre is called an apocalypse. An apocalypse means "an unveiling" or "a revealing." It's the Greek equivalent of the Latin word "revelation." Apocalypse and revelation are synonyms.

Revelation is given by God, and it is narrated by the prophet who is writing the text. This revelation is mediated by a heavenly mediator, for example, an angel will give the revelation and then explain it to the person who receives it. That is the third characteristic—heavenly mediator. Fourth characteristic; this revelation shows mundane realities on earth that can be explained in light of the ultimate truths of heaven. So the revelation tries to make sense of what's happening here on earth, in light of ultimate realities in the world above. Those are the characteristics of most apocalypses.

There are actually two kind of apocalypses that we find in the ancient writings, by both Jews and Christians. The first kind of apocalypse is one in which the prophet is shown a symbolic vision, which mysteriously describes the future fate of the earth when the forces of evil are overthrown and God's kingdom will come. So the prophet has a symbolic vision of future events on earth. An example of this actually does occur in the Hebrew Bible. The last book of the Hebrew Bible to be written was the Book of Daniel, which is an apocalypse. In Daniel chapter 7, there's a vision that the prophet has which is an apocalyptic vision. He sees four beasts rising fast out of the sea one after the other. These are terrible, horrible, powerful beasts who take over the world. The fourth is the worst of all, more terrible than all the beasts before him. Finally, though, the prophet sees coming from heaven, instead of from the sea, "one like the Son of Man." When this one like the Son of Man comes on the clouds of heaven, the beasts are destroyed; the kingdoms are taken over from the beasts and given to the one like the Son of Man, who then has rule, power, and dominion, for ever and ever.

This is an account of four kingdoms that will take over the world prior to the giving of the kingdom to God's own people, done in the Book of Daniel in the Old Testament, a book that is written pseudonymously in the name of a prophet allegedly living in the sixth century B.C., but probably actually written in the second century B.C. So this is the first type of apocalypse, a vision of the future fate of the earth.

A second type of apocalypse is one in which a prophet is actually taken up into heaven in order to see the heavenly realities that foreshadow the ultimate triumph of God here on earth. This second type, where a prophet actually goes up into heaven, is found in the New Testament Book of Revelation, in which a prophet, named John, is taken up through a window in heaven and goes up to the heavenly realm. He ascends through this window and observes the throne of God, on which is sitting God Himself; and then he has a vision of subsequent events that take place in heaven, reflecting events that take place here on earth.

It's a highly symbolic, highly metaphoric vision that he has. He sees seven seals of a large scroll that are broken, and after the seal is broken a set of catastrophes happen on earth. After the seventh seal is broken, instead of a final catastrophe on earth, we're introduced to seven angels who blow trumpets. Each time an angel blows a trumpet, more disasters happen on earth, until the seventh trumpet, after which there's a period of silence, followed by seven angels who appear with seven bowls of God's wrath, which are poured out on the earth one at a time.

After all of these series of judgments, and persecutions, and oppressions, and wars, and famines that take place on earth, finally the end comes, in which God sends Christ back to earth from heaven to set up a perfect kingdom on earth, a millennial kingdom. At the end of the book, the prophet sees a new heaven and a new earth, a

Jerusalem descending from heaven, alighting on the earth, a place where people who have followed God will live forever, where there will be no more tears, because God will wipe away every tear. There will be no more sin or hatred or war or death. This then is the Book of Revelation, describing the future fate of the earth by a prophet who has been taken up to the heavenly realm.

Both types of apocalypses—both those in which there is a vision given to the prophet and one in which the prophet is taken up into heaven—both of them are concerned with the fate of the earth and with people on it. The idea lying behind these books is that God had created this world; it had gone bad because of evil forces. But God would destroy these forces and redeem this world, so that life eternal would be lived here in this world. In short, these books are theodicies, explanations of God's justice. They try to explain how it is there can be evil and suffering, in a world created and maintained by an all-powerful and loving God. If God is all-powerful, surely He can stop the suffering people are experiencing. If He is loving, surely he wants to stop the suffering people are experiencing. Why, then, doesn't He stop it? According to these apocalypses, God is going to stop the suffering in this world. If people can hold on for just a little while, He will bring in his good kingdom.

Christians living somewhat later than the first century adopted this apocalyptic worldview over time. Christians eventually became less concerned with the salvation of this material world, and became more concerned with the salvation of each person's soul. This was a shift away from the teachings of Jesus, who appears to have thought that there was to be a real physical overturn of the forces of evil here on earth, when God brought in a good kingdom for His people. When this never happened—when God never did intervene and this world never was transformed—Christians began to transmute the original apocalyptic message of a future kingdom on earth into a spiritual kingdom in heaven. Rather than thinking in terms of what would happen here in the future, people began thinking in terms of what would happen up in heaven when a person died.

The original expectation of the overthrow of forces of evil here in this world, when it never occurred, led Christians to begin to emphasize the salvation of the individual soul in the world beyond. When this happened is when Heaven and Hell became centrally important categories for Christian theology. You look in vain, in most of the New Testament, for any discussion of Heaven and Hell as we think of it today, as a place that a soul goes to when it dies. That's a development that transpires later in Christianity, as soon as the apocalyptic vision of the earliest Christians failed to materialize.

This transformation of emphasis—from a future kingdom of God on earth to heaven after you die and hell after you die—this transformation of emphasis can be seen already in the Apocalypse of Peter. The Apocalypse of Peter was unknown throughout the Middle Ages, until it was discovered in modern times, in the year 1886. As it turns out, the Apocalypse of Peter was discovered in the same manuscript as the Gospel of Peter, which, as you know, was buried with a monk sometime in the early Middle Ages. The same manuscript which has the Gospel of Peter has the Apocalypse of Peter.

The book, though, was mentioned earlier, even though it wasn't known in manuscript form in the Middle Ages. It was mentioned by authors of the late second century, some of whom thought that this book, the Apocalypse of Peter, should have been included within the canon of the New Testament. There were debates over whether this book should be written; some of the debates had to do with whether Peter actually wrote the account or not. I mentioned in the previous lecture that people in antiquity realized that some works were forged, and there were debates over whether this particular book was forged or not. The Christians ended up deciding, of course, not to include it in the canon. So the Book of Revelations is the only apocalypse included in the New Testament.

This account is very interesting. It begins with Jesus teaching his disciples on the Mount of Olives. His disciples ask him when the end is going to come. Let me read you some excerpts from first chapter. It begins with a kind of title: "The second coming of Christ and resurrection of the dead, which Christ revealed through Peter." So this is a book that involves a revelation, an apocalypse, about the future, the second coming, which is given in a mediated way, through Jesus to Peter, who then is being portrayed as the prophet. This is fitting our categorization of what a genre of apocalypse looks like.

> When the Lord was seated upon the Mount of Olives, his disciples came to him, and we besought and entreated him separately.

"We," because the author is going to be claiming to be Peter himself.

> We implored him, saying, "Declare to us, what are the signs of your coming and the end of the world?

They want to know what the end is going to be like. Jesus then begins to tell them. He tells them in words that sound familiar to those who know their New Testament. Jesus says:

> "Learn a parable from the fig tree. As soon as its shoots have come forth and the twigs grown, the end of the world shall come." And I, Peter, answered and said to him, "Interpret the fig tree to me. How can we understand it?" The Master said to me, "Do you not understand that the fig tree is the house of Israel? Verily, I say to you, when twigs sprout forth in the last days, then shall come false Christs. They'll come, awake expectations and say, 'I am the Christ who has come before the end of the world.'"

This is a very interesting passage. It's like what we find in Matthew, Chapter 24, when Jesus describes the wars and the rumors of wars that will happen at the end of time, earthquakes, disasters in many places, and at the very end the moon will turn to blood, the sun will stop giving its light, the stars will fall from heaven. Then the Son of Man will come, send his angels to collect the people from every corner of the earth at the end of time. And the disciples want to know when this will be, and Jesus says, "Learn the lesson from the fig tree; when the fig tree puts forth its leaves, you know that summer is near. So, too, when you see these things you know that he is near, he is at the very gates."

This is a very interesting prophecy, in part because it's been a significant prophecy for fundamentalists in modern times. The best selling book of the 1970s in America, apart from the Bible, was a book that took this and other prophecies to indicate what was to transpire in our own future, when the world was going to come to an end. The book was written by an author named Hal Lindsey. It's a book that many of you may know of, called *The Late Great Planet Earth*, in which Hal Lindsey predicted that the world was going to end when Jesus returned in glory, sometime in the late 1980's. Hal Lindsey indicated that this had to happen by the year 1988.

Why 1988? Well, because of the parable of the fig tree found in Matthew. Jesus says, "When the fig tree puts forth its leaves you know the summer is near, so too when these things take place, you know the end is near." It goes on to say, "This generation will not pass away before all these things take place." Well, what does it mean, though? Well, Hal Lindsey interprets it the same way the Apocalypse of Peter does. The fig tree putting forth its leaves—well, in Scripture, fig tree refers to Israel in the Old Testament. What does it mean that the fig tree puts forth its leaves? Well, that's the fig tree coming back to life, after lying dormant through the winter. When does Israel come back to life? Well, when Israel retakes the land and establishes itself as a sovereign state, 1948.

"This generation will not pass away before all these things take place." How long is a generation in the Bible? It's forty years. So we know that's 1948 plus forty years—"this generation will not pass away"—Jesus must be returning before 1988. Or so Hal Lindsey said in the 1970s. He sold millions of books based on this declaration, a very interesting book, *The Late Great Planet Earth*, which spells out in considerable detail what will happen at the end of time, when Jesus returns. Of course, it didn't happen; and as typically happens when the predictions of the future don't transpire, then Hal Lindsey wrote other books which changed the predictions.

The Apocalypse of Peter did not give anything so precise as 1948 or 1988; we're simply told that this will happen at some time, when the fig tree puts forth its leaves. The book goes on to explain what will happen in the future judgment. What is most interesting is that the future judgment is concerned not so much with the fate of the earth, although that does come into play some. It involves, much more, the fate of the individual souls.

Christ shows Peter what it will be like in the afterlife for people who have disobeyed God. "He showed me in his right hand the souls of all peoples." Christ holds all people within his hands.

> On the palm of his right hand, the image of that which shall be accomplished on the last day and how the righteous and the sinners shall be separated and how those who are upright at heart will fare and how the evil doers will be rooted out to all eternity.

> Behold now what shall come upon them in the last days, when the day of God and the day of the decision of the judgment of God comes, says Jesus.

And he goes on and gives a description—a description of the glories of Heaven and of the torments of Hell. As typically happens in these Christian descriptions of Heaven and Hell, the bliss of the saved is described in very glowing terms. But bliss cannot be described in particularly graphic terms. There's only so many ways you can talk about somebody being happy. On the other hand, there are numerous ways you can talk about somebody being tormented, and so there are rather lurid and graphic descriptions of what it will be like in Hell. And we are given this description.

> Then shall men and women come to the place prepared for them by their tongues wherewith they have blasphemed the way of righteousness they shall be hanged up, there spread under them unquenchable fire so that they shall not escape it.

So the people who commit blasphemy are hanged by their tongues forever over flames of eternal fire.

> Again, behold, there were two women. They hung them up by their neck and by their hair. They shall cast them into the pit. Who are these women who are hanged by their hair? These are those who plaited their hair, not to make themselves beautiful, but to turn them to fornication, that they might ensnare the souls of men to perdition.

So women who have braided their hair to make themselves attractive will be hanged by their hair over eternal fire. The men who lay with them in fornication shall by hung by other bodily parts.

> They are hanged by their loins in the place of fire. They shall say to one another, "We didn't know that we shall come to everlasting punishment."

I guess they didn't. Had they known, they wouldn't have done that.

Besides those there are others—men and women gnawing their tongues.

> These they shall torment with red hot irons and burn out their eyes. These are those who slander and doubt my righteousness. Other men and women whose works were done in deceitfulness shall have their lips cut off.

If you deceive you have your lips cut off.

Fire enters into their mouth and their entrails. These are they who caused the martyrs to die by their lying. In another place full of filth they cast men and women up to their knees. These are ones who loved money and took usury.

So if you lend out your money at interest you end up in pits of filth.

There shall be another place very high. The men and women whose feet slipped shall go rolling down into a place where there is fear. And again, while the fire that is prepared flows, they mount up and fall down again and continually to fall down. They shall be tormented forever. These are those who did not honor their father and their mother, etc....

He goes through and describes how people will be punished for their sins, and in most cases the punishment corresponds to the sins they committed during their life. This is what people can expect during the afterlife, according to the Apocalypse of Peter.

Well, there are several major points this author wants to make. One obvious point that he's trying to make is that anyone who sides with God is going to reap a reward, but anyone who opposes God will pay an eternal and horrific price. Ultimately, appearances notwithstanding, this shows that God is in control of this world and all that happens in it. You may think that people are sinning, doing horrible things, oppressing other people, killing, doing all sorts of harmful, hateful things and they are getting with it. No. According to this account, they are not. God, ultimately, is going to have the last say. The last say, though, involves not just a future kingdom on earth. It actually involves the afterlife of Heaven and Hell.

These accounts—like the other earlier Christian apocalypses, they're not meant merely to scare people into avoiding certain kinds of behavior. They are also meant to explain how it is there is evil and suffering in this age, and how that evil and suffering will be resolved in the next age. What happens here will be overturned there; those who succeed in being wicked now will pay an eternal price later, whereas those who suffer for doing what is right in this age will be vindicated forever, as God shows once and for all that He alone is sovereign over this world. In any event, this Apocalypse gets to that idea, not by describing a future kingdom of God in this material world. Instead, it describes the torments and the blessings of the damned and the saved in the afterlife, in Hell and in Heaven.

Lecture Nineteen
The Rise of Early Christian Orthodoxy

Scope:

To this point in the course, we have considered a range of pseudepigraphical works, documents both "orthodox" and "heretical" forged in the names of the apostles, fabricated to authenticate one or another understanding of the Christian faith. In this lecture, we consider broader issues in the struggles for dominance among various forms of Christianity. The standard view of the emergence of orthodoxy was proffered by the fourth-century church father Eusebius, who maintained that orthodoxy was the view taught by Jesus and his apostles and was held by the majority of Christians at all times, with heresies representing deviations of the true faith, espoused by willful and demonically inspired persons intent on perverting the truth. That perspective was significantly challenged in the twentieth century by Walter Bauer, who argued that different forms of Christianity were dominant in different parts of Christendom in the early centuries, until one form, that best attested in the church of Rome, extended its influence and came to overpower all others, labeling its opponents heretics and rewriting, then, the history of the conflict.

Outline

I. We have covered a wide range of early Christian beliefs and practices in our lectures to this point.

    A. We have seen remarkable diversity among the Christian groups that we know of from the second and third centuries.

        1. Ebionites thought that Christ was a human being, a righteous man adopted by God at his baptism to be the Son of God (adoptionistic).

        2. Marcionites thought that Jesus was completely God and only seemed to be human (docetic).

        3. Gnostics thought that Jesus was a man, but Christ was a God (separationist).

        4. The proto-orthodox view agreed with the Ebionites that Jesus was a man but disagreed with them when they said that Jesus was not God. They disagreed with Gnostics, believing instead that Jesus was both God and man.

B. Each of these groups had authoritative books that claimed to represent the views of Jesus and his apostles.

    1. Ebionites used the Gospel of Matthew.

    2. Those who separated the Jesus from the Christ used the Gospel of Mark.

    3. Marcionites used the Gospel of Luke.

    4. Followers of Valentinus used the Gospel of John.

C. But only one of these early Christian groups emerged as victorious in the struggle to win converts and to establish the "true" nature of Christianity. This victorious group shaped for all time what Christians would believe and which Scriptures they would accept.

D. How, though, did this one group establish itself as dominant and virtually eliminate all traces of both its opponents and the various Scriptures they revered?

II. The traditional answer to this question derives from Eusebius, the fourth-century "father of church history."

A. Eusebius is one of the most important authors of Christian antiquity.

    1. He figured prominently in the theological disputes of his own day and was well connected politically.

    2. Most significantly, he wrote the first history of Christianity, discussing the course of the Christian religion from the days of Jesus down to his own time.

    3. Eusebius's *Ecclesiastical History*, as the book is called, was written in ten volumes and is still available today. The book is one of the most important writings of antiquity, the source of much of our information about early Christianity.

B. The book discusses numerous topics: the spread of Christianity, the rise of important Christian churches, opposition by Jewish authorities, persecution by governmental officials, and significant early Christian leaders and writers.

C. We owe our knowledge of numerous Christian writings to Eusebius, which he quotes at length and which otherwise have been lost.

D. And it is to Eusebius that we owe what was to become the classical view of the relationship of diverse Christian groups, or as he would put it, the relationship between orthodoxy and heresy.

1. According to this view, orthodoxy is and always has been the true view advocated by Jesus and his followers and by the vast majority of Christians, the "great church," ever since.

2. Heresy, in this view, is always a corruption of the truth, spawned by a malevolent apostate from the truth with only a small, if occasionally pestiferous, following. Heresy, in other words, is always a late, derivative, corrupt minority view.

3. Orthodoxy involves certain great truths: that there is one God who is the creator of the world; that Jesus is his son who is both God and man; that Jesus died for the sins of the world and was physically raised by God from the dead; that there is also a Holy Spirit who, with God and Jesus, forms one God; and that these views are taught by the books truly written by Jesus' own apostles. Heresies denied or corrupted one or another of these views.

E. This "classical view" of the relationship of orthodoxy and heresy held the field for sixteen centuries.

III. A major shift in thinking came only in modern times, with the discovery of other early Christian writings and a critical appraisal of the biases at work in Eusebius's account.

A. The bombshell was dropped in 1934 by Walter Bauer, a German scholar, in a groundbreaking book, *Orthodoxy and Heresy in Earliest Christianity*.

B. Bauer maintained that Eusebius had not given an objective account of the relationship of early Christian groups but had rewritten the history of Christian internal conflicts to validate the victory of the orthodox party that he represented. As evidence, he cited the letter of 1 Clement, which details the doctrine of apostolic succession.

C. Rather than being the original view always shared by the majority of Christians, what later came to be known as orthodoxy was just one of the numerous forms of Christianity in the early centuries, the one that ended up acquiring the majority of converts over time, then rewrote the history of the conflict to make it appear that this view had always been the majority one. Writings in support of other views were systematically eliminated from the historical record.

D. But traces of the earlier conflict managed to survive. Bauer's book proceeds by going region by region, examining these surviving traces and showing that virtually everywhere we look—Egypt, Syria, Asia Minor—the *earliest* attested forms of Christianity are in fact non-orthodox, for example, Gnostic or Marcionite.

E. There were, of course, pockets of believers who held the views that later became dominant, but these were not the majority everywhere.

    1. They *were*, though, the majority in the city of Rome.

    2. That ended up being significant because, as this group happened to be located in the capital of the empire, it was able to use its vast resources and administrative skill to exert influence on churches in surrounding areas and, then, throughout the world.

    3. Thus, by the beginning of the fourth century, it was the *Roman* form of Christianity that was dominant, with the *Roman* church, or the *Roman Catholic Church*, that determined the course of future Christianity.

IV. Today, nearly seventy years after Bauer's breakthrough, no one subscribes to his views wholesale, but his basic understanding of early Christianity is enormously influential.

A. We have since made additional discoveries—most significantly, the Nag Hammadi library—that appear to support his perspective.

B. Early Christianity appears now to be widely diverse, not basically monolithic, as Eusebius would have had us believe.

    1. This can be seen in our very earliest sources. The apostle Paul, for example, appears to be fighting *Christian* opponents in virtually every one of his letters—and these are addressed to churches that he himself founded! What of the churches he did not found?

    2. We have also become increasingly aware of other forms of Christianity not even dealt with much by Bauer (such as the Ebionites).

C. Moreover—and this is perhaps the most significant point in this discussion for the purposes of this course—each of these groups appears to have had its own literature, books allegedly written by apostles of Jesus (as we have seen throughout this course) authorizing the theological views of the group.

D. As Bauer recognized, the production and dissemination of literature was extremely important in the struggles between these various Christian groups.

    1. Christians on all sides wrote tractates supporting their own perspectives and attacking the perspectives of others.

    2. Christians used letters to various churches to urge them to ignore and remove teachers who taught beliefs and practices contrary to those thought to be true.

    3. Some Christians forged documents in the names of Jesus' apostles to support their own points of view.

    4. Some Christians who were copying the texts of earlier writings (by hand, necessarily) changed what they said to make them appear more orthodox (as we will see in a later lecture).

    5. And Christians of all sorts began compiling lists of books that they accepted as canonical authorities and excluded other books as being heretical forgeries.

V. In conclusion, we can say that the group that won these battles ended up deciding *which* books would be included in the Scriptures and which would be left outside, either as unworthy of canonical status (e.g., the Epistle of Barnabas) or as heretical forgeries (e.g., the Gospel of Peter).

A. How, though, can we be certain that they got it "right" (for example, about which books were actually written by apostles)?

B. And how did the process of forming the orthodox canon take place? Who decided which books should be included? On what grounds? And when?

C. We will address some of these questions in the following lectures.

Essential Reading:

Walter Bauer, *Orthodoxy and Heresy in Earliest Christianity*.

Bart D. Ehrman, *The Orthodox Corruption of Scripture*, ch. 1.

Supplementary Reading:

Glenn F. Chesnut, *The First Christian Histories*.

Robert M. Grant, *Jesus after the Gospels*.

Elaine Pagels, *The Gnostic Gospels*.

Questions to Consider:

1. Explain how such discoveries as the Nag Hammadi library might call into question Eusebius's understanding of the relationship of orthodoxy and heresy. Then, taking the other position, assume that Eusebius was right; how might you explain the existence of these gnostic books?

2. If the "winners always write the history," how can we *ever* be sure about what happened in the past?

Lecture Nineteen—Transcript
The Rise of Early Christian Orthodoxy

We've covered a wide range of early Christian beliefs and practices in our lectures up to this point. We've seen that there was a remarkable diversity among the Christian groups that we know of from the second and third centuries; for example, the Ebionites, the Marcionites, the Gnostics, the proto-orthodox.

We can see these differences in a number of different areas of theological reflection. One area to see it in is especially in the area of Christology. The Ebionites thought that Christ was a human being, a righteous man, more righteous than anyone else, a good Jewish man who followed the Jewish law and, as a result of being more righteous than anyone else, was chosen by God, adopted by God at his baptism, in order to be the Son of God. This stood in sharp contrast with the view of the Marcionites. Whereas the Ebionites though that Jesus was a righteous man, the Marcionites thought that Jesus was God, completely God, so much God that he wasn't human at all. Jesus only seemed to be human. So they had a docetic Christology, rather than the adoptionistic Christology of the Ebionites.

Most Gnostics had a different point of view. Gnostics thought that Jesus was a man, but Christ was a God, a divine aeon who came from above and came into Jesus at his baptism, empowering him for his ministry, allowing him to do miracles to deliver his fantastic teachings, but then leaving Jesus prior to his death, so that on the cross, Jesus cries out, "My God, my God, why have you left me behind?" because the divine aeon had left Jesus prior to his death. This, then, would be a separationist kind of Christology, one that separated the man Jesus from the divine Christ. This is different from the Ebionite adoptionism and the Marcionite docetism.

But there was also a proto-orthodox view, which denied what each of the other parties have said, while affirming some aspects of what the parties have said. The proto-orthodox agreed with the Ebionites that Jesus was a man, but they disagreed when the Ebionites said that Jesus was not God, because for the proto-orthodox Jesus was God. And so they agreed with the Marcionites that Jesus was God, but they disagreed when the Marcionites said he was not a man. They agreed with the Gnostics that there was Jesus and Christ. But they disagreed when they said they were two different beings. For the proto-orthodox there was one person, Jesus Christ, who was both

God and man. The proto-orthodox Christology emerged, in some respects, in response to the various groups that they were attacking.

These various groups, with their various Christologies, also had different views of God, different views of the world, different views of what human beings were, different views of most major theological issues. What is striking is that each of these groups had authoritative books that they claimed represented the views of Jesus and the apostles both, that they could use in support of their own perspectives. It's not just that the proto-orthodox had Scriptures that supported their views; all of these groups had Scriptures that could support each of their different views.

Strikingly, these various groups could use books that eventually made it into the New Testament canon. There's a very interesting passage from the proto-orthodox heresiologist, Irenaeus, writing around the year 180, in his five-book *Against the Heresies* that we've referred to earlier in this course. In this interesting passage, Irenaeus points out that the various heretical groups used one or the other of the gospels that made into the New Testament.

The Ebionites, he says, used the Gospel of Matthew. Why? Well, because Matthew is the most Jewish of the Gospels and the Ebionites were Jewish Christians. Those who separated the Jesus from the Christ, he says, use the Gospel of Mark; which makes sense, because as I've pointed out, in Mark's Gospel the spirit comes into Jesus at his baptism, then Jesus cries out, "Why have you forsaken me?" at the end, showing, possibly, a separationist view. According to Irenaeus, those who were Marcionite used the Gospel of Luke, the most Gentile of our Gospels, in their opinion. Moreover, those who were followers of Valentinus used the Gospel of John, because this endorsed a kind of understanding of Jesus as one who is a divine person, who comes down to reveal the truth that can set you free.

Each of these four groups, says Irenaeus, used one of the four Gospels; and where they went wrong, he said, is in using just one of the Gospels instead of having all four. Irenaeus, an advocate of proto-orthodoxy, maintained that there were four Gospels and that we needed all four to have a complete understanding of who Jesus was.

We know that there were other groups that had additional gospels, the Gospel of Thomas, the Gospel of Truth, the Gospel of Philip, and others. Some groups had more than one other gospel. Some groups probably had many gospels at their disposal to endorse their views.

It's striking that, despite the fact that there's such a range of Christian beliefs—so many different groups advocating so many different theologies with so many different kinds of Scripture—that there was, in the end, only one that emerged as victorious. There was one group that ended up winning the struggle to acquire converts and to establish the true nature of Christianity. This victorious group shaped for all time what Christians would believe, and they determined for all time which Scriptures would be accepted as canonical. How, though, did they do it? How did this one group establish itself as dominant and virtually eliminate all traces of both its opponents and the various Scriptures that they revered? This is the question that we'll be dealing with in the present lecture.

The traditional answer comes to us from Eusebius, the fourth-century "father of church history" whom we've met before. As we've seen, Eusebius was one of the most important authors of Christian antiquity. He was a highly educated and aristocratic a Christian who was well connected politically and well-situated in the theological disputes of his day. Most significantly for subsequent history of early Christianity is that he wrote the first account of the course of the Christian religion from the days of Jesus down to his own time, early fourth century. Eusebius's ten-volume *Ecclesiastical History*, as it's called, the ten-volume church history, was one of the most important writings to come to us from antiquity. It's the source of much of our information about early Christianity.

Eusebius's book discusses numerous topics: The spread of Christianity; the rise of important Christian churches in significant locations; the opposition to Christianity by Jewish authorities early on; internal Christian conflicts; heresy and orthodoxy; the persecution of Christians by governmental officials; also it discusses significant Christian leaders and writers.

It is to Eusebius that we owe our knowledge of numerous Christian writings that, otherwise, we don't have. He quotes many books that were available to him as sources, and when he quotes them, then we have them. In most cases, we don't have manuscripts of these other books, so it's to Eusebius that we owe much of our knowledge of what was written by Christians during the first three centuries. And it is to Eusebius that we owe what has become the classical understanding of the relationship between various diverse Christian groups, or as Eusebius would put it, the relationship between orthodoxy and heresy.

According to Eusebius's view—which became the standard view throughout the Middle Ages down to the modern period—according to Eusebius's view, orthodoxy is and always has been the teaching of the main Christian churches. Eusebius understood that theological doctrines were espoused by the majority of Christians; these theological doctrines were once actually taught by Jesus himself to his apostles. His apostles then wrote them down and handed them down orally, and they were the majority view throughout history.

Heresy, in this view, is always a corruption of this truth that was passed down by Jesus to his apostles. Heresy is a corruption of the truth, spawned, in almost every case, by a malevolent apostate from the truth. There's always an individual who comes along who decides to pervert or corrupt the truth. He acquires a small, if occasionally pestiferous, following, who become then a group of heretics. Heresy, in Eusebius's understanding, is always— necessarily, by definition—a late, derivative, corrupt, minority view. That's what heresy is. orthodoxy is the original truth that was held by the majority of churches at all time.

Orthodoxy, for Eusebius, involves certain great truths that were always espoused by Christians: that there is only one God who is the creator of this world; that Jesus is his son and that Jesus is both God and human; that Jesus died for the sins of the world and was physically raised from the dead; that there is also a Holy Spirit who is with God and who is God, just as Jesus is—a Holy Spirit that, with Jesus, forms with God the Father a Trinity. These views, according to Eusebius, are taught by the books that were truly written by Jesus' apostles. Heresies denied or corrupted one or another of these views. This classical view of the relationship of orthodoxy and heresy held the field among Christian thinkers for sixteen centuries. Of course, it's still held by many people today. Ultimately though, it goes back to Eusebius.

A major shift in thinking came only in modern times, with the discovery of other early Christian writings, and a critical appraisal of the biases that were at work in Eusebius's account. The bombshell was dropped, in 1934, by a prominent German scholar named Walter Bauer, in a book that was entitled *Orthodoxy and Heresy in Earliest*

Christianity. This is arguably the most important book written on early Christianity in modern times, Bauer's book on orthodoxy and heresy.

Bauer maintained that Eusebius had not given an objective account of the relationship of early Christian groups, but that Eusebius had rewritten the history of internal conflicts so as to validate the victory of the orthodox party that he himself represented. Rather than being the original view that had always been shared by the majority of Christians, according to Bauer, what later came to be known as orthodoxy was originally just one of the numerous forms of Christianity in the early centuries. It was the one form of Christianity that eventually ended up acquiring the majority of converts over time. Once it had done that, and once it had wiped out the opposition, then it rewrote the history of the conflict to make it appear that it had always been the majority view. Writings that had supported other views—for example, writings by Ebionites and by Marcionites and by Gnostics—were either systematically destroyed, or else simply not copied so that they didn't survive into the Middle Ages, down to today; so that we didn't expect, in fact, that there were larger groups of other people who had other views. All we had was the orthodox view by Eusebius and others like him, who said that their view had always been the view of the majority of the Christian churches.

But as it turns out, even though according to Bauer this is how it happened that orthodoxy emerged as victorious, traces of the earlier conflict managed to survive. Bauer's book proceeds by going region by region through the early church—geographical region by geographical region, examining these surviving traces and showing that virtually everywhere we look—for example, Egypt, Syria, Asia Minor—in virtually every region in which we know there were early Christians, the earliest attested form of Christianity are, in fact, non-orthodox. The Egyptian churches, for example, according to Bauer, were largely Gnostic; Asia Minor was largely populated by Marcionite churches in the second century; and so forth and so on.

There were, of course, according to Bauer, pockets of views that later became dominant. These would be people that I've been calling proto-orthodox. There were proto-orthodox Christians scattered throughout the empire, of course. But these were not the majority everywhere, the way Eusebius makes it out that they were.

©2002 The Teaching Company.

According to Bauer, these proto-orthodox, though, were the majority in the city of Rome, as it happens. And that ends up being significant. This happened to be the form of Christianity in the capital of the empire. As a church in the capital of the empire, it had certain advantages, and it made full use of these advantages that it had.

This church in Rome happened to be a fairly large church, as opposed to other places. Of course, Rome was larger than any other city, and so the number of Christians was larger than it was in other places. Moreover, Rome, the capital, had vast resources that were available to the people who were there. And the administrative skills that were found throughout the city, that helped it run the empire, trickled down into the church, as those who were in the upper classes converted. The church in Rome eventually ended up asserting its influence on churches in surrounding areas, and then throughout the world, according to Bauer. The church in Rome acquired more converts than others, because it used its vast resources and its administrative skills in order to influence other churches.

We have evidence that, in fact, this happened. One piece of evidence that Bauer points to is one of the earliest pieces of writing from outside of the New Testament—in fact, this may be *the* earliest writing from outside the New Testament—it's commonly known as the Letter of First Clement. First Clement is written by the church in Rome to another church, the church in Corinth. It's a rather long letter. The main point of the letter is to deal with a problem that had arisen, not in the church in Rome, but in this other church in Corinth.

What had happened is, there had been some kind of coup in the upper regions of the church in Corinth. There had been a coup in which the presbyters, the leaders of the church, had been kicked out and some other people had come in to take over the leadership of the church. The Christians in Rome were incensed at what had happened, and they write this letter in order to reverse the situation; it's in order to get the Christians in Corinth to reinstate the presbyters from their church. I'll quote parts of this letter, from Chapter 47.

"It is disgraceful," says the Roman church, "exceedingly disgraceful and unworthy of your Christian upbringing to have it reported that because of one or two individuals, the solid and ancient Corinthian church is in revolt against its presbyters." So they've heard about this coup and they're upset about it. They say in this letter that this was completely inappropriate. It's inappropriate, because the presbyters of this church had been appointed by those who had been appointed by apostles, who had been appointed by Jesus, who had come from God. In other words, this letter develops an understanding that later became known as the doctrine of apostolic succession. God sends Jesus, Jesus has his apostles, the apostles appoint the bishops over the churches, the bishops appoint their own successors. And so if you get rid of one of the successors, you are opposing then their predecessors, who were apostles, who were from Jesus, who was from God. By getting rid of the presbyters, in fact, you're opposing God.

This Letter of First Clement, then, is trying to change the situation in Corinth so that it will revert to a situation that the Roman church prefers. The Roman church clearly liked the other presbyters better, and wanted these other presbyters to be in control. Bauer argues that what's going on, then, in First Clement, is that Rome, unsolicited, has tried to intervene in the internal affairs of another church. And it appears from subsequent history that they were successful in doing so. This is the kind of thing that Rome started doing and, in fact, Rome became very good at.

Rome was able to assert itself over other churches. It could do this in a number of ways. It could write letters like this, trying to urge people to change the way they're acting. Rome could use the resources available to them; they had a lot of money available. They could give donations to the other churches, who would elect So-and-so to be their bishop. They could manumit slaves with this money, set slaves free. Well, then which church are the slaves going to go to? Are they going to go to the Marcionite church someplace, or are they going to go to the church that the Roman church says they should go to? Well, according to Bauer, the manumission of slaves allowed for increase of converts, within the churches that agreed with the Roman point of view.

Rome began asserting its influence at the end of the first century, as in the Letter of First Clement. It continued to assert its influence until Roman Christianity started spreading throughout the Roman Empire. Eventually, of course, the Roman emperor converts to Christianity, and that changes everything. Christianity had been growing bit by bit over the years, but when the Roman emperor converted, then there was an explosion in the spread of Christianity. What kind of

Christianity will the Roman emperor convert to? He'll convert to a Roman form of Christianity. Eventually, it's the Roman church that has control of the church throughout the world. The Roman Catholic Church determines the course of future Christianity.

Well, this is quite different from what you get in Eusebius. In Eusebius's understanding, orthodoxy started out as one big thing that everybody subscribed to, beginning with Jesus and his apostles. Heresies were little offshoots that came off of that occasionally. According to Bauer's understanding, Christianity did not start out as one big thing; it started out as a bunch of little things, different geographical regions having different forms of Christianity, only one of which ended up emerging as victorious. It declared itself orthodox, and then it rewrote the history of the engagement.

Many years have passed since Bauer's breakthrough in 1934. And I should say that no-one, to my knowledge, subscribes to his views wholesale. Yet nonetheless, his basic understanding of the relationship between what we call orthodoxy and heresy continues to be enormously influential. In part, that's because we've made additional discoveries since his day—most significantly, the Nag Hammadi library—that appear to support his perspective. Even in Nag Hammadi, there's a range of beliefs represented in the Nag Hammadi library. There's a lot of variety there. There's no monolith, even there. We have just happened to discover this library. This was not a form of Christianity or forms of Christianity that were preserved for us by orthodox writers. These are forms of Christianity that we just happened to find and, as it turns out, what we happened to find supports Bauer's view that there was a wide range of Christian beliefs.

Early Christianity appears, to most scholars today, to have been widely diverse, not basically monolithic the way Eusebius would have had us believe. This is, in fact, can be seen from our earliest sources, that weren't even dealt with by Bauer. Bauer begins his study with the second century. If you go back even into the first century, you are struck by the amazing diversity of Christianity.

Just think about the letters of the apostle Paul. Paul writes letters to Christian churches that he himself founded and, in virtually every letter, he has to oppose people who are taking views that he finds offensive. He writes his letter to the Galatians to attack people who think that to be Christian you have to first become Jewish. He writes his letters to the Corinthians in order to argue that people don't already have spiritual salvation, that full salvation won't be until the second coming of Jesus. There are writings in Paul's name to the Ephesians, to the Colossians, to the Second Thessalonians—letters in his name to First and Second Timothy and to Titus, the Pastoral Epistles, all opposing different forms of heresy, false teaching; later on, the letter of Third Corinthians and other pseudepigrapha. Everywhere Paul turned he had enemies. His enemies thought that they were right and that Paul was wrong. We only have Paul's side of the argument. What if we had all of the sides of the argument? Remember the Ebionites? They thought that Paul was the arch-heretic.

And what about the churches Paul didn't found? What points of view did they have? Well, we've become increasingly aware of other forms of Christianity not dealt with extensively by Bauer, including various groups of Gnostics and Jewish Christians that Bauer simply didn't know about. Moreover, and perhaps this is the most significant point in this discussion for the purposes of this course, each of these different groups appear to have had its own literature— books allegedly written by apostles of Jesus, authorizing the theological views of their group.

As Bauer himself recognized, the production and dissemination of literature was extremely important in the struggles between these various Christian groups. Christianity, unlike other religions in the world, was a literary religion. It's not that Christians could read and write more than other people in the world. In fact, Christians probably tended to be more from the lower classes, and probably could read and write less. Nonetheless, Christianity as a religion— for a reason that we will be examining in the next few lectures—was, in fact, more literary than other religions which simply didn't have religious texts as part of their religion's practices. Christians did, though, and they used literature extensively, especially in these debates between heresy and orthodoxy.

Literature was important in these struggles for five major reasons, in five different ways. First, Christians on all sides wrote tractates supporting their own perspectives and attacking the perspectives of others. That's one way they used literature in these disputes between heresy and orthodoxy, the disputes among the various Christian groups. We've seen this already in the heresiologists, heresy-hunters, like Irenaeus and Tertullian, who write lengthy treatises against the Gnostics, against Marcion, against others.

We've also seen it, though, from the other side. Luckily preserved for us from Nag Hammadi is the Coptic Apocalypse of Peter, which, as with another book found at Nag Hammadi, the Second Treatise of the Great Seth, attacks proto-orthodox Christians for being heretics. Groups on all sides are using literature in order to attack the perspectives of others. That's one way literature is important in these struggles.

Two, Christians use letters to various churches in order to urge them to ignore and remove teachers who taught beliefs and practices contrary to those thought to be true. Not just arguing against points of view and trying to convince people; there are a number of letters that we have that simply tell their readers to get rid of the false teachers. This happens already in the New Testament period. The Pastoral Epistles of First and Second Timothy and Titus, allegedly written by Paul to two of his pastor companions, tell them to get rid of false teachers. He doesn't argue with them. He doesn't say why they are wrong. He simply says, get rid of them. Same thing of Ignatius of Antioch, writing after the New Testament period in the early second century, writing to different churches, telling them get rid of the false teachers. It is simply understood that those who don't agree with Ignatius are false teachers, and are to be gotten rid of.

Three, some Christians, as we have seen throughout this course, forged documents in the name of Jesus' apostles in order to support their own points of view. This is a third way Christians are using literature, by forging apostolic documents. So somebody writes a gospel and says that it's Peter who is writing the gospel, even though it wasn't; somebody writes a gospel and says that it's Thomas that is writing the gospel, even though it wasn't. Somebody claims to be Paul and writes the Letter of First Timothy, which makes it into the canon of Scripture. Someone else writes a letter claiming to be Paul; it's called Third Corinthians, and it doesn't get into the canon of Scripture. Christians are forging documents in the name of apostles—some of them become scriptural; others do not—in order to explain their points of view. This a third way the Christians are using literature in these conflicts.

Four, some Christians who are copying the texts of earlier writers, copying them by hand—they didn't have Xerox machines yet, they didn't have moveable type, they had to copy them by hand—sometimes when they copied these books by hand, they changed the texts that they copied in order to make the texts appear to be more orthodox than they originally were. This happened even with the texts that made it into the canon. I'm going to be devoting an entire lecture to this interesting question of scribes changing their texts, in order to make them say what they wanted them to mean. I'll be devoting a lecture to that later. So that's a fourth way Christians were using literature.

Fifth, Christians of all sorts begin to compile lists of all books that they accept as canonical authorities, and exclude other books as heretical forgeries. In other words, Christians are using literature by compiling canons of sacred texts. Only one canon ends up surviving. Those are the five ways that Christians used literature in their struggles of heresy and orthodoxy.

In conclusion, we can say that the group that won these battles ended up deciding which books would be included in the Scriptures and which books would be left outside, either as unworthy of canonical status, or as flat-out heretical forgeries. How, though, can we be certain that they got it right? How can we be certain that the decisions about what to include in the canon—based on who wrote these books, that they were apostolic authorities—how can we be certain that these decisions were right? For example, how can we know that the Gospel of Thomas was a forgery in Thomas' name, but that the Gospel of John actually was written by the son of Zebedee? And how did the process of forming this orthodox canon actually take place? Who decided which books should be included, on what grounds and when? These will be some of the questions we will be addressing in the following lectures.

Lecture Twenty
Beginnings of the Canon

Scope:

The canon of the New Testament emerged in the context of the struggles among different forms of Christianity. Christianity was unique among the religions of the Greco-Roman world in emphasizing the importance of doctrine (that is, proper belief) instead of cultic practice and in its exclusivity (that is, its insistence that it was the only true religion). The different versions of the "truth" among various Christian groups, though, required some means of arbitration. To establish the credentials of their claims, all early Christian groups appealed to the writings of the apostles. When no such writings existed, they were forged. The formation of the New Testament canon, then, represents a sensible development among Christians to root their understandings of God, Christ, the world, salvation, and so on in the teachings of Jesus and his apostles.

Outline

I. Up to this point, we have been exploring the wide diversity of early Christianity. It is out of this context of varying beliefs and practices that the canon of the New Testament emerged.

   A. Given the wide range of gospels, epistles, acts, and apocalypses produced by early Christians, how is it that these twenty-seven books, and only these books, came to be recognized as Scripture?

   B. This is the question we will begin to address with this lecture.

II. First, we need to consider some fundamental aspects of early Christianity.

   A. Christianity, of course, was simply one of many religions in the Roman world.

   B. In the Roman Empire, religion was prominent in society.
      1. Religion was needed, it was felt, because people knew they could not control the forces of life that could harm them.
      2. Religion was a way of getting what people needed that they couldn't provide for themselves.

3. Ancient religions were almost entirely polytheistic. The only exception was Judaism.
4. As a rule, ancient religions were ways of worshiping the gods. They emphasized cultic acts (sacrifices and prayers) but did not at all emphasize the importance of belief. *Cult*, in this context, meant "care of the gods." What one believed about the gods was a private matter, not a necessary component of religion itself.
5. As odd as it might seem to us, these ancient religions had no beliefs to affirm, theologies to embrace, or creeds to recite. There was no such thing as heresy and orthodoxy in ancient religions. There were no ethics; ethics was a matter for philosophy, not religion.

C. Judaism was partially an exception, in that one needed to believe in only the one true God who called Israel to be his people and instructed them how to live in community and to worship him.

D. Christianity emerged out of Judaism and was, from the outset, a religion that emphasized belief. It stressed that Jews needed to believe that Jesus was the messiah promised from God who could save people from their sins.
1. Early on, then, Christianity was structured as a religion not so much of cultic act as of proper belief. Christians believed that Jesus was the sacrifice.
2. Unlike the other religions, Christianity was exclusivistic. Christians insisted that to worship *their* god, you could not worship any other gods. This is probably one of the reasons Christianity spread as far as it did.
3. As it developed and spread, Christianity refined more and more what it meant to believe in Jesus. And as different opinions emerged over who Jesus was and what it meant to believe in him, different theologies developed and came to be embraced, and controversies emerged and creeds came into being, with different Christian groups affirming different things.
4. Each group needed its own authority for what it believed, and each claimed that its beliefs were rooted in the teachings of Jesus' own apostles and, through them, to Jesus himself.

5. In particular, each group stressed that its authorities could be found in its own sacred writings, allegedly produced by the apostles of Jesus. The canonization of the New Testament is the end result of this set of controversies over apostolic authority.

III. The Christian idea of having written authority for beliefs about God goes back to Jesus himself because, as a Jew, Jesus himself had a sacred set of authorities, the Hebrew Bible.

  A. There was not a universally accepted canon of Jewish Scriptures in Jesus' day, but there was a widely agreed upon group of sacred books, especially the Torah, the Law of Moses, sometimes called the *Pentateuch*.

  B. Jesus, as a Jewish rabbi, accepted the authority of these sacred Scriptures and interpreted them for his followers.

  C. After his death, his followers continued to accept these Scriptures (although some, including such groups as the Marcionites and some Gnostics, maintained that they were not really inspired by the one true God).

  D. But for their particular beliefs about Jesus and the new relationship with God that he had effected, his followers soon started turning to new authorities.

IV. The development of a distinctively Christian set of authorities was under way already during the New Testament period itself.

  A. The words of Jesus were soon taken to be authoritative (1 Cor. 7:14; 1 Tim. 5:18).

  B. So, too, the writings of his own apostles soon came to be seen as authoritative (2 Pet. 3:16).

  C. This movement to consider apostolic writings as sacred authorities makes considerable sense. Christianity was rooted in the life and teachings of Jesus, but Jesus left no writings. His apostles, then, were the link back to Jesus, whether for the Ebionites, the Marcionites, the Gnostics, or the proto-orthodox.

V. These apostolic links were made more plausible by the existence of written documents allegedly produced by the apostles themselves. There are four kinds of writings that should be differentiated: genuine, anonymous, homonymous, and pseudonymous books.

A. Books that were actually written by apostles.

    1. The writings of Paul would be included in this group.

    2. Critical scholars are not confident that any of the other books of the New Testament can be placed in this category (and even six of the thirteen letters allegedly written by Paul are debated).

B. Anonymous books that were later attributed to the apostles (e.g., the four gospels of the New Testament).

C. Homonymous books, that is, those written by someone with the same name as an apostle (e.g., the Book of James).

D. Pseudonymous books, that is, those forged in the name of an apostle or group of apostles (e.g., 2 Peter, the Gospel of Peter, and the Apocalypse of Peter).

VI. All four kinds of books were in wide circulation in the early centuries of Christianity. All were claimed as having apostolic authority to settle disputes over what to believe and how to act. But only twenty-seven of them eventually were included in the canon of the New Testament. How did those books eventually acquire sacred status? Who made the decisions? When did they make them? And on what grounds? Those are the questions we will consider in our next lecture.

Essential Reading:

Harry Gamble, "Canon: New Testament," *Anchor Bible Dictionary*, vol. I, pp. 852–861.

Supplementary Reading:

Harry Gamble, *The New Testament Canon: Its Making and Meaning*.

Bruce Metzger, *The Canon of the New Testament*.

Hans von Campenhausen, *The Formation of the Christian Bible*.

Questions to Consider:

1. Many Christians today find it difficult to imagine a religion that is not based on proper "belief." Can you think of religions in our world of that kind?

2. If all the ancient groups of Christians maintained that they had ties back to Jesus through the apostles, is it possible for us today to decide, historically, which of the groups, if any, was *right* in its claims?

Lecture Twenty—Transcript
Beginnings of the Canon

Up to this point, we've been exploring the wide diversity of early Christianity. It is out of this context of varying beliefs and practices that the canon of the New Testament emerged. Given the wide range of gospels, epistles, acts, apocalypses produced by early Christians, how is it that these 27 books of our New Testament, and only these 27 books, came to be recognized as Scripture? This is the question that we'll begin to address with this lecture.

First, we need to consider some fundamental aspects of early Christianity, to set the historical context for the discussion of the emergence of the Christian canon. Christianity, of course, was simply one of the many religions of the Roman Empire. In Roman antiquity, religion was prominent throughout society. Virtually everybody was religious in one sense or another. Very rare was it that anyone in the ancient world would declare themselves an atheist. Virtually everybody accepted the existence of the gods. Some people may not worship the gods extensively, but virtually everybody agreed that the gods at least existed—except for the rare philosopher who might come along, who might deny the existence of the gods. But virtually everybody agreed that there were gods, and that they were to be worshipped. Religion was ubiquitous in that world, and widely felt to be needed.

Why needed? People in the ancient world recognized the need for religion, because they knew that they themselves, as mere mortals, were not able to control the forces of life that could harm them. They could not control drought or war or disease. Moreover, they couldn't control things in their personal lives that they might think would benefit them. They couldn't control if the neighbor next door would fall in love with them. They couldn't control whether their child would get sick. They couldn't control whether the crops would grow, whether their cattle would survive. Religion was a way of getting things that people needed, when otherwise they couldn't provide them for themselves. They needed somebody more powerful than themselves, to give them what they need. Who is more powerful than us? The gods. The gods provide what we need in our daily lives.

Ancient religions were almost entirely polytheistic. The only major exception, of course, was Judaism. Virtually everybody in the Roman world worshipped many gods, thinking that there were many gods, involved with many aspects of human life. There were the national state gods; the great gods who were the gods of Greek and Roman mythology, Zeus and Athena and Ares. There were the gods of localities. Cities had their own gods that they would worship. There were gods of different places, gods of forests, gods of meadows, gods of rivers, gods of houses. There were gods over all sorts of functions in human life, gods to help the crops grow, gods to bring the rain, gods who would bring healing if somebody were sick, gods of childbirth, gods of the pantry, gods of the heart, gods for virtually everything in human life.

Religion in the ancient world was a way of worshipping these gods. The gods were worshipped by cultic acts, especially acts of prayer, showing submission to the gods, making requests to the gods and, in particular, cultic acts of sacrifice. The word cult, in this context, does not refer to what we normally think of as a "cult," as some kind of wild offshoot of religion. Cult, in this context, actually comes from the Latin term *cultus deorum,*, which literally means "care of the gods." Just as in English *agriculture* means "care of the fields," *cultus deorum* means "care of the gods."

Cult, then, was a way of worshipping the gods, taking care of their needs so that they would take care of your needs. How does one take care of the needs of the gods? By sacrifices of either animals or things that have been grown, vegetable and animal sacrifices. Sacrifices could be performed in the home, for example; before somebody would eat they would normally pour our a little bit of wine, maybe offer a bit of grain on a family altar before eating. Sacrifices in a big way, though, usually animal sacrifices, were performed in temples located in cities and towns, some small, some large—many run by priests who were often appointed, in the major religions, as political appointments. People who had political aspirations were appointed to the priesthood, to take care of the sacrifices to the gods.

There were special festivals where people would celebrate the birth of a god or some great thing that the god had done. Many of the festivals were sponsored by the state. Throughout these ancient religions—and there were many of them scattered throughout the Roman empire; in addition to the state Roman religion, every region had its own religion in every city and town, each family had their own personal gods that could be worshipped—throughout all of these religions, through all of these cultic expressions of adorations and worship, what is striking to modern people is that there is very little evidence of the importance of belief in any of these systems.

As it turns out, when you read the ancient sources you discover that ancient people did not think that belief about the gods was a significant matter for personal and public religion. What mattered was that the god was taken care of, through cultic sacrifice and prayer. So, of course, you had to believe enough about the gods to believe that they existed, and that they wanted the sacrifices. But beliefs about important aspects of the gods—who they were, what they demanded, what they wanted, what they wanted in terms of your personal ethical life, what they wanted you to believe about them, what they wanted you to believe about what they had done— these were matters of mythology perhaps, matters of stories to be told about the gods, and they were matters for philosophers to talk about; but they simply did not enter into personal religion. As odd as it might seem to us, ancient Roman religions had no beliefs to affirm, no theologies to embrace, no creeds to recite. When people went to worship the gods in the temple, they performed sacrifices; they didn't recite creeds or state their theological beliefs. These were irrelevant to religion; they were private matters or philosophical matters.

As a result, in ancient Roman religion, and Greek religion, and every other religion we know from this period, there was no such thing as heresy and orthodoxy, because there was no insistence on right belief and wrong belief. There was only an insistence that people perform the cultic rituals that were necessary to appease the gods. Interestingly, there were no ethics, either, normally associated with religion. These religions did not promote particular forms of morality. There were some things that you could do that would be offensive to the gods; it was quite offensive, for example, to commit patricide. There were a few things that were prescribed by these religions. But by and large, these religions were not about ethics. It didn't matter if you had just committed adultery with your next door neighbor and went to perform sacrifice. Zeus didn't care about that. Zeus himself was, in fact, often committing adultery. This wasn't an issue for these ancient religions. It didn't matter if you cheated on your taxes. It didn't matter if you stabbed your colleague in the back so you could get up to the top of the heap in your business. None of those things mattered for religion. They mattered for philosophy; but these were not matters that the gods were overly concerned about.

The one exception to what I'm laying out as religion was Judaism. In key respects, Judaism differed from other religions in the world. It wasn't a majority religion, of course. As I've pointed out, possibly at this time period, second to third century, Jews were probably something like seven percent of the empire's religion. But they were different, and everybody recognized them as different. The Jews, unlike other religions, maintained that there's only one God to worship—the God of Israel, Who chose Israel to be His people. This is the only God that Jews choose to worship. The Jews don't say everybody should worship this one God; the Jews thought this is our God, this is the God that we worship. You can worship whatever God you want to, but this is the God that we're worshipping, and we're not worshipping other gods.

Since God had chosen them to be His people, He had given them His Law, which was to be followed so that people could continue to be in a close covenantal relationship with this God. This Law was written, a written text that Jews considered to be sacred. This will be significant for our understanding of the development of the Christian canon, because Christianity, of course, emerges from Judaism. The ancient Jews believed in only the one true God, Who called Israel to be His people and instructed them on how to live in community and how to worship Him. Christianity started out as a sect within Judaism and was, from the outset, a religion that, unlike other religions, emphasized belief. Christianity, from the outset, emphasized belief. It stressed, in the early stages, that Jews needed to believe that Jesus was the Messiah promised from this God, Who had given the sacred Law. Jesus was the Messiah whom God had promised in the Scriptures, who would save his people from their sins.

We see this in our earliest authors, this emphasis on the need to accept, by belief, Jesus. For example, the apostle Paul. Paul is our earliest Christian author. He was writing before the Gospels were written. His letters were written probably about twenty to thirty years after Jesus' death. In them he explains that Christ is the fulfillment of the written law of the Jews. Paul is a Jew, who sees Jesus Christ as the fulfillment of a law God had given to Moses; that one needed to believe in Jesus; that, in fact, belief in Jesus was everything. It's the only way to be right with God, is by having faith in Jesus. Early on, then, Christianity was structured as a religion, not so much of cultic acts as of proper belief. Christians did not perform sacrifices to their God, because they believed Jesus was the sacrifice. Their religion was based on accepting the sacrifice of Jesus, rather then performing their own sacrifice. It was a religion of belief rather than of cultic act.

Moreover, unlike the other religions of the Roman Empire, Christianity was exclusivistic. This made Christianity stand out. None of the other religions insisted that if you were to worship their God, you couldn't worship other gods. The ancient religions, in fact, were inclusivistic. They included one another. If you decided to worship a new god—suppose you moved to a new town and you decided to adopt the deity of that town—that didn't mean you had to give up your other gods. All the gods exist. They all deserve cultic worship, and so people throughout the empire would worship all the gods they wanted to. None of these religions was exclusivistic, until Christianity came along.

Christianity insisted that the only way to be right with God is by believing in Jesus, that if you didn't believe in Jesus you could not be right with God. The other religions, therefore, were wrong, so that Christianity could be right. This was a unique thing in the ancient world. It's also one of the reasons Christianity probably spread as quickly and as far as it did, because when Christianity's missionaries would go out and convert people, when they converted people, they not only acquired followers to Christianity, they took away followers to the other religions.

In other words, suppose you have got two evangelists, for two different gods. You have a pagan evangelist trying to get people to believe in Zeus, and you've got a Christian evangelist who is trying to get people to believe in Jesus, and they are talking to a crowd of a hundred pagans. Suppose both of these speakers are equally persuasive, so that people who previously didn't worship Zeus, suppose half of them start worshipping Zeus, but the other half start worshipping Jesus. What happens? They all started out as pagans, but paganism loses half of its followers and doesn't gain anyone. Christianity gains fifty and doesn't lose anyone. Christianity destroys the other religions in its way, precisely because it's exclusivistic and it's the only religion that's exclusivistic.

The exclusivism of early Christianity exaggerated the need for early Christians to be correct in what they believed. Christians ended up having to refine more and more what it meant to believe in Jesus: Who was he; who was he really? What did he stand for? What did he teach? What are we to believe if we are to be right? If salvation is based on being right and what you believe, then you better know what it is that you believe. As it turns out though, different opinions emerged over who Jesus was, and what it meant to believe in him. Different theologies developed and came to be embraced, and controversies emerged, and creeds came into being, with different Christian groups affirming different things. Each group needed its own authority for what it believed, and each claimed that its beliefs were rooted in the teachings of Jesus' own apostles and, through them, to Jesus himself.

In particular, each group stressed that its authorities could be found in its own sacred writings, allegedly produced by the apostles of Jesus. The canonization of the New Testament is the end result of this set of controversies over apostolic authority. The Christian idea of having a written authority for beliefs about God goes back to Jesus himself, since, as a Jew, Jesus himself had a sacred set of authorities, the Hebrew Bible.

I should say that there was not yet, in Jesus' day, a universally accepted canon of Jewish Scriptures. Eventually there is going to a set canon within Judaism that—in English Bibles, the Old Testament is 39 books. In the Jewish Scriptures, in the Hebrew, it's 22 books. It's the same books, actually; they just number them differently. There is a set canon. In Jesus' day, though, there was not a set canon; except to the extent that in the first century, every Jew that we know about did accept the first five books, the Law of Moses, sometimes called the *Pentateuch*—the first five books: Genesis, Exodus, Leviticus, Numbers, Deuteronomy—as being sacred and having come from God. Eventually, they would also accept other groups of writings; prophets, and a group of writings called, "the writings," which included the wisdom and poetic books of the Hebrew Bible.

The canon was in formation, probably, during the days of Jesus, different groups arguing that different books should be included. But everybody accepted the text of the Torah as being authoritative. Jesus, as a Jewish rabbi, himself accepted the authority of these sacred Scriptures, and he interpreted them for his followers. He had a sacred text, a written authority for what he taught.

There's not much doubt about this, when you study the traditions about Jesus found in the Gospels. Time and again, Jesus quotes the text of Scripture as sacred authority. For example, a man comes up to him in Mark's Gospel, our earliest Gospel, and says, "Master, what must I do to inherit eternal life?" And Jesus says, "Keep the commandments." And the man says, "Well, which ones?" And Jesus enumerates on them; he starts giving the Ten Commandments. Don't kill, don't commit adultery, don't bear false witness, honor your father and mother. In other words, Jesus is affirming that these written texts, these commandments, in fact, are authoritative for how one can stand in a right relationship with God.

An expert in the law comes up to Jesus and says, "What are the two greatest commandments?" And Jesus quotes the Scriptures to show what God really wants. "The first and greatest commandment is that you shall love the Lord your God with all your heart, soul and strength. And you shall love your neighbor as yourself. On these two commandments hang all the law and the prophets," says Jesus.

Jesus isn't the one who makes up the idea, "you shall love your neighbor as yourself." He is quoting Scripture, Leviticus, Chapter 19, Verse 18. He doesn't make up the idea that you should love God with all your heart and soul and strength. He's quoting Scripture, Deuteronomy, Chapter 6. Jesus accepted the Scriptures as authoritative for how people ought to live. He gave his own interpretation of these Scriptures.

> You have heard it said that you shall not commit murder. But I say to you, you shouldn't be angry with somebody. You have heard it said that you shall not commit adultery. But I say to you, you shouldn't lust after a woman in your heart. You have heard it said, "An eye for an eye, a tooth for a tooth." But I say to you that when someone strikes you on the right cheek, turn to him the other also.

These so called antitheses, found in Matthew's Sermon on the Mount—they're called antitheses, because they seem like contrary statements—they are not contrary statements to the law. Jesus here is not denying what the law says, he is interpreting the law.

The law of murder is that you're not supposed to take life away from somebody who is your neighbor. Well, in fact, you should take it a step further; you shouldn't even be angry with your neighbor. The law of adultery is that you shouldn't take your neighbor's wife; well, Jesus interprets this to say, you shouldn't want to take your neighbor's wife. The law of "an eye for an eye, a tooth for a tooth," is a law that the punishment should fit the crime. Jesus is saying that, in fact, you should show mercy and go beyond what the law says. These are interpretations of the law, that presuppose that the law itself is authoritative.

Jesus, then, had written texts that he accepted as authoritative, of importance for one's standing before God. Immediately after his death, Jesus' followers continued to accept the Scriptures. Most of his followers eventually accepted the Scriptures in their Greek translation, which was read more widely throughout the world among Jews who didn't read Hebrew; they could read the Jewish Bible in Greek. But for their particular beliefs about Jesus and the new relationship with God that Jesus had effected, his followers soon had to start turning to other authorities. They had to turn to other authorities to support their beliefs in Jesus. Belief is extremely important to them; they're exclusivitic; they need authorities for these new beliefs, not just the Hebrew Scriptures.

The development of a distinctively Christian set of authorities is what starts the ball of the canon rolling. This development of a distinctively Christian set of authorities, in fact, was already underway during the New Testament period itself, in two ways. First, the words of Jesus soon come to be taken as authoritative—as authoritative, in fact, as the Hebrew Scriptures. We get this early on in one of Paul's letters, First Corinthians. In First Corinthians, Paul will occasionally quote a saying of Jesus and attribute to it the same kind of authority that one would attribute to the text of the Hebrew Bible. For example, First Corinthians, Chapter 7, Verse 10; Paul is talking to people who are married and he says, "To the people who are married I give this command, not I, but the Lord, that the wife should not separate from her husband and the husband should not divorce his wife." Paul comes out against divorce, and he says this command comes not from him, but from the Lord. He's talking about Jesus' words, in which Jesus said that divorce is not to be permitted.

Later on, an author writing in Paul's name, writing in a book that we now call First Timothy, actually calls one of Jesus' sayings "Scripture." This is a very interesting passage in First Timothy, Chapter 5, Verse 18. First Timothy is one of those books in the New Testament that claims to be written by Paul, that scholars are fairly convinced—for reasons that I don't have time to go into now—that Paul himself actually did not write. In Chapter 5, Verse 18, the author is talking about whether you should pay your preacher or not, and he says that you should. You should honor those that labor in preaching and teaching among you, for the Scripture says, "You shall not muzzle an ox while it's treading out the grain;" and it says, "The laborer deserves to be paid."

Well, that's very interesting, these two quotations that he gives. The first is actually from the book of Deuteronomy, "Don't muzzle an ox while it's treading out the grain." In other words, if one is working with you, they should be allowed to eat. But the second quotation that he quotes, that he calls "Scripture," that labor deserves to be paid, is a quotation of the words of Jesus, Matthew, Chapter 10, Verse 10. "The workman is worthy of his hire." In other words, this author, writing near the end of the first century, calls Jesus' words "Scripture."

Interestingly, also within the New Testament period, the writings of Jesus' apostles begin to be accepted as authoritative, just as authoritative as the Scripture. An interesting passage in the Book of Second Peter—which, again, appears to be pseudonymous; it looks like Peter didn't write this book, but somebody else wrote it, probably at the beginning of the second century, say around the year 120—this author is talking about the writings of the apostle Paul. He says, "So also our beloved brother, Paul, wrote to you according to the wisdom given him, speaking of this as he does in all of his letters. There are some things in these letters that are hard to understand," says the author with a bit of understatement, "which the ignorant and unstable twist to their own destruction;" people who are misusing Paul's writings, "as they do," he says, "to the other Scriptures." This author counts Paul's writings among the Scriptures.

Already then, during the New Testament period, we have a bipartite canon developing, in which the words of Jesus and the writings of his apostles are taken as sacred authorities. That bipartite canon is going to emerge eventually in our canon of Scripture, in which we have the Gospels on the one hand and the accounts of Jesus' death and Resurrection, and the writings of his apostles, the Acts, the Epistles and the Apocalypse on the other—a bipartite canon which emerges. We can see its emergence already, within the New Testament period itself.

This movement to consider apostolic writings as sacred authority makes considerable sense. Christianity was rooted in the life and teachings of Jesus. But Jesus left us no writings himself. If Jesus had left us writings, I suppose those would be the Scriptures. But Jesus didn't write anything that we know of. His apostles, then, are the only link that people had back to Jesus. If they want access to Jesus, they have to go through the apostles. This is true of every Christian group. This is true of the Ebionites, the Marcionites, the Gnostics, the proto-orthodox; and so all of these groups claimed links back to Jesus. The Ebionites claimed to follow the teachings of James, who was the brother of Jesus. The Marcionites claimed to follow the teachings of Paul, who was the apostle of Jesus. The Valentinian Gnostics claimed that they followed the teachings of Valentinus and they claimed that Valentinus got his teachings from a guy named Theudas, who was allegedly a follower of Paul, who was the apostle of Christ.

All of these groups are making apostolic links, trying to trace their views through a kind of a genealogy, that traces the teachers back to the teachings of the apostles and, through them, to Jesus. These apostolic links were made more plausible by the existence of written documents, allegedly produced by the apostles themselves. There are four kinds of writings that we probably should differentiate, among these apostolic writings. We've seen this in passing up to this point. Now I want to be explicit about the four kinds of books that we should differentiate among apostolic writings.

First, books actually were written by apostles. We have some genuine apostolic writings, that these apostles actually wrote. As it turns out, we don't have anything written not only by Jesus, but we don't have anything written by any of his twelve disciples, that we know about. It's true that in the New Testament, First Peter, Second Peter claim to be written by Peter; but so, too, does the Coptic Apocalypse of Peter and the other Apocalypse of Peter and the Gospel of Peter. Lots of books claim to be written by Peter. Most scholars think that these books are pseudonymous. We don't have any books that probably were written by Jesus' disciples. But we do have writings written by Paul, who was considered by the early Christians to be an apostle. Thirteen of the books in the New Testament claim to be written by Paul. Scholars are confident that at least seven of these actually were written by Paul; there are debates about the other six.

So the first types of apostolic books are the ones actually written by apostles, and we can at least include the seven undisputed Pauline epistles. A second kind of books are books that are not authentic, but are anonymous, that later came to be attributed to apostles; for example, in the New Testament, Matthew, Mark, Luke, and John. These books don't claim to be written by people called Matthew, Mark, Luke, and John. They were attributed to Matthew, Mark, Luke, and John only in the second century, decades after they were written. Well, why do people say that Matthew, Mark, Luke, and John wrote them? Because they wanted these books to be tied to apostles; Matthew and John being two of Jesus' disciples, Mark and Luke being companions of apostles—Mark, the secretary of Peter, Luke, the companion of Paul. These books were attributed to apostles, even though they themselves were anonymous. They never claim to be written by apostles, and give no hint within their texts that they were written by apostles.

So you have authentic books, you have anonymous books. The third category, you have homonymous books—an unusual word, but a homonym, somebody who has the same name as someone else. There are some books that are written by somebody who is just writing in his name, but he happens to have the name of somebody who's famous. For example, the name James was very common. Jesus' brother was not the only one named James. There were lots of people named James. The book of James in the New Testament is written by somebody named James, but he doesn't claim to be Jesus' brother. It's homonymous. It was included in the canon, not because it actually was written by James, brother of Jesus, but because people thought it was written by James, brother of Jesus. There are good reasons for thinking otherwise. So that's a third category.

Fourth and finally, books which we've seen already, pseudonymous books; books that are forged in the name of an apostle or a group of apostles. For example, Second Peter, the Gospel of Peter, the Apocalypse of Peter, the Coptic Apocalypse of Peter. All of these are

129

pseudonymous books, written by somebody claiming to be famous, knowing full well that he is not that person but someone else.

In conclusion, all four of these kinds of books were in wide circulation in the early centuries of Christianity. All of them claimed to have apostolic authorities, so as to settle disputes about what to believe and how to act. But only 27 of them came to be included in the canon of the New Testament. How did these books eventually acquire sacred status? Who made the decisions and when did they make them? On what grounds? These are the questions that we'll consider in our next lecture.

Lecture Twenty-One
Formation of the New Testament Canon

Scope:

Contrary to what many people may imagine, the canon of the New Testament—the twenty-seven books that were eventually considered Christian Scripture—did not emerge at the very beginning of the Christian movement. Even though the books that became part of the New Testament were all written during the first century, or soon thereafter, it was not for another 300 years that anyone declared that these books, and only these books, were canonical. The debates about which books to include and which to exclude were long and hard. Some of the earliest "canonical lists," such as the famous Muratorian canon, reveal the criteria involved. For a book to be admitted into the canon, it had to be ancient, attributed to an apostle, used widely, and orthodox. Many of the books that were excluded, of course, were deemed "heretical," even though they had once been considered scriptural authorities by some early Christian groups.

Outline

I. Throughout the course of these lectures, we have seen the wide-ranging beliefs and practices evidenced among various groups of early Christians and looked at some of the sacred authorities different groups appealed to in support of their views.

   A. Many, perhaps most, of these books were either anonymous, only later attributed to the apostles, or blatantly forged in the names of the apostles.

   B. Why did some of these books finally come to be included in the New Testament canon when the others came to be excluded? Who decided which books to include? On what grounds? And when?

II. We will begin with the question of when the canon came into being.

   A. The formation of the New Testament canon was a long, drawn-out process, involving many long years of hard debates and controversy. The debates, in fact, lasted for centuries.

B. During the first 400 years of Christianity, various Christians argued for different collections of books as "the" New Testament, many of them including some or most of the books we are familiar with as the New Testament, but often, other books, as well.

C. It was not until 367 A.D. that *anyone* put forward our twenty-seven books, and only these twenty-seven books, as the New Testament.

D. This was the list first proposed by Athanasius, the powerful bishop of Alexandria, in a letter written to the churches under his jurisdiction.

    1. Even then, the matter was not resolved. Christians in different parts of the world sometimes accepted other books as canonical.

    2. Eventually, Athanasius' view became the almost universally accepted view of Christendom.

III. What led up to this closure of the canon? Probably the best way to get to the issue is to move back closer to the beginning of the process.

    A. We have already seen the leading motivation for the formation of the canon: the conflicts between various Christian groups over what to believe. Among other factors was the need for Christians to differentiate themselves from Jews, who also had a canon of Scripture.

    B. But the need to define "orthodoxy" was, no doubt, the leading motivating factor for the formation of the canon.

        1. Strikingly, one of our best attested authors of the mid-second century, Justin Martyr (c. 150 A.D.) speaks at length about the authority for his views but does not cite specific gospels or insist on a closed canon of Scripture.

        2. Soon after Justin wrote his books in Rome, Marcion began converting large numbers of people to his understanding of the religion.

        3. Only then, did proto-orthodox Christians begin to speak of a fixed canon of Scripture.

        4. Thus, the church father Irenaeus (c. 180 A.D.) argues that just as there are four corners of earth and four winds of heaven that have spread the gospel over the earth, so, too, there must be four and only four gospels!

IV. Some of the factors leading to the formation of the canon can be seen by examining the earliest canonical list that we have from earliest Christianity: the Muratorian canon.

A. The Muratorian canon is a list of books that the anonymous author considered to be part of the New Testament Scripture.

B. It is named for the eighteenth-century scholar L. A. Muratori, who discovered the document in a library in Milan in 1740.

C. This is a seventh-century document, written in ungrammatical Latin. It is a translation of a much earlier Greek original.

D. Scholars have debated when and where the document was produced, but the best evidence indicates that it was written in or around Rome sometime near the end of the second century.

E. The document begins in mid-sentence; all we have is a fragment of the earlier work.

    1. But the first full sentence is suggestive of how the work actually began: "Now the third book of the gospel is that according to Luke." Given that the next, and last, gospel it discusses as part of the canon is John, the Muratorian canon appears to have accepted all four of the gospels now in the New Testament.

    2. It goes on to indicate the other books that it accepts as canonical, in all, twenty-two of the twenty-seven books of our New Testaments. Not mentioned are Hebrews, James, 1 and 2 Peter, and 3 John.

    3. But it accepts additional books, as well: the Wisdom of Solomon and the Apocalypse of Peter.

    4. Moreover, it rejects some books as heretical: Paul's letters to the Alexandrians and the Laodiceans are said to be Marcionite forgeries; other forgeries are attributed to Gnostics.

    5. Further, the Muratorian canon rejects the Shepherd of Hermas, because it was written only "recently" by the brother of the bishop of Rome.

    6. Clearly, for the anonymous author of the Muratorian canon, a book needed to be ancient, apostolic, and orthodox to be accepted as canonical.

V. Thus, we can consider the criteria proto-orthodox Christians used in deciding which books to include in their canon.

   A. A book needed to be ancient: Nothing written long after the time of Jesus could be accepted.

   B. A book needed to be apostolic: written by an apostle or one of their companions.

   C. A book needed to be orthodox: Nothing that advocated a false view of the religion could, of course, be accepted into the canon.

   D. A book needed to be widely recognized throughout the church.

VI. Using these criteria, the proto-orthodox Christians debated which books should belong in the canon.

   A. As we have seen, these debates lasted for centuries.

   B. Even after Athanasius' pronouncement of 367, the matter was disputed; eventually, though, it was this canon that came to be accepted, copied, and read.

   C. Excluded, then, were all the books that embraced alternative points of view, many of which, including most of the pseudonymous writings that we have looked at in this course, were labeled as heretical and forged. Others were orthodox, but not seen as canonical.

   D. One can only imagine what Christianity may have become had some of these other books been included in the canon of Scripture.

Essential Reading:

Harry Gamble, "Canon: New Testament," *Anchor Bible Dictionary*, vol. I, pp. 852–861.

Supplementary Reading:

Harry Gamble, *The New Testament Canon: Its Making and Meaning*.

Bruce Metzger, *The Canon of the New Testament*.

Hans von Campenhausen, *The Formation of the Christian Bible*.

Questions to Consider:

1. In your judgment, should the canon of the New Testament still be considered an open question? That is, should it be possible to include other works in the New Testament (such as the Gospel of Thomas or the Epistle of Barnabas)? And to exclude some that made it in?

2. With the historical information available to us, if we were to apply the criteria used by the proto-orthodox Christians to establish the canon, what books would now be accepted?

Lecture Twenty-One—Transcript
Formation of the New Testament Canon

Throughout the course of these lectures, we've seen the wide range in beliefs and practices evidenced among the early groups of Christians, and we've looked at some of the sacred authorities that different groups appealed to in support of their views. Many, perhaps most, of these apostolic books were either anonymous, only later attributed to the apostles, or blatantly forged in the name of the apostles. Why did some of these apostolic books finally come to be accepted in the New Testament canon when the others came to be excluded? Who decided which books to include, on what grounds, and when? Those questions will be the subject of the present lecture.

As it turns out, and as you may have surmised, the New Testament canon did not drop from the sky, one day in June, soon after Jesus died. The formation of the canon was the result of many years, decades, or even centuries of hard-fought debates and controversies among various Christian groups, and various Christians within each group. This was a long, drawn-out process. We've seen the beginnings already within the New Testament period, when the sayings of Jesus and the writings of his apostles are beginning to take on sacred authority. Jesus' own words, which originally had circulated purely by word of mouth, are taken to be of equal weight to the Scriptures of the Hebrew Bible. The writings of the apostles, soon thereafter, are taken themselves to be authoritative. Eventually, these two kinds of authority will be put together into a canon, the words and teachings and life of Jesus in a set of Gospels, and the writings of the apostles in the other books—a kind of bipartite canon.

During the first 400 years of Christianity, various Christians argued for various types of books and collections as the New Testament, many of them including some or most of the books we're familiar with today as the New Testament, but often including other books as well. We've seen this already, for example, with the Ebionites, who accept a form of Matthew but along with another book, so that they have the Gospel of the Nazarenes, which is an Aramaic translation of Matthew, but they also have the Gospel of the Ebionites; with the Marcionites, who have some truncated version of the Gospel of Luke, and truncated versions of ten of the Pauline Epistles. These are canons that were being formed early on.

Even the proto-orthodox Christians, though, debated about which books to include in their canon. This wasn't a settled issue, early on, even for the proto-orthodox. Which Gospel should be included as canonical? Early on, each community had its own Gospel, so that the gospel that originally had Mark didn't also have Matthew, Luke, and John; they hadn't been written yet. Even after they had been written, though, different geographical regions used one or another, two or maybe three, of these Gospels. At the beginning, all four were not used by the same community.

Some proto-orthodox communities used other Gospels; for example, the Gospel of Peter, used in the village of Rhossus that we know about from Eusebius's discussion of Serapion. This was a proto-orthodox community, evidently, that used Peter, possibly in addition to other Gospels they had available to them. In the region of Syria, none of the four Gospels was used as a separate text, beginning near the end of the second century. In Syria, the gospel consisted of a single book that was called, or is called today, the *Diatessaron*. The *Diatessaron* is a book that is a kind of conflation of the four Gospel accounts into one account. The word *Diatessaron* itself literally means "through the four." It was put together by a writer named Tatian. Tatian lived in Rome for a time, and then moved back to his native Syria and constructed a single book, taking what's found in all four Gospels, making them into one big gospel. And this one big gospel, the *Diatessaron*, was used then by churches in Syria for centuries, even though they were completely proto-orthodox.

The proto-orthodox debated about other books as well. What about the Epistle of Barnabas, included in our earliest complete manuscript of the New Testament as Scripture? As was another book, The Shepherd of Hermas, an early- or mid-second-century text, which is a kind of apocalypse written by an author named Hermas, who lived in Rome, which was accepted as canonical by many Christians, including the famous manuscript Siniaticus—this fourth-century manuscript that included Barnabas as one of Scriptures.

Some Christians thought that First Clement, which we looked at in our previous lecture, was canonical and should be accepted as part of the Scripture. Proto-orthodox Christians, as well as Christians of other groups, had long debates and hard debates about which books should be included in the canon. As odd as it might seem, it was not until the year 367 A.D. that anyone that we know about put forward our 27 books, and only these 27 books, as belonging to the New Testament Scriptures. 367—that's almost 300 years after many of these books were produced, that anyone chose these 27 books as being canonical.

The person who chose the books was Athanasius. Athanasius was a powerful bishop of the city of Alexandria, which was one of the major seats of Christianity in the early centuries. Athanasius was a powerful bishop who, as a young man, had been present at the Council of Nicea, that we've already referred to and we'll talk about in our final lecture in the course as an important council that helped decide many of the theological disputes of its day. As a young man, he had been at the Council of Nicea. When he became older, he became the bishop of Alexandria, and every year he would write a letter to his churches that were under his authority throughout Egypt in order to instruct them when the date of Easter was to be for that following year. They didn't have calendars that told them these things years in advance. It had to be determined every year based on astronomical considerations. In his thirty-ninth such "Festal Letter," as they were called, written in the year 367, Athanasius, in addition to saying when Easter needs to be celebrated, used the occasion, as he always did, to give some pastoral advice to his congregations. This particular year, he wrote out which books should be read as scriptural authorities and which books should not be read. This letter, then, written in the year 367, listed the books that we have as our New Testament, our 27 books.

Some scholars have said that this settled the matter, that when Athanasius wrote this letter, that was the end of the story. In fact, that's not the case. Even in Athanasius' own day and even in his own place, Alexandria, there were other Christian leaders who thought that other books should be included as scriptural. For example, there was a famous Christian teacher in Alexandria, during Athanasius' day, a man named Didymus. Didymus, as it turns out, was blind, so he is commonly known as Didymus the Blind. Didymus the Blind was a famous teacher. He taught the church leader Jerome; he taught Athanasius; he taught a number of other people. He thought that there were other books that should be included in the canon; at least, he quotes other books, such as the Shepherd of Hermas, as being a canonical authority. In other parts of the church, for decades, even centuries, there were disputes about some books that might be considered to be the fringes of the canon. But eventually Athanasius' view became the almost universally accepted view of Christendom. These are the 27 books of the canon.

What led up to this closure of the canon? People today sometimes debate whether the canon is closed or not. Can we add books if we want to? Can we get rid of books we don't like? And, I suppose, technically speaking, the canon's not closed; nobody is going to stop the Christian church at large from deciding to get rid of a book, or add a book. But practically speaking, the reality of the case is they're not going to be any other books added and there aren't going to be any books taken away. For all practical purposes, the canon is closed. Well, what led up to this closure?

We've seen some of the original motivations for this formation of the canon, already in the course. Christians in the early stage needed to have authorities for their views, apostolic authorities, written authorities when the apostles had died. Moreover, there were a number of forged documents going under the names of apostles, that were being used to claim authority from variant views. So one needs to close the canon, and to decide which books are in and which books are out, in order to exclude heretical documents. Moreover, Christians were motivated to formulate a canon precisely in order to differentiate them from the mother religion from which they had emerged. Judaism was developing its own canon of Scripture, and Christians needed to differentiate themselves from the Jews.

In this connection, it's worth making a historical note that Christians appear to have preferred for their books the codex form of a book, which is similar to the books we use today, in which you have a piece of papyrus, in this case, in which you write on both sides of the papyrus. You have a number of pages like this, that end up being sewn together into a book between bindings, so you read both sides and you turn the page. Most ancient books, in fact, almost all books prior to Christianity, were written on scrolls, which were rolled up, and they would simply write on one side and then roll up the scroll; and then to get to a place you would unroll the scroll with one hand and roll it up with the other. Jews, of course, used scrolls for their Scriptures. Some people think that Christians preferred the codex form, they used codices rather than scrolls, precisely in order to differentiate them from the sacred books of the Jews. It's a possibility. It is quite clear that the popularity of the codex form emerged with the emergence of Christian writing in the early centuries of Christianity. And eventually, then, it became popular even for pagan authors.

The need to define what was orthodox and what was not is, no doubt, the leading motivation factor for the formation of the canon. There is some interesting evidence for this view, that the reason the canon got formed was because proto-orthodox Christians wanted to establish orthodoxy and wanted to exclude heretical books. This striking piece of evidence comes to us from the second century.

There is an author that I've mentioned before in this course, named Justin Martyr. As I've indicated, he is called Justin Martyr, not because Martyr is his last name, but because he experienced martyrdom in the second century for his faith. His name was Justin. Justin Martyr, around the year 150, was a popular teacher and speaker in the church of Rome. He wrote down a number of his views. He wrote out several books, of which we have three that survive. These books are usually labeled as *Apologies*. They are called *Apologies*, not because Justin is saying that he's sorry for something that he has said or done; they are Apologies in the technical sense—an *apologia* is literally "a defense," a defense of one's beliefs. So these Apologies are reasoned defenses of Christianity written for their culture despisers.

In the *Apologies* of Justin Martyr, he speaks at length about the authority for his views. Interestingly, he talks about the apostles' writings about Jesus, and he actually quotes what became our Gospels. But he doesn't cite specific Gospels. He doesn't say, for example, "as you can find in the Gospel of Matthew." He doesn't name these books. He calls them "memoirs of the apostles." And he doesn't designate how many of these memoirs are available; he doesn't talk about a closed canon of these Gospels. He simply talks about the authority that is provided by these memoirs written by apostles.

He does quote Matthew, Mark, and Luke—what is now Matthew, Mark, and Luke. So presumably he had these available to him. In two places he may quote the Gospel of John, but scholars are divided on whether he actually knew John or not. It's interesting that Justin never quotes the writings of the apostle Paul. That's interesting, because he's living a hundred years after Paul in Rome; that's interesting, because one of Paul's letters were written to Rome; and it's interesting because we know Paul was known in Rome, because at the same time as Justin, Marcion was in Rome, who advocated that Paul was the apostle to be believed and his canon consisted largely of Paul. Justin never quotes Paul at all. It's not clear why. Maybe it's because he's opposing Marcion.

What is clear is that Justin had no set canon of Scripture, even for the Gospels that he quotes. Soon after Justin wrote his books in Rome, Marcion was beginning to acquire a large number of followers to his understanding of the religion. Strikingly, it was only after that, after Marcion starts acquiring large numbers of converts, after he begins propagating his closed canon of Scripture, that proto-orthodox Christians did begin to speak of a fixed canon. So you see, the piece of evidence is that Justin—writing before Marcion proposed a closed canon, or at least before he was successful in proposing this to a lot of people—Justin didn't have a closed canon, even though he was proto-orthodox. But afterwards, proto-orthodox Christians did start speaking about a closed canon, and started insisting on it.

In the year 180, the Church Father Irenaeus wrote his famous five books *Against the Heresies*, in which he makes a very strong claim that in fact there are and must be four Gospels. His logic may not strike many of us as being overly convincing, even though it is interesting. Irenaeus says, "It is not possible that the Gospels can be either more or fewer in number than they are, for since there are four zones of the world in which we live, and four principal winds, while the church is scattered throughout the world and the pillar and ground of the church is the gospel and the spirit of life, it is fitting that she should have four pillars." So why four Gospels? Well, you have four corners of the earth and four winds. You've got to have four Gospels. As I said, this may not strike us as overly convincing. But his point is that there are four, and only four—Matthew, Mark, Luke, and John. This is just thirty years after Justin was fairly lax in saying what the Gospels were and how many there had to be. This shows that Christians had to formulate their views, probably in response to heretical groups.

How, though, did the proto-orthodox Christians decide which books to include and which books to exclude? What were the factors that led to the formation of a canon as we now have it? One of the best ways to get to that question, to resolve the issue of what criteria the proto-orthodox used to decide what's in and what's out, is by looking at the earliest canonical list that survived from the early church.

The earliest canonical list that we have is a list of Scriptures that is called today the Muratorian canon. This is a list of books that an anonymous author considered to be part of Scripture. Scholars debated when the Muratorian was produced. I will give an argument, after a bit, that it was probably produced near the end of the second century, the second half of the second century. The Muratorian canon is named after the scholar who discovered it, a guy named L.A. Muratori, who then put his name to this canon that he discovered. He discovered this document in a library in Milan in 1740. The document was written in the seventh century, and it's written in highly ungrammatical Latin. It's somewhat difficult to read, because the Latin is not grammatically correct in many places. It looks pretty clear that this was originally written in Greek. So what we have is an ungrammatical Latin translation of a Greek original, probably from the second half of the second century.

It's a very interesting document, even though it's only fragmentary. The entire document didn't survive. The beginning of this shows quite clearly that it didn't survive, but it also gives hints as to what happened preceding the portion that we still have. The Muratorian begins with these words: "But he was present among them. And so he put the fact down in his Gospel. The third book of the Gospel is that according to Luke." Then he goes on to describe that Luke was a physician who after Christ's ascension, ended up writing this gospel. "The fourth book of the Gospels is that of John, one of the disciples." Then he gives the account about how John went about writing his Gospel, the Gospel of John.

Now, since the account begins by saying, "The third book of the Gospel is Luke, the fourth book of the Gospel is John," then it goes on to talk about the Acts and the Epistles, it's pretty clear how this thing originally began. It began by describing two other Gospels. Since the rest of this Gospel canon consists of Luke and John, the third and fourth Gospels, then it's pretty clear that this author had as his first and second Gospels Matthew and Mark. There's no definitive evidence of that. I mean, it could have been, you know, the Gospel of Truth and the Gospel of Peter. But it seems pretty unlikely. This is a proto-orthodox text, as we'll see. So it appears that he's got four Gospels—Matthew, Mark, Luke, and John.

Let me read you excerpts from the rest of this, to give you a sense of what this author considered to be canonical Scripture. He intersperses a number of his comments about what belongs, with comments about how the book came to be written and by whom. I won't read all of it.

"The Acts of the apostles," he says, "were written in one volume." He mentions this after Matthew, Luke, and John—the Acts were written in one volume. The Epistles of Paul he goes on to talk about; "written by Paul, imitating the example of his predecessor John, who wrote to seven churches, only by name and in this order." He's referring to the Book of Revelation, which allegedly was written by John. Chapters 2 and 3 of the Book of Revelation are letters addressed to the churches of Asia Minor. This author is saying Paul, like John, wrote to seven churches. Then he explains, "He wrote first to the Corinthians, second to the Ephesians, third to the Philippians, fourth to the Colossians, fifth to the Galatians, sixth to the Thessalonians and seventh to the Romans."

He goes on to say, "He wrote twice to the Corinthians and the Thessalonians." So, in other words, he has all of these epistles that we have in the New Testament—First and Second Corinthians, First and Second Thessalonians. He goes on to say that "He wrote one letter to Philemon, one to Titus, but two to Timothy for the sake of affection and love. There is extant also," he says, "an epistle of Paul to the Laodiceans and another to the Alexandrians. These are forged in the name of Paul, according to the heresy of Marcion. There are also many others which cannot be received in the general church, for gall cannot be mixed with honey."

He goes on to say that he has an Epistle of Jude and two with a superscription of John. So he has two letters of John. We don't know if they're First and Second John, or Second and Third John or First and Third John, but he's got two of the Johannian epistles. Also are accepted "the Wisdom of Solomon, which was written by friends in his honor. And we accept only the Apocalypses of John and Peter." He goes on to say, "Hermas composed the 'Shepherd' quire recently in our times in the city of Rome, while his brother Pius, the bishop occupied the episcopal seat of the city of Rome. It cannot be published for the people in the church," he says. It should be read, he says, but it cannot be published for the people in the church.

"Finally," he says, "we accept nothing at all of Arsinous, or Valentinus or Miltiades. These also are rejected, who composed the New Book of Psalms from Marcion, together with Basilides and Cataphrygians of Asia…" and then it breaks off in mid-sentence.

This is a very interesting work. In it we're told which books this author accepts as canonical. Strikingly, he accepts 22 of the 27 books of the New Testament. He does not mention the Book of Hebrews or James or First and Second Peter, or Third John, assuming that's the John he doesn't have. But he does accept some books that did not make it into the canon, the Wisdom of Solomon and the Apocalypse of Peter—we've already seen The Apocalypse of Peter. He accepts another book that we haven't discussed here, called the Wisdom of Solomon.

He rejects some books as being heretical. He rejects the letters of Paul to the Alexandrians and to the Laodiceans because, he says, these are Marcionite forgeries. He attributes other forgeries to Gnostics. Moreover, it's interesting that he rejects the Shepherd of Hermas. He says it can be read, so it's not heretical, but he rejects it from the canon because it was written only recently, and it was written by the brother of the bishop of Rome; so it wasn't written by an apostle and it's not very old. So he doesn't accept it as canonical. Clearly other people are accepting it as canonical, and that is why he has to exclude it.

I've mentioned that I think this list came from the second half of the second century. My evidence for that is that, if he's right that Hermas was the brother of the bishop of Rome, we know when his brother Pius was the bishop of Rome; it was around the year 150. Moreover, when you look at the heresies that he's concerned about— he's concerned about Marcionite forgeries and Gnostic forgeries and the people that he names, Valentinus, Arsinous—these are all people living in the second century, so his ultimate concerns are about things going on in the second century. So I think probably he was writing at the end of the second century, possibly around the city or Rome.

This list can be used as a springboard to consider the criteria that became standard fare among proto-orthodox Christians in deciding what to include in their canons of Scripture. There are four major criteria that these proto-orthodox Christians appear to have used, to decide what gets in and what gets out.

First, a book had to be ancient. Nothing written long after Jesus' time could be accepted. That's why this author could say that the Shepherd of Hermas can't be included, "because it was written recently in our time," he says. So it's not ancient. That shows that antiquity was an important consideration.

Second, a book had to be apostolic. If a book was not written by an apostle or by a companion of an apostle, then it was not going to be accepted into the proto-orthodox canon of Scripture. This ended up leading to big debates among the proto-orthodox. For example, the Book of Hebrews. Hebrews is anonymous; the author doesn't give his name. There are some people who think that the Book of Hebrews was written by the apostle Paul, because Timothy is actually mentioned in this book and Paul, in his letters, mentions Timothy on a number of occasions. So some people thought that Hebrews was written by Paul. Others said, no, Hebrews was not written by Paul. So there was this debate. It ended up that people decided that yes, Paul did write the book, and so they included it, but only because they had the apostolic authority of Paul.

So, too, with the Book of Revelation. The Book of Revelation was widely debated, because it claims to be written by somebody named John. But we're not told that it's John the son of Zebedee. There were disputes. Some scholars in the early church pointed out that whoever wrote the Book of Revelation could not have written the Gospel of John. That's a view that scholars continue to hold today, because the writing style of John and Revelation are strikingly different. Whoever wrote the Book of Revelation did not have Greek as his first language. The Book of Revelation is written by someone who appears to know Aramaic, or some other Semitic language, principally as his first language. He actually makes grammatical mistakes in the Greek. Not so the Gospel of John, which is written by somebody who is completely fluent in Greek. Well then, people eventually decided that John the son of Zebedee did write the Book of Revelation, and so it was included.

So a book first had to be ancient and then had to be apostolic; and there were debates about what was and wasn't apostolic. Third, a book needed to be orthodox. Any book that did not advocate a correct understanding of religion, in the opinion of the proto-orthodox, was obviously not going to be included in the canon. Remember the debates over the Gospel of Peter. Serapion excluded the Gospel of Peter because it contained docetic Christology, in his opinion. Well, that's how he concluded Peter did not write it, because Peter obviously could not have a docetic Christology. But it was because it wasn't orthodox that he knew Peter did not write it. Only books that could be understood in an orthodox way could be included.

That was another thing that got the Book of Revelation into trouble, because revelation teaches a literal one-thousand-year Age of Christ at the end of the age, a literal millennium. And by the time people were forming the canon, they began to think that, in fact, it was not going to a literal millennium here on earth. On those grounds, it almost got excluded.

Fourth, the book needed to be widely recognized throughout the church. It needed to be catholic; it needed to be universally used. So those are the four criteria that proto-orthodox Christians used to decide which books belonged in the canon and which did not. As we've seen, these debates, even among the proto-orthodox, lasted for centuries. Even after Athanasius' pronouncement in the year 367, the matter was disputed. Eventually, though, it was this canon—the canon of Athanasius—that came to be accepted, copied, and read by Christians.

Excluded were all of the books that claimed alternative points of view, many of which, including most of the pseudonymous writings that we've looked at in this course, were labeled heretical and forged. Others were orthodox, but they weren't seen to be canonical. For example, the Apocalypse of Peter, the Epistle of Barnabas. They are orthodox, but they're not canonical. One can only imagine what Christianity might have become, had some of these other books been included in the canon of Scripture.

©2002 The Teaching Company.

Lecture Twenty-Two
Interpretation of Scripture

Scope:

Even deciding which books to include in the canon of Scripture was not enough to ensure the proto-orthodox understanding of the Christian faith. Accepting a book is not the same thing as interpreting a book, and as early Christians recognized, there were numerous ways to interpret the books of Scripture. The early Christian centuries, then, saw numerous debates over proper interpretive strategies. In particular, the debates involved the appropriateness of figurative, as opposed to literal, methods of interpretation, as proto-orthodox Christians found themselves in constant debate with Gnostics and others who were thought to read their views "into" the text instead of "out of" it. Even though proto-orthodox Christians championed literal modes of interpretation, they used figurative approaches, as well, as long as their resulting interpretations could be seen as theologically acceptable.

Outline

I. We saw in the last lecture that the canon of Scripture was formed in the context of the struggles between orthodoxy and heresy in the first Christian centuries.

   A. The New Testament developed as a set of books that proto-orthodox Christians could use to provide them with "apostolic" authorities for their views against the views of other Christian groups.

   B. But establishing a list of authoritative books is not the same as establishing their *meaning*. It is one thing to have a book; it is another thing to interpret it.

   C. Proto-orthodox Christians from the earliest of times realized that, in addition to promoting authoritative books, they needed to promote authoritative interpretations of those books.

II. The importance of interpreting texts was recognized at the very beginning of Christianity.

A. Jesus himself was an interpreter of the Hebrew Scriptures. Interestingly, his approach to interpretation became controversial in later centuries.

    1. Jesus clearly affirmed that the Hebrew Scriptures came from God.

    2. But sometimes he appeared to contradict their teaching: for example, in his claim that God did not really intend the *lex talionis* (an eye for an eye, a tooth for a tooth) or the law on divorce (which the Torah allows, but Jesus disallowed).

    3. Early Christians also believed that Jesus himself had "fulfilled" the law (Matt. 5:17–20). Does that mean, then, that the law was no longer in force? If it was in force, then don't Christians have to follow it (even, for example, kosher food laws)? If not, why does Jesus say that his followers need to keep the entire law—even better than the scribes and Pharisees?

B. The apostle Paul also was an interpreter of Scripture.

    1. He again read many texts of Scripture literally.

    2. On occasion, however, he would interpret these texts in a figurative sense, making them mean something other than what they said when read literally. An example can be found in the allegory of Hagar and Sarah in Gal. 4, which he interprets as referring not to the two partners of Abraham, but to Jews (Hagar) and Christians (Sarah).

III. Later proto-orthodox Christians then had to decide how to interpret their Scriptures, and the matter became increasingly important, with different teachers interpreting the same texts in different ways, then claiming that these texts supported their points of view.

A. Marcion, for example, insisted on a literal interpretation of the Old Testament, which led him to conclude that the God of the Old Testament was inferior to the true God because he was sometimes ignorant, changed his mind on occasion, and was wrathful and full of vengeance.

B. Marcion's proto-orthodox opponent Tertullian insisted that passages speaking about God's ignorance and emotions were to not to be taken literally but figuratively. He took other passages figuratively, as well, to illustrate his own theological system.

C. In this, he was following solid precedent (cf. the use of figurative interpretation to attack Jews in the Epistle of Barnabas).

D. But when proto-orthodox fathers faced opponents like the Gnostics, who interpreted Scripture figuratively, they insisted vehemently that only a literal interpretation of the text would do.

IV. The proto-orthodox attacks on gnostic figurative modes of interpretation are particularly interesting.

    A. The second-century church father Irenaeus, bishop of Gaul, is a key figure in these debates. Irenaeus recounts a number of interpretive strategies used by Gnostics to support their points of view and gives specific instances of their interpretations that he finds to be completely willful, in that they overlook the literal meaning of the texts.

        1. Gnostics who believed in thirty divine *aeons* appealed to the claim of the Gospel of Luke that Jesus started his ministry when he was thirty.

        2. They also found support that these thirty *aeons* were divided into three groups—the final twelve of which were completed with the creation of Sophia, an *aeon* who fell from the divine realm, leading to the creation of the universe—in the fact that Judas Iscariot, the twelfth of the disciples, fell away to become a betrayer.

    B. Irenaeus considered these interpretations ludicrous.

        1. In his view, the Gnostics were simply making texts mean what they wanted them to mean and ignoring what the texts actually said.

        2. He likened the gnostic approach to interpretation to someone who takes a beautiful mosaic image of a king and rearranges the stones into the likeness of a mongrel dog, then claims that is what the artist meant all along.

    C. The problem, though, is that the proto-orthodox engaged in similar modes of interpretation when it suited their own purposes.

        1. For Irenaeus, the kosher food laws of Leviticus refer not to unacceptable foods but to unacceptable kinds of people: Not eating animals that chew the cud but do not have cloven hooves means not being like Jews who have the word of God in their mouths but do not move steadily toward God.

2. Generally, though, the proto-orthodox claimed that literal interpretations were to be primary, with figurative interpretations useful only to support views established by literal interpretation.

3. Thus, Origen of Alexandria widely used figurative modes of interpretation but only when the literal meanings appeared to be contradictory or ridiculous.

V. It may seem to us today that the proto-orthodox view is fairly obvious, that the way one should read a sacred text is the same way one should read any text, taking the literal meaning as primary.

A. But we should always remember that the ways of reading texts that we ourselves have inherited and learned are not necessarily "obvious" or "right" or "commonsensical."

B. We should be especially aware of the circumstance that our commonsensical ways of reading texts are now common sense because of these ancient debates over interpretation, which proto-orthodox Christians won.

Essential Reading:

Karlfried Froehlich, *Biblical Interpretation in the Early Church*.

Robert M. Grant and David Tracy, *A Short History of the Interpretation of the Bible*.

Supplementary Reading:

Walter Bauer, *Orthodoxy and Heresy in Earliest Christianity*.

Questions to Consider:

1. Explain how insisting on a "literal" approach to interpretation could both help and hinder the proto-orthodox Christians in their struggles with alternative forms of early Christianity.

2. If "literal" interpretations of a text were simply a matter of letting the text speak for itself, why is there such an enormous range of different interpretations of any given text (for example, the Bible, Shakespeare, the Constitution)?

Lecture Twenty-Two—Transcript
Interpretation of Scripture

We saw in the last lecture that the canon of Scripture was formed in the context of struggles between orthodoxy and heresy in the first Christian centuries. The New Testament developed as a set of books that the proto-orthodox could use to provide them with apostolic authorities for their views, over against the views of other groups. The canon did not simply drop from heaven one day, soon after Jesus died. And it was not decided, ultimately, by an authoritative church body that voted to make the big decision by show of hands. No, the canon emerged over a long period of time on the basis of widespread usage in proto-orthodox churches, churches that decided which books to include based on whether they were apostolic, ancient, orthodox, and catholic.

But establishing a list of authoritative books is not the same thing as establishing their meaning. It's one thing to have a book; it's another thing to interpret it. Proto-orthodox Christians, from the earliest times, realized that if they wanted to fend off false understandings of their faith, in addition to promoting authoritative books, they needed to promote authoritative interpretations of these books. And so, this lecture will now shift gears away from the question of how the 27 books of the New Testament were gathered into a canon, and on to the question of how the sacred books, both the Christian Old Testament and the New Testament, were to be interpreted.

The importance of interpreting texts was recognized at the very beginning of Christianity. Jesus himself was an interpreter for the Hebrew Scriptures. Interestingly, his approach to interpretation became controversial in later centuries. On the one hand, it was clear that Jesus affirmed that the Hebrew Scriptures had come from God. At least, that was clear to proto-orthodox Christians and those who took the Gospels that now survive seriously, because in these Gospel traditions, Jesus time and again affirms the sanctity of the Scriptures, and himself interprets these Scriptures for his followers.

As we saw previously, for example, a man comes up to Jesus, in the Gospel traditions, and says, "What must I do to inherit eternal life?" Jesus' initial response is to turn to the Scriptures and say, "Keep the commandments," and start listing, then, some of the Ten Commandments. Jesus sometimes opposed the Pharisees because they held traditions which led them to violate the commandments of the written Scriptures. An example found in the Gospels; the Pharisees have a tradition that if something is *Korban*, which means set apart for a sacrifice in the temple—a material that can be used by their father and mother, that their father and mother needed—the Pharisaic tradition allowed the person to use what was needed by their parents, and give it for the temple sacrifice. Jesus says, "This tradition that you have is a violation of the law. Your human traditions are causing you to violate God's written law," showing once again that Jesus affirmed the Hebrew Scriptures as having come from God. Or as Jesus is recorded as saying in the Gospel of John, "Scripture cannot be broken."

Jesus then, on the one hand, appeared quite firmly to affirm the Scriptures, saw himself as their interpreter. But other times, Jesus appeared to contradict the teaching of Scripture. A couple of examples; the *lex talionis*, "An eye for an eye, a tooth for a tooth." Jesus says, "I say to you, rather than 'An eye for an eye, a tooth for a tooth,' turn the other cheek. If somebody strikes you on the right cheek, turn to him the other also." Isn't this a contradiction of the law of retaliation? If you turn the other cheek then, in fact, you don't implement the law that the punishment should fit the crime. In fact, you get rid of this law. Hasn't Jesus abrogated the law, then, by his teaching on mercy?

Or the teaching of divorce; according to the Law of Moses, a man can divorce his wife by giving her a certificate of divorce. But Jesus says, "This law was only given for the hardness of your heart. In fact, from the beginning it was not meant to be this way. A man should not divorce his wife, a woman should not divorce her husband." Does he not abrogate the law of divorce, given by Moses?

Or take the kosher food laws. In the Gospel of Mark, we are told that Jesus is being opposed by Pharisees, who are offended that he and his disciples are not washing their hands before they eat. Ancient Jews washed their hands, not because they knew that there were germs and that you needed to get rid of them, but in order to show a kind of outward ritual purity before God, and before the taking of the food that God had provided. Jesus and his disciples did not follow this Pharisaic tradition. And Jesus maligned the Pharisees for cleaning the outside without being concerned about the inside. Jesus says, "The problems come, not from what is external to a person, but from what is internal to a person." Mark interprets this to mean that

Jesus therefore declared all foods clean; Mark Chapter 7. Declaring all foods clean means that you can eat any foods you want, because it's an external thing; it doesn't matter what you put in your body. What matters is what comes out. Jesus says, "It doesn't matter what you put in; it matters the sorts of things that you say, that come out of your mouth." Didn't Jesus declare all foods clean? That would be a violation of the kosher food laws.

On the one hand, Jesus seems to affirm the Scriptures. On the other hand, Jesus appears to abrogate the Scriptures. It's easy to understand why different understandings of the Scriptures could emerge, given this ambiguity. Moreover, early Christians believed that Jesus himself had fulfilled the law. Matthew Chapter 5, Jesus says, "Don't think that I came to abolish the law. I came to fulfill the law. Truly I tell you not one jot not one tittle,"—not one stroke of the law, not one little piece of the law—"will pass away before all is fulfilled. "

Well, if Jesus fulfilled the law, then it's already fulfilled. Doesn't that mean that it's no longer enforced? But if it's no longer enforced, does that mean Christians don't have to follow the law, even the Ten Commandments? If it is enforced, then don't Christians have to follow it, including the kosher food laws? If Christians do not have to follow the law, then how is it that Jesus can say that his followers need to follow the law even better than the scribes and Pharisees (Matthew Chapter 5)? You can see the confusion that results from this entire idea. What are Christians supposed to do with the Old Testament Scriptures? How are they to interpret them? Are they to keep these laws and interpret them literally? Are they to give figurative interpretations of these laws? How does one go about doing it?

The problem emerged not just because of Jesus, but because of the apostles. Take the apostle Paul, who was also an interpreter of the Scripture. Paul, like Jesus, read many of the Scriptures of the Hebrew Bible completely literally, taking them to be literal truths. For example, in the Book of Romans, Paul is trying to show that all people are sinful before God, and he does this by quoting a long string of Scriptures that he takes to be literally correct. "As it is written," says Paul. And then he starts quoting texts. "There is no-one who is righteous, not even one." The Book of Ecclesiastes. "There is no-one who is understood. There is no-one who seeks God.

All have turned aside. Together they become useless. There is no-one shows kindness. There is not even one;" quoting Psalm 14. "Their throats are open graves. They use their tongues to deceive. The venom of vipers is under their lips;" quoting Psalm 140. "Their mouths are full of cursing and bitterness;" quoting Psalm 10. "Their feet are swift to shed blood. Ruin and misery are in their paths;" quoting Isaiah 59. Paul quotes all these Scriptures and takes them quite literally to refer to the human condition. So Paul accepts the Scripture literally.

This can be seen quite clearly in one of the Scriptures that Paul quotes the most often, Genesis Chapter 15, Verse 6. Paul is trying to understand whether a person is made right with God by works of the law, by doing as the law commands, or by having faith in God. He quotes, on several occasions, Genesis Chapter 15: 6—a reference to the father of the Jews, who is Abraham himself. Genesis 15: 6 says, "Abraham believed God and it was reckoned to him as righteousness." So Abraham is made right with God by his faith, because he believed God.

Moreover, as Paul points out in one place, this happened to Abraham—that he believed God and was made right with God—this happened before Abraham was given the sign of circumcision. Abraham is given the sign of circumcision in Genesis, Chapter 17. But he's declared to be right with God because of his faith in Genesis, Chapter 15. So in a very strict literal understanding of things, in which the chronology is very important, Abraham is made right with God before he does any works of the law, before he is even given the sign of circumcision. This, then, is a literal understanding of Scripture.

On other occasions, though, Paul would interpret the Scriptures in a figurative, symbolic sense, making the Scripture mean something other then what it means when read literally. The most famous example of this in Paul is in Galatians Chapter 4, in which Paul talks about another incident that happened with Abraham involving his wife Sarah and her handmaiden Hagar. The deal is this. Abraham was promised by God to have a son; in fact, a host of descendants, that outnumbers the stars in the sky. Unfortunately, Abraham didn't have any children, and he had grown to be an old man. He decides that in order for God to fulfill this promise—apparently Sarah, his wife, can't get pregnant—so he works it out that he's going to get her handmaiden pregnant, so that he'll have descendants through Hagar, the slave of Sarah, rather then through Sarah. So he gets Hagar pregnant. Hagar then bears the child Ishmael. After which, God says, "No, that's not what I had in mind. Sarah was the one who you were supposed to get pregnant." Abraham says, "Well, Sarah is not getting pregnant, and I'm an old man." He is 100 years old at this time, Sarah is in her upper 90s, and it doesn't look likely. Well, God says "No, in fact, Sarah is to conceive." And Sarah does conceive miraculously. Sarah bears a child. And the child, then, is named Isaac. Isaac and Ishmael, the two children of Abraham.

This is a very interesting story, on its own terms, in the Book of Genesis. It can be taken quite literally simply referring to how the children of Israel came into being, that they were born as the children of the promise to Abraham. Paul, though, wants to interpret this story in a figurative sense. Paul wants to emphasize that people who are committed to following the Jewish law are enslaved to the law, whereas Christians who believe in Christ are set free from having to follow the law. He does this by referring to the story of Sarah, Abraham and Hagar. He says that "It's written that Abraham had two sons." This is in Galatians Chapter 4. "One of them by a slave woman, the other by a free woman. One of them, the child of the slave, was born according to the flesh." This was just his idea, and he went ahead and did it. "The other one, the child of the free woman, was fulfilled through the promise," the fulfillment of God's promise.

"Now," he says, "this is an allegory, because these women, in fact, stand for two covenants. One woman, in fact, is Hagar from Mount Sinai, bearing children for slavery. Hagar is Mount Sinai in Arabia, and corresponds to the present Jerusalem, for she is in slavery with her children. But the other woman, the one who's free, Sarah, corresponds to the Jerusalem above. She is free and she is our mother." In other words, Christians are the children of the promise to Abraham, because like Abraham, they believe God and it is reckoned to them as righteousness, so they are the children of the free woman, Sarah. Jews, who are enslaved to the law, descend from Ishmael. Figuratively, they are the children of the slave, because they too are enslaved.

This is a remarkable reading. Of course, Jews trace their lineage back to Isaac, not to Ishmael. But Paul turns this interpretation on its head, by taking it figuratively to show that, in fact, that it's the Christians who are the children of the promise—because they're the ones who, like Abraham, have faith—rather than Jews, who follow the words and are enslaved to the law.

Well, there you have it, then; an early apostle who reads some texts literally and some figuratively. What were later proto-orthodox Christians to do? How were they to interpret their texts to guarantee that the texts yielded the right interpretations to support the proto-orthodox points of view? This became increasingly important when different teachers began interpreting the same texts in different ways, all of them claiming that the texts supported their own points of view.

I'll give you some examples that we've seen already. Marcion; Marcion insisted on a literal interpretation of the Old Testament. He took the text quite literally. He refused any figurative interpretation at all. This led him, this literal interpretation led him, to conclude that the God of the Old Testament was inferior to the true God. The God of the Old Testament is occasionally ignorant. In the Garden of Eden, Adam has eaten the fruit, and he realizes he is naked, and he is hiding. God comes and he says, "Adam, where are you?" Where are you? God doesn't know? Well, what kind of God is that?

Sometimes the God of the Old Testament changes his mind. Abraham—to turn to Abraham for a second—is in a conversation with God, when God has decided he'll destroy Sodom and Gomorrah. And Abraham says, "But God, what if there are 100 people who are righteous, would you destroy it then?" "No, not if there are 100." "What if there are only 10, would you destroy it then?" He starts bartering with God, and God can't decide what he's going to do; and it appears that he's changing his mind.

Well, what is that? God decides not to punish people in the Old Testament, occasionally, because they repent, so he changes his mind. What kind of God is this, that he changes his mind? Well, according to Marcion, he's an inferior God. In fact, he's a God full of wrath and vengeance. Surely the true God isn't wrathful. Surely, he's above human emotion. This literal interpretation, then, is what leads him to understand that the Old Testament God can't be the true God.

How do the proto-orthodox oppose Marcion? After all, he's just taking the text literally. They oppose Marcion by arguing that these passages are not meant to be taken literally; they're to be taken figuratively. We best know the opposition of Marcion from the writings of Tertullian, who insisted the passages in Scripture that speak about God's ignorance and emotions were to be taken figuratively—not really referring to the actual passions and actions and emotions of God. Tertullian took lots of passages figuratively, in order to illustrate his own theological system. There are hundreds of examples in Tertullian's voluminous writings. Let me just give you one.

There's a story in the Old Testament of when the people have come out of Egypt, and Moses is leading the people through the wilderness. They engage in battle with another tribe named Amalek. Moses is directed by God to stand on a hill during the battle and to raise his arms up, stretched out by his side. As long as he can hold the position, the Israelites win the battle with the Amalekites. But when his arms get tired, he puts them down, so they hang down loose, they start losing the battle with the Amalekites. Eventually, he manages to keep his arms up for long enough for the Israelites to win. It's a very interesting passage. Tertullian takes it figuratively, because when Moses reaches out his arms straight up from his shoulders and they win the battle, well, Moses has assumed the position of the cross. This is showing that it's the cross of Jesus that brings victory. The passage is taken figuratively.

So Tertullian will—in order to support his own views and attack the views of others—will insist that texts should be taken figuratively. And in this he is following, quite solidly, the precedent among proto-orthodox writers. Remember the Book of Barnabas, that says that the law of circumcision didn't mean that Jews were meant to cut the flesh off of their baby boy's penis; that is a reference to the cross of Jesus. The Sabbath didn't refer to the need to take one day out of seven off; it was a reference to the future thousand-year reign of Christ. Kosher food laws weren't about what to eat. Kosher food laws were about what kind of people to avoid and to avoid being. So that, according to these writers, many texts should be taken figuratively.

The problem with figurative interpretation is, where does one draw the line, and what are the restraints? How, if you allow for a figurative interpretation of text, do you control the interpretation? How do you keep somebody from saying that the text means something that it obviously doesn't mean? This is a problem that the proto-orthodox had to face—not against somebody like Marcion, who wanted to interpret the text literally, but against people like the Gnostics, who interpreted Scripture figuratively. Against Gnostics, the proto-orthodox authors insisted, with some vehemence, that only a literal interpretation of the text would do.

The proto-orthodox attacks on Gnostic figurative modes of interpretation are particularly interesting. We turn now to the second century church father, Irenaeus, the heresiologist we've met on a number of occasions, the bishop of Gaul in France. Irenaeus is a key figure in these debates against the Gnostics, because as we've seen he wrote a five-volume work that still survives, against the Gnostics—we today generally call it, *Against the Heresies*. These five books were used extensively by Irenaeus's intellectual successors, people who were also attacking heresies, who would simply take what Irenaeus had to say and regurgitate it, and add on some of their own ideas. But his influence was quite substantial. He wrote extensively against the interpretive strategies used by the Gnostics, which they used in order to support their points of view.

He sometimes gives specific instances of their interpretations, in order to show why he thinks these are willful interpretations that overlook the literal meaning of the text. Therefore, in his opinion, these interpretations can't be right, because they overlook the literal meaning of the text. A couple of the examples that he appeals to; the Valentinian Gnostics believed that there were thirty divine aeons in the Pleroma. You get the one true God, who emanates some divine aeons, and eventually the number is thirty that come out. So the Pleroma is made up of thirty aeons. Gnostics could turn to Scripture to support that there were thirty aeons. They pointed, for example, to the Gospel of Luke, where it says that Jesus started his ministry when he was thirty years old. Well, what's the significance of him starting when he was thirty? Well, this is when he receives the divine aeon into himself. He was thirty, because there were thirty of these aeons; and so this is used as a support for the view that there were thirty aeons.

These Valentinian aeons were put into three different groups. The final group was a group of twelve aeons, the last of which was Sophia. Sophia—if you remember, Sophia means wisdom—was the final aeon who fell from the divine realm, which led ultimately to the creation of the universe; because she ended up giving birth to a creature, not from within the Pleroma, but from outside. And so her fall from the divine realm led to the creation of the material world. The Valentinian Gnostics found support for this view of Sophia, the twelfth of the final group of aeons, in the fact that Scripture indicates that Judas Iscariot, the twelfth of the disciples, fell away from Jesus' following to become a betrayer. This is a symbolic story, they thought—Judas Iscariot falling away, because he's the twelfth and he's representing Sophia, the twelfth of the final set of aeons who fell away, leading to a material world. So this is support for this view.

Irenaeus, who is attacking these points of view, considers these interpretations to be completely ludicrous, because they violated the literal sense of the text. These texts about Jesus being thirty when he starts his ministry and Judas being the betrayer—these aren't about the divine Pleroma, they're not about Sophia falling, they're not about the creation of the material world. No, these are about Jesus being thirty years old when he starts his ministry and Judas being one of the twelve disciples. It has nothing to do with the Pleroma. It's the literal meaning that matters, not the figurative meaning. He attacks these Gnostics for making these texts mean what they want it to mean, and ignoring what other texts actually say.

In an effective image, he likens this Gnostic approach to somebody who has in front of him a beautiful mosaic image of a king. A mosaic is made out of finely colored and polished stones that are carefully arranged to make an image. Well, Irenaeus says that this person who has this mosaic of a king in front of them takes the stone and rearrange them into the likeness of a mongrel dog. By rearranging this image into a mongrel dog, they then have recreated what the image is, obviously, but then they come along and claim that that is what the artist meant to portray all along. For Irenaeus, that is what these Gnostics are doing. They are rearranging what the texts say to make them mean what they want them to mean, to make them appear what they want them to appear, and then claiming that's what the text meant all along. For Irenaeus, that's completely unacceptable; you have to take the literal meaning of the text as primary.

What's striking, though, is that for Irenaeus and others of his ilk, like Tertullian, it is legitimate to take the text figuratively, when it met their own purposes. Even within Irenaeus, for example, the kosher food laws of the book of Leviticus are not meant to be taken literally. The kosher food laws do not refer to unacceptable foods. For Irenaeus, they refer figuratively to unacceptable kinds of people. For example, in the kosher food laws, Jews are told they cannot eat animals that chew the cud, but do not have cloven hooves. Well, one might take that to means that there are certain kinds of animals that you can't eat. Well, no; not for Irenaeus. What this really means is that people should not be like Jews, who have the word of God in their mouth, so that they chew the cud, but do they do not move steadily towards God; they do not have cloven hooves. Well, that's his interpretation of what the kosher food laws means. One wonders how different it is from a Gnostic interpretation that takes its text figuratively rather than literally.

The proto-orthodox had a problem, because they were opposing people who would take the text figuratively. The proto-orthodox didn't want them to do that, and so they forbad the figurative interpretation—unless they themselves were doing the figurative interpretation. Generally speaking, it's safe to say that the proto-orthodox claimed that literal interpretations of the text were to be primary. This is where the proto-orthodox drew the line. Literal interpretations were to be primary; the text was to interpreted literally, to come away with the literal truth—that figurative interpretations could be used only to support views that were established by literal interpretations.

Probably the best known interpreter from the proto-orthodox was a Church Father from the early third century, named Origen, who was from the city of Alexandria. Origen was a brilliant scholar, who was probably the most prolific author of early Christianity. He wrote hundreds and hundreds of books, and was known for his interpretation of Scripture. His view was that the text of Scripture was to be taken literally, except when the text appeared to contradictory or ridiculous. For example, when Jesus says, "When you look upon a woman with lust in your eye; if your right eye offends you, then it's better for you to take your eye out and to cast it away, because it's better for you to enter into heaven with one eye then to sent into hell with two eyes." Origen says, well, that's ridiculous. I mean, if you're looking at somebody and your eye is offending you, how do you know that it's your right eye? Maybe it's your left eye. You never just have one eye that offends you. So for him, the text was not to be taken literally, because God had intentionally put something ridiculous into it.

God occasionally put contradictions and ridiculous statements in the text. Those contradictions and ridiculous statements were indications that the text was not be taken literally, but figuratively. Whenever you don't have those contradictions and ridiculous statements, though, you are to take the text literally. That generally was the proto-orthodox view. Texts needed to be construed literally, in order to avoid the heresies that come about when the texts are interpreted figuratively. It may seem obvious to us today that this proto-orthodox view is right—that one should read a sacred text like one reads any text. A text is a text, and it makes sense that you simply read texts literally for what they have to say.

It's important for us to remember, though, that the way we read texts today has been conditioned by the history of the interpretation of texts. Our commonsensical, our literal, construal of texts, where we start with a word and then read the next word, and the next word, until we make sense of these words in their own context by reading them sequentially and we are taking their meaning literally—this kind of approach to texts makes obvious sense to us, and it's how we read texts. But the reason we think this is such an obvious, or right, or commonsensical view, is because this is the way of interpreting texts that we have inherited.

We should also be aware of the circumstance that our commonsensical ways of reading texts are now "common sense" because of these ancient debates that we've been discussing, and that it was the proto-orthodox Christians, who insisted on this literal interpretation of texts, who won these debates. These debates determined how Christians were going to be reading their texts. People who read texts through the Middle Ages were Christians reading their sacred texts, so that the debates over how to interpret texts go all the way back to early Christianity, in their controversies with other groups who were construed as heretical, who took the text figuratively.

Lecture Twenty-Three
Orthodox Corruption of Scripture

Scope:

Early Christian disputes involved not merely knowing how to interpret the words of Scripture, but even knowing what the words actually were. The reason for this is that all the available texts were copied by hand and were, as a result, different from each other, because copyists inadvertently or intentionally changed the words they copied. Of the nearly 5,400 copies of the New Testament writings that survive today (in the original Greek), no two are exactly alike; all have mistakes, to a greater or lesser degree. Some of the changes appear to have been made intentionally by scribes concerned to make the texts say what they were already known to mean, making the texts less susceptible to "heretical" interpretation and more clearly orthodox. This is a phenomenon that scholars have come to call, somewhat ironically, the orthodox corruption of Scripture.

Outline

I. In previous lectures, we have seen that proto-orthodox Christians who were engaged in theological controversies decided which books to include in their sacred Scriptures and which to exclude.

 A. Many other kinds of Christians—Jewish Christian Ebionites, Gnostics, and Marcionites—had other sacred books, but also used these books that made it into the canon.

 B. Thus, the proto-orthodox developed ways of interpreting these books that provided some assurance that they would be understood as promoting explicitly proto-orthodox Christianity.

 C. Some of the early theological controversies, however, were not simply over how to interpret these books but, on a more basic level, were about what was actually *in* these books. That is to say, there were disputes not just about how to interpret the words of these texts but also about which words actually were found in these texts.

D. Christians on all sides of these debates accused their opponents of changing the words of the texts they were arguing about, modifying the wording of important passages to make them say what they wanted them to say.

E. This is not a kind of argument that happens nearly as much today in religious or political disputations, but it was common in antiquity.

   1. There was no such thing as electronic distribution of texts, desktop publishing, photocopy machines, typewriters, or moveable type; books had to be produced by hand, by human scribes who created copies of a text by copying its words, one letter at a time.

   2. Unlike our world, where every copy of a book is exactly the same, in the ancient world, every copy of a book was different.

   3. They were different because the copyists who produced the books made mistakes—different mistakes by different copyists in different places. And sometimes the mistakes were not accidental slips of the pen but intentional alterations, affecting the very meaning of a text.

   4. In this lecture, we will be looking at some of the intentional alterations created by scribes who were invested in the theological disputes waging over the meaning of their texts, who sometimes changed their texts to make them say what they wanted them to mean.

II. We do not have the original texts of any early Christian book (or of any literary work from antiquity).

A. Instead, we have copies made much later—not the first copies or the copies of the copies—but copies from hundreds of years after the fact.

B. At present, we have nearly 5,400 copies (or manuscripts) of the New Testament (in Greek), from extremely small fragments to entire massive tomes containing all the books.

   1. The earliest copy of any book of the New Testament is called P52 and is the size of a credit card. A fragment, written on both sides on papyrus, it dates to around 125 A.D. and preserves some words from John 18.

2. The first full manuscript of the entire New Testament is the Codex Sinaiticus, dating from the second half of the fourth century.

3. Most of the manuscripts we have date from the Middle Ages.

C. These copies date from the second to the sixteenth centuries.

D. The New Testament is also preserved in different versions (for example, Latin, Syriac, Coptic, Old Georgian, Armenian).

E. Strikingly, no two of these copies, except for the smallest fragments, are exactly alike in their wording.

F. No one knows how many differences of wording there are among these manuscripts. It is safest to put it in comparative terms: There are more differences among our manuscripts than there are words in the New Testament.

G. Most of these differences are pure accidents, misspelled words, words or lines accidentally dropped out or accidentally written twice.

H. But some of the changes appear to have been made intentionally, as scribes tried to make sense of the texts they were copying and sometimes changed the text to change the sense.

I. Textual critics decide what the original text said and what changes have been made.
    1. They look at what kinds of manuscripts have a particular passage and the wording of the passage.
    2. They consider whether the writing style, vocabulary, and theology are consistent with the presumed author.
    3. Textual critics tend to prefer a reading that is more difficult, as an easier reading could have been "corrected" by a scribe.

J. There are very few instances in our surviving manuscripts in which Gnostic or Marcionite scribes altered a text to make it coincide with their point of view. If such alterations *were* made, they did not survive the copying practices of orthodox scribes over the centuries.

K. But there are numerous proto-orthodox changes of the text, where the text has been changed in line with its orthodox interpretation, making it harder to be used in support of other views.

III. Examples of this kind of scribal change can be readily categorized and illustrated.

    A. Some texts copied by proto-orthodox scribes were changed to counter the Jewish-Christian adoptionist claim that Jesus was a man but not divine.

        1. For example, Luke 2:33, which calls Joseph Jesus' father, was occasionally changed (because, for the proto-orthodox, Jesus was not Joseph's son).

        2. Or Luke 3:22, where the voice of God at Jesus' baptism was changed so that it no longer said to Jesus, "today I have begotten you."

    B. Other texts were changed to counter the idea among Marcion and other docetists that Jesus was fully God, but not a human, and that he could not, therefore, really suffer. For example, a famous scene was inserted into Luke's account of Jesus' final prayer before being arrested, in which he is shown really to suffer, sweating great drops of blood in agony before his coming fate (Luke 22:43–44).

    C. Other texts were changed to counter the gnostic idea that the divine Christ came into Jesus before his baptism and left him before his death (because the divine cannot suffer); for example, in Mark 15:34, where Jesus' cry "My God, my God why have you forsaken me" (literally: left me behind) was altered to "My God, my God, why have you mocked me?"

IV. Many other examples of this phenomenon could be readily adduced, but these are enough to make the point.

    A. Proto-orthodox scribes concerned about the use (or abuse) of their scriptural texts occasionally changed them to make them more useful for the orthodox cause and less available to non-orthodox Christians.

B. This kind of alteration of the text sometimes had a permanent affect on Christian interpretation of these texts, because in some cases, it was the altered text that came to be copied more than the original text. Even today, people sometimes base their understandings of the New Testament on passages that we do not have in the original wording.

Essential Reading:

Bart Ehrman, *The Orthodox Corruption of Scripture*.

David Parker, *The Living Text of the Gospels*.

Supplementary Reading:

Eldon Jay Epp, "Textual Criticism, New Testament," *Anchor Bible Dictionary*, vol. VI, pp. 412–435.

Bruce M. Metzger, *The Text of the New Testament: Its Transmission, Corruption, and Restoration*.

Questions to Consider:

1. In what ways is the scribal alteration of a text like and unlike the forgery of a text?

2. If there are so many changes in the surviving manuscripts of the New Testament, how do you suppose we can discern, in every case, what the New Testament authors actually wrote?

Lecture Twenty-Three—Transcript
Orthodox Corruption of Scripture

In previous lectures, we've seen the proto-orthodox Christians, who were engaged in theological controversies, decide which books to include in their Scriptures and which to exclude. Many other kinds of Christians, for example Jewish Christian Ebionites, had other sacred books, but they also used these books that made it into the canon. And so the proto-orthodox developed ways of interpreting these books that provided some assurance that they would be understood as promoting explicitly proto-orthodox Christianity. Even though figurative interpretations were allowed, it was literal interpretations that were given primacy by these proto-orthodox Church Fathers. This was even in later times, when figurative modes of interpretation were developed more extensively by the orthodox. Even then, it was a literal interpretation that must be used in order to establish major doctrines of the church.

As it turns out, though, some of the early theological controversies were not simply over how to interpret these books, but on a more basic level, they were about what was actually in the books. That is to say, there were disputes, not just about how to interpret the words of these texts, but also about which words were actually to be found in the texts. That will be the subject of the present lecture.

How can we know what the words of these ancient texts were? And how can we know when these words were sometimes changed by the scribes who copied them? Christians on all sides of the debate of theology accused their opponents of changing the words of the texts that they were arguing about, modifying the wording of important passages, so as to make them say what they wanted them to say. We've seen this already, in particular with reference to Marcion, who believed that the texts of Paul's letters that he had inherited, the text of Luke that he had inherited, had been corrupted by earlier copyists, that they had put their own understandings back into the text; so that when these texts of Paul and Luke affirmed the Old Testament or affirmed the material world, or claimed that the God of the Old Testament who created this world was the one true God, that all of these passages that said such things were, in fact, put into the texts, after they had been originally written, by later scribes. Marcion's solution, then, was to remove these passages so as to make them say what they had originally said. He didn't think that he was changing the text; he thought that he was restoring the text to its pristine original.

This is not the kind of argument that happens nearly as much today in religions or political disputations, although it occasionally happens; who said what, when? In antiquity, though, this kind of argument was extremely common. There was no such thing as electronic publication, desktop publishing, photocopy machines, typewriters, removable type of any kind. Books had to be produced, in the ancient world, by hand, by human scribes who created copies of a text by copying its words one letter at a time. Unlike our world, where every copy of a book is exactly the same, in the ancient world every copy of a book was different. They were different because the copyists who produced the books made mistakes. Even trained copyists made mistakes; different mistakes by different copyists in different places. Sometimes the mistakes were not accidental flips of the pen, but intentional alterations affecting the very meanings of a text.

In this lecture, we'll focus on some of the intentional alterations created by scribes who were invested in the theological disputes waging over the meaning of their texts; scribes who sometimes changed their texts to make them say what they wanted them to mean.

First, I need to provide some important background. When you go to the bookstore today, you can buy a New Testament, and you generally assume that the New Testament you are reading, comprised of these 27 books, is a translation of the words written by the original authors. That's our natural assumption of any book we read from antiquity, whether we are reading Tacitus, Suetonius, Cicero, Pliny, the books of the New Testament. We assume the translations we're reading—knowing full well that they're translations—but we assume that they're translating the original text written by an author. In point of fact, we don't have the original texts of any early Christian book or, for that matter, of any literary work from antiquity. We don't have any originals. Instead, what we have are copies that ultimately descend from the original. We don't have the first copies of any of the books of the New Testament; nor do we have copies of the copies; nor copies of the copies of the copies. What we have are copies that come from hundreds of years after the books themselves first were produced.

Let me give you an example of how the process worked, just so you can get an idea of what I'm talking about. When an anonymous author produced the Gospel of Mark—let's say he was writing in the city of Rome, as many people think that Mark was written in Rome—this anonymous author wrote his Gospel based on oral traditions that he heard, possibly on some written sources available to him. He wrote his book and, in the ancient world, the way he would have produced his book, or published his book, was by putting it in circulation. Normally books were published by giving them to friends or acquaintances, who would read the book. When this happened with the Gospel of Mark, say, in the city of Rome, presumably somebody wanted a copy of the book for themselves. They didn't want the original; they wanted their own copies, so they could give the original back. And so they either copied out the Book of Mark by hand themselves, or they had a scribe do it for them.

Suppose another church in town wanted a copy of this Gospel for their worship services. Well, then, they made a copy. And another house-church in town—these churches, by the way, were meeting in houses in the early period; they weren't meeting in their own buildings. So there are churches in different houses throughout Rome—another house-church wants a copy, so they make a copy. Somebody is visiting Rome from Ephesus. They hear about this book and decide, in fact, that they want a copy to take back to their church in Ephesus. So they take a copy back to Ephesus. The copy in Ephesus gets copied, in Ephesus, and then it goes over to Philippi, goes over to Corinth. Pretty soon the thing is circulated by individuals writing down copies.

What happens when somebody writes out a long text by hand? Well, if you don't know what happens, then do it sometime yourself. Sit down with the Gospel of Mark and try and copy it by hand, and then have somebody check for your accuracy. Even though you are far more highly literate, probably, than most people in antiquity—because people in antiquity could not read or write at all—you are far more literate than people in antiquity who are doing this copying, you would have made mistakes. I can assure you, you would have made mistakes. These ancient copyists made mistakes.

Suppose the first copyist made mistakes, and then somebody came along and copied the copy that he made. What would happen? Well, the second copyist would include the mistake that the first copyist had made, and would make some mistakes of his own. The only exception would be is if the second copyist realized that the copy that he's copying has mistakes. He may want to try and correct the copy. Now if he corrects the copy, he may correct the copy correctly, or he may make the correction incorrectly, in which case he's made a second mistake. A third copier comes along and uses the copy of the second copyist, which has its own mistakes and that of its predecessor. And the third copyist makes mistakes, in addition to the ones that he's inherited. And so it goes, every generation of copying—and a generation might just be a week apart—introducing its own mistakes and replicating the mistakes of its exemplar, the copy that it's using to copy. This goes on for years and years, decades, even centuries.

We have a number of copies of the New Testament that have survived, all of which were made in this way. The term "manuscript" is used for these copies. The term "manuscript" literally means "written by hand," so it is used to refer to any copy of a document made before the invention of movable type. We have, in fact, something like 5,400 copies, manuscripts, of the New Testament in the original Greek. All of these 27 books were written, originally, in Greek. We have copies of them in Greek—5,400 of these copies. When I say we have 5,400 copies, I don't mean complete copies. Many of these copies, especially the earliest ones, are highly fragmentary.

The very earliest copy of any book of the New Testament that we have is written on papyrus. Most of the earliest copies, from early centuries of Christianity, are on papyrus; from the first four centuries, almost all of the surviving copies are on papyrus. Later people started using parchment or leather—parchment is refined leather that they processed for writing. Later copies, especially done from the seventh century onward, are done on parchment. The earlier material used was papyrus. The earliest copy we have of the New Testament is on papyrus. It's the fifty-second papyrus to have been discovered of the New Testament—it was discovered probably at the end of the last century—it is therefore called P52. This is a very important little manuscript of the New Testament. But it's not a complete manuscript. It's nowhere close to being a complete manuscript. In fact, it's the size of a credit card. It has writing on both sides of the page. It's made out of papyrus, and it's a fragment with ragged edges. The fact that it's written on both sides is important because it shows it came from a codex, rather than a scroll.

The scholars who study ancient manuscripts are able to date manuscripts on the basis of their handwriting. This is the art or science of paleography, study of ancient writing. Paleographers date P52, this earliest fragment that we have, to sometime in the first part of the second century. So say, roughly 125, give or take 50 years. So it could have been written in 110, it could have been written in 140. As it turns out this has portions of John, Chapter 18 on it. It preserves some words from John, Chapter 18, on the front and the back, of the trial before Pilate; from about the year 125.

The first full manuscript of the entire New Testament that we have is Codex Siniaticus, dating back from the first half of the fourth century. Most of the manuscripts that we have date from the Middle Ages. And so, the 5,400 copies that we have date from the second century up through the sixteenth century. We have some manuscripts that were produced after the invention of printing. In addition to these 5,400 copies—the early ones are fragmentary—we also have the New Testament preserved in versions. In antiquity, when somebody in a Latin speaking area wanted a book of the New Testament, of course, somebody translated it into Latin, or if they lived in Syria, in Syriac, or in Egypt, into Coptic, into various languages. We have thousands and thousands of copies of the Latin New Testament, since Latin became the language of the Roman church; probably more than 10,000 copies of the Latin version, and copies of Syriac, Coptic, old Georgian, Armenian and other ancient languages.

Sticking for the moment with the Greek copies, which are of most importance to us, because they are in the language of the original authors. What is striking is that, among the 5,400 copies that we have, no two of them are exactly alike in their wording, except for the smallest fragments. Scribes changed the text so extensively that no two of these copies are exactly alike.

Well, how many differences are there among these manuscripts? How many changes did the scribes make? The fact is, we don't know. Nobody has been able to count all the differences among the manuscripts yet, even using computers. We do know that the differences number in the hundreds of thousands. Possibly it's safest to put the matter in comparative terms. There are more differences among our manuscripts of the New Testament, than there are words in the New Testament.

Now it must be admitted that most of these differences among the manuscripts are pure accidents and completely immaterial for any thing; by far the most common mistakes that scribes make simply show that scribes in antiquity could spell no better than people can today. Most of the differences are misspelled words, which doesn't matter at all, for the most part, for the meaning of a passage. Sometimes there are other accidents; for example, words that drop out accidentally, when a scribe got lazy or tired or inattentive. Sometimes an entire line will drop out. When two lines happen to end with the same words, sometimes the scribe will copy the first line and then when his eye came back to the page, instead of coming to the words that he had just copied, his eyes would skip down to the next line which ends with the same words and he'd think that was the line he just copied. And so then he would go to the line below that. As a result he would leave out an entire line in the copying. Sometimes scribes dropped entire pages or more. Sometimes scribes accidentally recopied a line or recopied a paragraph or recopied a page. These were all kinds of accidental mistakes, but fairly easily detected by people trained to look for such things.

But there are other changes that have been made intentionally. As scribes tried to make sense of the texts that they were copying, sometimes they changed the text in order to change the sense. Two of the most famous kinds of changes like that are well-known passages in the New Testament.

If you watch any movies about Jesus, the one story from the New Testament that gets into every Jesus movie is the story of the woman taken in adultery; John, Chapter 7 and 8, where a woman is caught in the act of adultery and they bring her to Jesus for judgment and they say, "The law says we are to condemn such a one; what do you say?" Jesus stoops down and starts writing on the ground, and then he looks up and says, "Let the one among you who has not committed a sin be the first to cast a stone at her." Then he writes some more on the ground and they start leaving one by one, realizing they too have sinned, until no-one is left. Jesus looks up, sees the woman and says, "Is there no-one left to condemn you?" She says, "No, Lord, no-one." He says, "Neither do I condemn you. Go and sin no more."

It's a terrific story, and it's found in not only every Jesus movie, but also in any book about Jesus of a novelistic sort. Unfortunately, this story, found in the Gospel of John today, in the King James translation, was not originally found in the Gospel of John. It's in none of our early manuscripts. Greek Church Fathers who talk about the Gospel of John don't mention this story being in the Gospel of John until the twelfth century. Moreover, when you look at this passage in Greek, the style of writing is considerably different from the style of the rest of the Gospel of John. Scholars, therefore, are convinced that this wasn't originally part of John's Gospel, that somebody had written the story as some kind of marginal note perhaps, and that a later scribe then put it in to the Gospel of John.

Another famous passage that probably was not original involves the Gospel of Mark; in fact, the last twelve verses of Mark. In Mark's Gospel, the women go to the tomb after Jesus has died. They are going to anoint him for his burial three days later. But the tomb is empty, and they are told by a man in the tomb that Jesus had been raised and that he'll meet his disciples in Galilee. And we're told that the women flee the tomb and they don't say anything to anybody, "for they were afraid." That's probably where Mark's Gospel actually ended, with the line that the women fled the tomb and said nothing to anybody, for they were afraid. Scribes who didn't like that ending very well added twelve verses, in which Jesus actually appears to his disciples and tells them that he's been raised from the dead, tells them to go forth and preach the gospel. These twelve verses, though, are not in our oldest and best manuscripts. They don't coincide with the writing style of Mark otherwise. They probably are not original.

Textual critics are scholars who are involved in deciding what the original text actually said, deciding where changes have been made. Textual critics of the New Testament utilize a number of pieces of evidence to help them decide what the original text was, and what the corruption was. They look at what kind of manuscripts, for example, have a particular passage, and what the wording of the passage is in the oldest manuscripts and in the manuscripts that are generally judged to be superior in quality. They consider things like, is the passage consistent with the writing style and vocabulary and the theology of this author otherwise?

They consider passages that look like they would have been amenable to what scribes would have produced. Sometimes, if you've got a passage that's worded in two different ways, one way is highly problematic, maybe contains a contradiction or a difficult theological idea, or a difficult grammatical construction, and the other passage is very easy to read, no deep theological conflict, no contradiction, the wording is not a problem; then they suspect that the one that actually reads pretty well, maybe the scribe has changed—the idea being that a scribe is more likely to "correct" a problem, rather then to create a problem. So textual critics tend to prefer a reading that is more difficult, than a reading that is easier.

I don't have time to go into all of the ins and outs about how textual critics go about their work. What I'm interested in is detailing some instances in which proto-orthodox scribes appear to have changed their texts, in order to make their text more useable for the proto-orthodox purpose and less amenable to heretical use. There are very few instances in our surviving manuscripts in which it appears that Gnostic or Marcionite scribes, for example, altered the text to make it coincide with a point of view. I'm sure that such scribes did such things, but those manuscripts haven't survived from antiquity. What have survived are the copies made by the proto-orthodox scribes, in which there are changes that appear to support a proto-orthodox cause. These are places where the manuscript will have different readings, and it appears that the oldest form of the text, the original form of the text, has been changed in a lot of proto-orthodox theological interests. Let me give you a few examples of how it works.

Some texts copied by proto-orthodox scribes were changed in order to counter what we would understand to be Jewish-Christian adoptionistic claims. The Jewish-Christian adoptionists claimed that Jesus was a man, but he wasn't God. And so sometimes proto-orthodox Christians would change the text in light of these adoptionistic claims. I'll give you an example; Luke Chapter 2, Verse 33. This is a story we've talked about before. Jesus is a twelve-year-old in a temple. His parents have been there for a festival. They've gone home. Three days later in a caravan they realized that Jesus isn't with them. So they come back to try and find Jesus. They finally find him in a temple. His mother locates him and his mother says to him in Luke, Chapter 2, Verse 33. "Why are you here? Your father and I have been looking all over for you."

Your father and I? This is a problem for proto-orthodox scribes, because it presupposes that Joseph was Jesus' father. That is what the adoptionists said. But the proto-orthodox believed that Mary was a virgin, that Joseph was not his father. So, what did the proto-orthodox scribes do? Well, some of them left the text as it was. But some of the scribes changed the text to say, "We have been looking all over for you," Or "Joseph and I have been looking all over for you,"—changing the text so it could not be used by an adoptionist to say, "See, Joseph really was his father."

For a second example, consider Luke Chapter 3, Verse 22, the baptism of Jesus. Jesus gets baptized. According to Mark's Gospel, our earliest account, when Jesus gets baptized, the heavens rip apart, the spirit descends upon him as a dove, and he hears a voice from heaven that says, "This is my beloved son in whom I am well pleased." In Luke's Gospel, though, when Jesus is baptized, the heavens open up, the spirit descends upon him in bodily form as a dove, and a voice in Luke's Gospel says, "You are my son; today I have begotten you," a quotation of Psalm, Chapter 2, Verse 7.

Today I have begotten you? Jesus becomes God's son at the baptism? That's what all of the earliest witnesses to Luke's Gospel have the voice say at the baptism. Interestingly, the later manuscripts have something else. The later manuscripts have the voice from heaven say, "You are my son, in whom I am well pleased." It appears that scribes had gotten rid of the text that could have been used by adoptionists, so that they could make the text more amenable to their own theological understanding.

And so, first, some texts are changed by proto-orthodox scribes in an anti-adoptionistic move. Second, some texts are changed in anti-docetic ways, to counter Marcion and other docetists who say that Jesus was fully God, but he was not really human. Docetists insisted that Jesus was not a real human being and, therefore, he did not really suffer, he did not really shed blood and die.

One very famous instance, in which it appears that proto-orthodox scribes have changed their text to oppose these docetists, comes in a passage in Luke's Gospel in which Jesus is praying prior to his arrest. We're told that Jesus has had his last supper with his disciples, and he goes out to pray. In Luke's Gospel, when he's praying he seems very calm, unlike he seems in Mark's Gospel. In Mark's Gospel, he says that his soul is troubled unto death. He prays three times that God will take this cup away from him. He falls on his face before God. He's clearly quite disturbed.

In Luke's Gospel, though, he never says, "My soul is troubled unto death." Instead of praying three times that this cup will be removed, he only prays once and says, "If it is your will, take away this cup." Rather then falling to his face, he actually kneels down before God. It appears that in Luke's Gospel, Jesus is not being portrayed in deep agony—except two verses that are found in some manuscripts, but not others, the famous verses that recount Jesus sweating blood. Jesus is said to be in such agony, in these two verses, that he begins sweating great drops of blood, falling to the ground, and then an angel comes and ministers to him. The account of Jesus sweating blood.

Unfortunately, this account of Jesus sweating blood is not found in our earliest and best manuscripts of Luke's Gospel. Moreover, these verses seem to contradict Luke's portrayal of Jesus as being calm and in control going to his death. How did the verses get there? It's very interesting that the first Church Fathers to quote this verse, Justin Martyr and Iranaeus, quote the verses in order to oppose docetists, like Marcion, by showing that Jesus really did suffer; he really did bleed; in fact, he was in such agony that he sweated blood. These verses are used to show that Jesus was a full human being. The verses, though, aren't in our oldest and best manuscripts. It appears that scribes put them into the manuscripts, in order to make an anti-docetic statement about Jesus being fully human.

So some changes are anti-adoptionistic, others are anti-docetic. Other changes appear to be designed to counter the Gnostic idea that the divine Christ came into Jesus before baptism, and then left him prior to his death. A verse that I've given repeatedly in this course, Mark Chapter 15, Verse 34; Jesus hanging on the cross, cries out, "*Eloi, Eloi, lema sabachthani?*" "My God, my God, why have you forsaken me?" The text is originally given in Aramaic, and then Mark translates it into Greek for us. "My God, my God, why have you forsaken me?" It's very interesting, though, that in one of the earliest Gospel manuscripts, the translation is not, "My God, my God, why have you forsaken me?" In one early manuscript, the translation is, "My God, my God, why have you mocked me?"

It's an interesting change, because everybody else in this text has mocked Jesus. His disciples have fled, the passers-by have mocked him, both robbers have mocked him in Mark's Gospel, and at the end he says, "My God, my God, why have you mocked me?" That would make sense, except the Aramaic, "*Eloi, Eloi, lema sabachthani?*" doesn't mean, "Why have you mocked me;" it means, "Why have you forsaken me?"

Why would scribes change the text? Remember, Gnostics used this text in a literal sense, "My God, my God, why have you left me behind?" Gnostics used the text to show that the divine element had left Jesus and gone back to the Pleroma, to leave the man Jesus to die by himself. In order to counter that interpretation, scribes have then changed the Greek text so that Jesus doesn't complain about being left behind; he complains about being mocked. So now the text can no longer be used to support a Gnostic Christology.

Well, lots of other examples of this phenomenon could be readily adduced. But these are probably enough simply to make my basic point. Proto-orthodox scribes, who were concerned about the use or the abuse of their Scriptural texts, occasionally changed them to make them more useful for the orthodox cause, and less available to non-orthodox Christians. I'm not claiming that this was necessarily an insidious practice; it may be the motives of these scribes, changing the text was pure as driven snow. But nonetheless it's true, they did occasionally alter their texts, and these alterations of these texts had a permanent affect on Christian interpretation, since in some cases, it was the altered text that came to be copied more often than the original text, so that even today, people sometimes base their understandings of the New Testament on passages that do not have the original wording.

Be that as it may, I can quickly summarize the point of the lecture. It was not simply the collection of the New Testament books into a canon and the insistence on a literal interpretation of these books that furthered the proto-orthodox agenda against various kinds of heretics. On occasion, proto-orthodox scribes modified their texts in order to make them say what they were already thought to mean, and so to prevent their use by their heretical opponents.

Lecture Twenty-Four
Early Christian Creeds

Scope:

This final lecture brings our course to closure by considering the formation of the creeds in early Christianity, statements of faith to be made by all believers to affirm what was considered to be true (that is, "orthodox") and to deny what was false (that is, "heretical"). The well-known creeds of the fourth century, such as the Nicene Creed, developed from earlier formulations known as the "rule of faith" and from confessions made by converts before baptism. In large measure, these creedal affirmations emerged from the controversies within Christianity, representing orthodox responses to such groups as the Ebionites, Marcionites, and Gnostics. Because the orthodox were fighting on several fronts simultaneously, some of the creedal statements about the nature of Christ (as God and man) and God (as three but one) were quite consciously set forth as paradoxical, mysteries to be celebrated rather than intellectual puzzles to be solved.

Outline

I. To begin this final lecture in our course, we might do well to consider the big picture of what we have seen with respect to Christianity in the second and third centuries.

   A. Different groups of Christians had different beliefs: about the nature of God and about how many gods there were; about who Jesus was, whether he was human, or divine, or something else; about the world we live in, whether it was inherently good, the creation of God, or inherently evil, the creation of a malevolent deity; about what humans are, about how they can understand the world and be right with God; about the nature and extent of the Scriptures; and so on.

   B. There were, in fact, so many different groups of early Christians, who believed so many different things, that many scholars have come to prefer to speak not of early Christianity but of early *Christianities*.

C. As we have seen, one of these groups of early Christians eventually emerged as victorious in the struggles to acquire dominance and to determine once and for all the nature of Christianity as it was to evolve in a variety of ways down to the present day.

D. This struggle involved, among other things, deciding which books should be counted as sacred Scripture and how these books ought to be interpreted. It also involved deciding who should be in control of the churches and make major decisions about church life, worship, and belief. As we will see further in this lecture, on a very basic level, the struggles involved what it was that should and must be believed by those who converted to this faith.

E. In short, the struggles to establish orthodoxy by the fourth Christian century involved issues of the canon (which books should be included), the clergy (who should be in charge), and the creed (what should be believed).

F. We will consider this final aspect of the struggle, the development of a creed, in this last lecture.

II. One of the things that made Christianity so unusual in the ancient world was its insistence, from the outset, that what a person believed mattered religiously.

    A. In none of the other religions in the Greco-Roman world did theology or proper belief figure at all prominently.

        1. Pagan religiosity was almost entirely a matter of cultic activity.

        2. Judaism is a partial, but only partial, exception. Being Jewish was far more about doing God's will than belief.

    B. Christianity was different from the beginning in stressing the importance not only of belief but of correct belief. This insistence was rooted in two major factors.

        1. Christianity was, from the beginning, a religion as focused on cognition as on action, in that it insisted that a person was put into a right standing with God by accepting what God had done by having his son die on the cross. This was not a religion of cultic act to appease God but of accepting in faith what God had done.

2. Moreover, Christianity uniquely insisted that its understanding of the relationship with God was the only true one; there was no other way to salvation.

3. Both of these aspects—the stress on an act of cognition and an exclusivistic claim— made Christianity virtually unique among the religions of the Greco-Roman world in stressing the possibility of false belief (heresy) or correct belief (orthodoxy).

III. It is no surprise that different groups developed statements of what proper and improper beliefs were.

A. Already in the Letter to the Galatians, Paul stresses that anyone adhering to a form of Christianity different from the one he proclaimed stands under God's curse.

B. It became important, then, to know what counted as proper belief. Even before Paul, creed-like statements were developed to affirm the true beliefs (Rom. 1:3–4; 1 Cor. 15:3–5).

C. In the second century, proto-orthodox leaders devised more elaborate statements of faith, indicating not only positive statements of what was to be believed, but also negative statements of what must not be believed (cf. Ignatius of Antioch, Ign Eph. 18:2).

D. In the second century, a set of beliefs called the *regula fidei*, "the rule of faith," developed, which included the "basics" that all Christians were to believe, as taught, according to the proponents of the rule, by the apostles themselves.

1. There were various proto-orthodox authors who propounded the *regula fidei* (such as Irenaeus and Tertullian). It was not in a set form.

2. But it was always clearly directed against those (such as Marcion or the Gnostics) who opposed one or another aspect of it.

3. Typically, it included belief in only one God, the creator of the world, who created everything out of nothing; belief in his Son, Jesus Christ, predicted by the prophets and born through the Virgin Mary; belief in Jesus' miraculous life, death, resurrection, and ascension; and belief in the Holy Spirit, who is present on earth until the end, when there would be a final judgment in which the

righteous would be rewarded and the unrighteous, condemned to eternal torment.

IV. In addition to the *regula fidei*, there developed early on, actual creeds that were to be recited, possibly by the convert at the time of baptism.

A. These began as catechetical questioning in three parts, in conformity with the threefold immersion under the water, as suggested by Matthew 28:19–20 ("baptize in the name of the Father, the Son, and the Holy Spirit").

B. The creeds then became tripartite, stressing proper doctrines about Father, Son, and Spirit.

C. They were directed against the improper doctrines espoused by other groups.

D. Thus, we have the creeds that have come down to us today, most notably the Apostles' and Nicene Creeds, both of which reached something like their modern-day form in the fourth century.

1. Noting that these are formulated against specific heretical views; for example, "I believe in one God, the Father almighty, maker of heaven and earth. And in his one Son, Jesus Christ our Lord." These formulations were made not simply because they sounded good, but because there were other groups of Christians that disagreed with them (who thought, for example, that there was more than one God, that the true God was not the creator, that Jesus was not the creator's son, that Jesus Christ was two beings, not one, and so on).

2. Moreover, it is worth nothing that the views that ultimately developed were necessarily paradoxical in nature. Is Jesus God or man? Both! If Jesus is God and his father is God, are there two Gods? No, there's one!

3. Why the paradoxes? Because proto-orthodox Christians had to fight adoptionists on one side and docetists on the other, Marcion on one side and Gnostics on the other, and so on.

E. The result is the highly paradoxical affirmations of faith that have come down to the present day, about God who is the creator of all things but not of the evil and suffering found in all things; of Jesus who is both completely human and completely divine, not half of one or the other, but who is only one being, not two; of the Father, the Son, and the Spirit as three separate beings that make up only one God.

F. By its very nature, then, orthodox belief has to claim cognitive truth, but the way that truth developed and evolved over the centuries means that it needs to defy cognitive categories. This is why Christian theologians from the earliest of times have insisted that the ultimate truths of the faith are to be understood as divine mysteries, mysteries that must be acknowledged as true, but that defy full understanding as wrapped in the mystery of God himself, who must be known, but who is beyond all knowledge.

V. Despite the development of these creeds, Christianity, of course, has continued to be wildly diverse.

A. The differences among denominations is still mind-boggling, between the Pentecostals and the Greek Orthodox, the Mormons and the Southern Baptists, the Roman Catholics and the Plymouth Brethren.

B. But these are differences that all emerged from the triumphs of orthodox Christianity of the fourth century.

C. We can only imagine what might have happened if things had turned out differently; if different books, such as the Gospel of Thomas or the Apocalypse of Peter, had made it into the Bible; if different groups, such as the Valentinian Gnostics or the Marcionites, had won more converts than their proto-orthodox contemporaries.

D. But whether we like it or not, for the most part, these other views became marginalized, castigated as heresies, then destroyed, along with their sacred books. Now, rather than being a matter of interest for the religious claims they made, they are interesting only historically, as we think not only on how Christianity developed but also on how it might have developed differently if these other forms of faith had not been so effectively countered and, for all practical purposes, lost.

Essential Reading:

Bart Ehrman, *After the New Testament*, readings 73–76.

Jeroslav Pelikan, *The Christian Tradition*, vol. 1.

Supplementary Reading:

Walter Bauer, *Orthodoxy and Heresy in Earliest Christianity.*

Richard Norris, *The Christological Controversy.*

William G. Rusch, *The Trinitarian Controversy.*

Questions to Consider:

1. What might be seen as the difference between "faith" in God and having the right "beliefs" about God?

2. If the later creeds, such as the Nicene Creed, were products of their own time, developed over a long period of conflict, why is it that mainstream Christian churches today continue to affirm *those* creeds instead of devising ones appropriate to the conflicts of their own time?

Lecture Twenty-Four—Transcript
Early Christian Creeds

To begin this final lecture in our course, we might do well to reflect on the big picture of what we've seen, with respect to Christianity in the second and third centuries. Different groups of Christians had different beliefs—about the nature of God and how many gods there were; about who Jesus was, whether he was human or divine, whether he was one being or two beings; about the world we live in, whether it's inherently good, the creation of God, or inherently evil, the creation of a malevolent deity; about what humans are, about how they can understand the world and be right with God; about the nature and extent of the Scriptures, etc, etc.

There were, in fact, so many different groups of early Christians, who believed so many different things, that many scholars have come to prefer to speak, not of early Christianity, but of early Christianities. As we've seen, one of these groups of early Christians eventually emerged as victorious in the struggles to acquire dominance and to determine, once and for all, the nature of Christianity as it was to evolve, in a variety of ways, down to the present day. This struggle for dominance involved, first, deciding which books should be counted as sacred Scripture and how these books ought to be interpreted. Second, it involved deciding who should be in charge of the churches, and to make major decisions about church life, worship, and belief. And third, as we'll see further in this lecture, on a very basic level, it involved the struggle over what should and must be believed by those who converted to this faith.

In other words, the struggles to establish orthodoxy, by the fourth Christian century, involved issues of the canon, which books should be included; the clergy, who should be in charge; and the creed, what should be believed. It's this final aspect of this aspect of the struggle, the development of a creed, that we'll consider in the present lecture.

As we've seen, one of the things that makes Christianity so unusual in the ancient world was its insistence, at the very outset, that what a person believed mattered religiously. In none of the other religions in the Greco-Roman world did theology, or proper belief, figure at all prominently. Pagan religiosity was almost entirely a matter of cultic activity, performing the proper prayers and sacrifices at home and in the temple in order to appease the gods, in order to provide the gods what they needed, so the gods could provide the worshipers with what they needed. These ancient pagan religions were a matter of cultic activity.

Judaism is a partial—but only a partial—exception to the rule for the ancient world. Being Jewish was far more about doing God's will than it was about belief. And, of course, in the Torah, a good deal of the Torah involves how to make sacrifices in the temple, as God has prescribed. Judaism emphasized activity as much, or even more, than belief. Christianity, however, was different from the very beginning, in that Christianity stressed the importance not only of belief, but also of correct belief. In some respects, correct belief was the major focus of this new religion.

The insistence on correct belief was rooted in two major factors. First, Christianity was, from the beginning, a religion that was focused as much on cognition as it was on action, in that it insisted that a person was put into a right standing with God, not by what he or she did, but by accepting what God had done by having His son die on the cross. This was not a religion of cultic act to appease God, but of accepting in faith what God Himself had already done; so that it's an act of cognition and commitment to what God has done, rather than a cultic act to appease God. That's the first major factor.

Second factor; Christianity uniquely insisted that its understanding of the relationship with God was the only true one. There was no other way to salvation. Both of these aspects, the stress on an act of cognition and an exclusivistic claim, made Christianity virtually unique among the religions in the Greco-Roman world, in stressing the possibility of false belief, or heresy; or correct belief, orthodoxy. As I've indicated, in the other religions in the Greco-Roman world, orthodoxy and heresy were not even possibilities, because correct belief, theological statements, creedal formulae, were virtually absent from other religions. Not so Christianity.

Given the importance, not just of belief, but of correct belief, it's no surprise that different Christian groups developed statements of what proper and improper beliefs were. We find the beginnings of the movement towards establishing statements of proper belief in our earliest Christian author, the apostle Paul. Most particularly, you can find aspects of the importance of proper belief in Paul's letter to the Galatians in the New Testament.

This is a very interesting letter. It is a letter in which Paul is engaged in a very heated controversy with some opponents. Paul is not pleased with the situation of his churches in the region of Galatia, which was one of the Roman provinces in Asia Minor, modern day Turkey. Paul is not pleased at all with what happened in this church. You can tell this from the outset of this letter. The letter to the Galatians is the only letter in the entire Pauline corpus in which Paul does not begin by thanking God for the congregation. Instead he begins by reprimanding the congregation, because they have departed from his preaching of the gospel, to follow another gospel.

Paul had started this church in this region in Galatia, apparently in a variety of villages and towns, possibly cities, in Galatia. His proclamation had been what it was in other places that he'd established churches; he proclaimed that one needs to believe in the one true God, not the gods of the pagans; that one needs to accept the death and resurrection of Jesus for salvation, and that one is made right with God by believing in Jesus' death and resurrection; that Gentiles don't have to become Jewish or keep the Jewish law in order to be right with God. After Paul had left the community, though, to go off and start churches in other areas, there were missionaries who came in his wake, missionaries who proclaimed a Jewish-Christian message, who said that God had instituted the rite of circumcision to make people members of the covenant. They could quote the Scriptures, the Torah itself, in which God give s circumcision to the father of Jews, Abraham, and says everybody who is to be a member of the covenantal community, whether born Jewish or coming into the Jewish family from outside, needs to be circumcised. If somebody is not circumcised, they are to be cut off from the community.

Moreover, this passage in the Book of Genesis says that this is an eternal covenant; it will never pass away. These missionaries who came in Paul's wake insisted, if people in Galatia wanted to be right with God, of course, they needed to believe in Jesus who died for their sins; they also had to join in God's covenantal community. The men had to be circumcised. Men and women had to have followed the Jewish law.

When Paul found out that this was the message being brought by these other Christian missionaries, he was incensed. He insisted that, in fact, these Galatians had misunderstood, and that if they accept this alternative gospel, they are in danger of losing their salvation. It wasn't just a matter, to Paul, of doing something that one doesn't need to do. It wasn't just, for him, that you don't have to follow the law and if you do it, you are doing something extra. For Paul, if you are a Gentile and you're following the law, you have misunderstood, because you appear to think that you have to follow the law for salvation, but salvation comes apart from the law. So Paul is quite incensed. He begins this letter:

> I am astonished that you are so quickly deserting the one who called you in the grace of Christ, and are turning to a different gospel. Not that there is another gospel, but there are some who are confusing you and want to pervert the gospel of Christ. But even if we or an angel from heaven should proclaim to you a gospel contrary to what we proclaimed to you, let that one be accursed. As we have said before, so now I repeat, if anyone proclaims to you a gospel contrary to what you have received, let that one be accursed.

There is only one gospel message for Paul; it is the message that he has proclaimed. People have to believe the right gospel. If they believe any variation on this, then they stand accursed. These are very strong words, but they become the kind of statement that becomes prominent in Christianity as people began to insist on the importance of believing the right things and rejecting teachings, even Christian teachings, that are false.

And so, proper belief becomes of essential importance, from the earliest stages. In fact, even before Paul was writing his letters, we know that Christians were developing creed-like statements, in order to affirm their true beliefs. We know this is happening before Paul, because there are passages in Paul's writings in which he appears to be quoting an earlier creedal statement that he himself has inherited. An example of this comes in Paul's Letter to the Corinthians, the First Letter to the Corinthians, in Chapter 15, where Paul indicates that he's passing on a creedal statement that he himself has inherited. It's a statement about what one must believe in order to be right with God. Paul says, First Corinthians 15, Verses 3-5, "For I handed on to you, as of first importance, what I in turn had received;"—basically, he's passing on a tradition that he has received—"that Christ died for our sins in accordance with the Scriptures and that he was buried, and that he was raised on the third day in accordance with the Scriptures and that he appeared to Cephas and then to the twelve."

This statement in First Corinthians 15:3-5, is a carefully crafted statement that you can actually put into lines, almost as a modern creedal statement, or as a poem. It stands rather well. and it seems to indicate that this is a quotation of a creed that Paul, in fact, is giving to the Corinthians, something that they themselves confessed, possibly during their baptism services. He indicates that it's a statement that he himself has inherited, and that it involves two parts; that Jesus died for their sins, according to the Scriptures, and that he was raised from the dead, according to Scriptures, so that he fulfills Scripture by his death and resurrection. This a kind of creedal statement that people would have proclaimed early on in Christianity from the very early stages, even before Paul's writings.

Over time, Christian leaders devised more elaborate statements of faith, such as we begin to find later, after Paul's day, down into the second century. One of the more interesting statements that we find, a statement of faith, is found in the writings of this early second-century Church Father, Ignatius of Antioch. If you recall, Ignatius of Antioch was a bishop who had been arrested for Christian activities, and was being sent under armed guard to Rome, where he was to face the wild beasts. He was going to be martyred for his faith, in the arena in Rome. En route to his martyrdom, Ignatius wrote seven letters that still survive.

These letters are concerned with a number of issues in the churches that he'd become familiar with on his travels to Rome. In particular, Ignatius is concerned about false teachings that he knows about in these churches. Sometimes he describes these false teachings. Some of them sound like Jewish-Christian Ebionite sorts of teachings; others of them sound like what developed into Gnosticism. He's concerned about false teachings. He's also concerned about the unity of the churches that he's addressing, and he's concerned that these churches line up behind their individual bishops who can lead them in the right way, so that they will stay faithful to the gospel.

The first letter of his that we have—it's a letter that happens to be written to the Christians of Ephesus, so this is Ignatius's Letter to the Ephesians. At one point he's talking about the false Christians, and he gives a kind of creedal statement that he sets up over against the statements of the false teachers. The statement is—this is in Ignatius letter to the Ephesians, Chapter 7: "There is one physician," says Ignatius; he's referring to Christ:

> … in other words, one who can heal your soul of both flesh, yet spiritual, who was born and yet is unbegotten. He is God incarnate. He is genuine life in the midst of death. He sprung from Mary as well as from God. First he was subject to suffering, then he was beyond suffering; Jesus Christ our Lord.

This is a highly paradoxical statement. The Christ is spirit, but he's flesh. He's born, yet he's not begotten. He is in life, yet he's in the midst of death. He's from Mary, yet he's from God. He first suffered, then he was beyond suffering. These are paradoxical statements. This kind of paradox is something that developed in the early Christian creeds, as we'll see later in this lecture.

Eventually, in the second century, there developed a set of beliefs that was known, even in the early church, as the *regula fidei*. The *regula fidei*; that's a Latin term that means "the rule of faith." Christian leaders insisted that all Christians should subscribe to the *regula fidei,* which included the basics of what all Christians were to believe, as taught, according to the proponents of the rule, by the apostles themselves. So these were sets of beliefs that everybody was to subscribe to. There are various proto-orthodox authors who propound the *regula fidei,* who say what it was; it's never given in the same form by two different authors. So there wasn't a set of form, the way that there developed an Apostles' Creed and a Nicene Creed that is recited the same way in all the churches. These proto-orthodox Church Fathers agreed that there were these set rules of faith, but they weren't in any set wording yet.

This *regula fidei* was always, clearly directed against those who opposed one or another aspect of these beliefs, for example, Marcion or the Gnostics. Typically, the *regula fidei* included belief in only one God, the creator of the world, Who created everything out of nothing. That kind of belief would be set against, for example, Marcion who thought there were two gods, or the Gnostics who believed in many gods. The *regula fidei* included belief in God's son, Jesus Christ, predicted by the prophets of the Old Testament, and born through the Virgin Mary—again, beliefs that became standard in proto-orthodox Christianity were directed against the views of other Christian groups. The *regula fidei* included belief in his, Jesus', miraculous life and death and resurrection and ascension. He was physically raised from the dead. He had actually died. He really ascended into heaven.

Finally, the *regula fidei* included belief in the Holy Spirit—the Holy Spirit who was present on earth until the end, according to this rule of faith, the end where there will be a Final Judgment in which the righteous will be rewarded and the unrighteous will be condemned to eternal torment. So the proto-orthodox Church Fathers insisted that the Holy Spirit was here, and that eventually he would bring about a Final Judgment, which would be a literal Final Judgment of the dead. People are going to be rewarded or punished depending, on how they live their lives, depending on what they believe. So that, then, is the *regula fidei* that developed in proto-orthodox circles, directed against various sorts of heretics.

In addition to the *regula fidei*, there developed, in early Christianity, actual creeds that were to be recited, possibly by those who had converted at the time of their baptism. So that creeds were statements that would affirm a certain understanding of the faith, recited when a person is baptized and, at that moment, when they're baptized, joining a Christian community. Probably, these creedal statements began as a kind of catechetical questioning in three parts. Somebody who converted to Christianity had to go through a catechesis—a time of learning about the faith. So these catechetical sets of instruction would involve questions that would be asked of the person being baptized, and these questions would come in three parts, in conformity with a three-fold immersion under the water when they're baptized.

In the earliest church, it was adults who were baptized. They were baptized by being immersed in water. We have some texts that indicate how this is to be done. One of our earliest Christian texts is a text called the Didake. The Didake gives instructions on how one is to be baptized, and we're told that they're to be baptized in running water, if it's available. If running water isn't available, well, then they can use water that isn't running; in other words, you can use a pool. If that's not available, you can pour water on the head three times.

There is a three-fold immersion under the water of adults in these early churches. And apparently, these catechetical questions would come to people in three parts. They'd answer one of the questions. It would be something like, "Do you believe in God the Father?" "Yes, I believe in God the Father, creator of heaven and earth, maker of all things," and then they'd be baptized. "Do you believe in Jesus Christ?" "Yes, I believe in Jesus Christ, His only son our Lord." Then they'd be baptized. "Do you believe in the Holy Spirit?" They'd recite the third part of the catechetical instruction.

This three-part instruction and baptism is probably rooted in a very early tradition, found now in the Gospel of Matthew. In the Gospel of Matthew, after Jesus is raised from the dead, he appears to his disciples and he sends them out with what is now called the great commission, Matthew, Chapter 28, Verses 19 and 20, where Jesus tells the disciples, "Go make disciples of all the nations, baptizing them in the name of the Father, and of the Son, and of the Holy Spirit, and teaching them to obey everything that I have commanded you. And lo, remember I am with you always, to the end of the age."

And so there developed a tri-part creed, stressing proper doctrines about the Father, Son, and Spirit. These doctrines that were developed were espoused in order not only to affirm what was right, but also to oppose beliefs that were wrong. So we have creeds that have come down to us today, most notably the Apostles' Creed and the Nicene Creed, both of which took their final formulation in the fourth century and later, both of which continue to be recited, in these later forms, still in churches today—the Apostles' Creed and the Nicene Creed.

It is noteworthy that even these Creeds that continue to be recited today are directed against specific heretical beliefs. For example, in the Creed that's still recited in churches, when it says, "I believe in one God, the Father almighty, maker of heaven and earth, and in His one Son, Jesus Christ our Lord," virtually every statement is directed against a second- and third-century heretical belief. "I believe in one God," as opposed to Marcion, who believes in two, the Gnostics who believe in many. "The Father almighty," so that the one God is the almighty Father, "Who made heaven and earth." Heaven and earth didn't come about by cosmic disaster, or isn't made by a wrathful God who's not the true God. It's the one God Almighty who made it; and so forth. These formulations of these Creeds were made, not simply because they happened to sound good, but because there were other groups of Christians who disagreed with them.

It's worth noting that the views that ended up being embodied in these Creeds were necessarily paradoxical in nature. As I've already intimated with respect to the creed found early in Ignatius's Letter to the Ephesians. The Creeds that become orthodox are necessarily paradoxical. Is Jesus God or is he man? Is he divine or is he human? Some early Christians said, well, he's God, but since he's God he obviously can't be man. You can't be both God and man; he's one or the other. Others would say, no, he's man, therefore he's not God. The proto-orthodox wanted to oppose both groups. So they had to affirm that Jesus was both God and man. But he wasn't two beings. He was one being. It is a paradox. If Jesus is God, then, well, does that mean that there are two gods? If you've got the Father as God and Jesus as God, that's two Gods. The proto-orthodox replied, No, there aren't two Gods. There is one God. Jesus is God; his Father is God; and, in fact, the Spirit is God. There are three beings that are God, but there's only one God—necessarily a paradox.

Why the paradox? Because proto-orthodox Christians had to fight adoptionists on the one side and docetists on the other. They had to fight Marcion on one side and then Gnostics on the other, etc. Their own creedal statements come about in opposition to views that were being propounded by people that they considered to be heretical. And so what has resulted is the highly paradoxical affirmations that have come down to us today, in the Christian creeds about God, Who is the creator of all things, but not the creator of evil and suffering that's found in all things; confessions about Jesus, who is both completely human and completely divine, not half one and half the other, but completely both, and yet who is only one being, not two. Paradoxical statements about the Father, the Son, and the Spirit as three separate beings, and yet comprising only one God—the doctrine of the Trinity. There is only one God, but there are three beings, and they are not all the same beings, they are three separate beings, but there aren't three Gods, there's one God.

By its very nature, then, orthodox belief has had to claim cognitive truth, but the way that truth developed and evolved over the centuries means that it needs to defy cognitive categories. It's cognitive, but it has to defy cognitive categories. That's why Christian theologians, from the earliest of times, have insisted that the ultimate truths of the faith are to be understood as divine mysteries—mysteries that must be acknowledged as true, but that defy full understanding, as wrapped in the mystery of God Himself, Who must be known, but Who is beyond all knowledge.

So these are to be affirmed as mysteries that can't really be understood, and if you think you have a handle on it, if you think you really do understand it, then you don't understand it; because it's a mystery. That's why analogies that try to explain the Trinity simply don't work, because these are set up so you can't really understand them. They are mysterious.

Despite the development of these Creeds, Christianity, of course, has continued to be wildly diverse. The fourth century didn't end the controversies. The differences among denominations, still today, are mind-boggling—between the Pentecostals and the Greek Orthodox, between the Mormons and the Southern Baptists, between the Roman Catholics and the Plymouth Brethren. But these are differences that all emerged from the triumphs of orthodox Christianity of the fourth century. Every form of Christianity that we know today ultimately goes back to the victory of the fourth century over heretical groups, that we've been examining in this course of lectures.

We can imagine what might have happened if things had turned out differently. If different books, like the Gospel of Thomas, or the Epistle of Barnabas, or the Apocalypse of Peter, had made it into the Bible; if different groups, like the Valentinian Gnostics, or the Marcionites, or the Ebionites had won more converts than their proto-orthodox contemporaries; we can only imagine what would have happened. But whether we like it or not, for the most part these other views became marginalized, castigated as heresies, and then destroyed along with their sacred books.

But now, rather than being a matter of interest for the religious claims that they made, these other groups are interesting only historically, to historians who want to know what happened in early Christianity, who want to know about the conflicts between groups that were later castigated as heretics. These groups, now, are interesting, not because people genuinely think of adopting their religious views—although there are still some groups that claim to be representing these older views, now that they've become more widely known, groups that want to say that they, in fact, are Ebionites, we have Jewish-Christian groups today, or some groups that claim that they actually are Gnostics—but these groups are really basing their knowledge on historical understandings of what these groups used to be. There isn't historical continuity with these groups.

For the most part, these ancient groups of the second and third century are interesting to us only historically, as we think, not only on how Christianity developed, but also on how it might have developed differently, if these other forms of faith had not been so effectively countered and for all practical purposes, then, made to disappear—until modern scholars became interested in uncovering these lost Christianities and the sacred Scriptures that they revered.

Timeline

333–323 B.C.	Conquests of Alexander the Great.
145 B.C.	Book of Daniel, final book of Hebrew Bible.
140 B.C.	Rise of Jewish Sects: Pharisees, Sadducees, Essenes, Fourth Philosophy.
63 B.C.	Conquest of Palestine by Romans.
44 B.C.	Assassination of Julius Caesar.
40–4 B.C.	Herod, King of the Jews.
27 B.C.–A.D. 14	Octavian Caesar Augustus as emperor.
4 B.C.–A.D. 65	Seneca.
4 B.C.?	Jesus' birth.
A.D. 14–37	Emperor Tiberius.
A.D. 26–36	Pilate as governor of Judea.
A.D. 30?	Jesus' death.
A.D. 33?	Conversion of Paul.
A.D. 37–41	Emperor Caligula.
A.D. 41–54	Emperor Claudius.
A.D. 50–60?	Pauline epistles.
A.D. 50–60?	Q source.
A.D. 50–70?	M and L sources.
A.D. 50?–110?	Ignatius of Antioch.
A.D. 54–68	Emperor Nero.
A.D. 56–117?	Tacitus.
A.D. 61/62–113	Pliny the Younger.
A.D. 65?	Gospel of Mark.

A.D. 66–70	Jewish Revolt and destruction of the Temple.
A.D. 69–79	Emperor Vaspasian.
A.D. 79–81	Emperor Titus.
A.D. 80–85?	Gospels of Matthew and Luke, Book of Acts.
A.D. 80–100?	Deutero-Pauline epistles, 1 Peter, Hebrews, James.
A.D. 81–96	Emperor Domitian.
A.D. 85–105?	Pastoral epistles.
A.D. 90–95?	Gospel of John.
A.D. 95?	Book of Revelation.
A.D. 98–117	Emperor Trajan.
A.D. 100–165	Justin Martyr.
A.D. 100–160?	Marcion.
A.D. 100–160?	Valentinus.
A.D. 110–130?	Gospels of Peter and Thomas.
A.D. 120?	2 Peter.
A.D. 130–200	Irenaeus.
A.D. 135?	Epistle of Barnabas.
A.D. 150–220?	Clement of Alexandria.
A.D. 160–225	Tertullian.
A.D. 170–230?	Hippolytus of Rome.
A.D. 185–251	Origen of Alexandria.
A.D. 190	Melito of Sardis.
A.D. 249–251	Emperor Decius.
A.D. 260–340	Eusebius.
A.D. 285–337	Constantine.
A.D. 300–375	Athanasius.

Glossary

3 Corinthians: Part of the Apocryphal Acts of John, a letter allegedly by Paul to the Corinthians warning against *docetic* teachers and emphasizing that Jesus was a real flesh-and-blood human being and that there could be a future resurrection of the body.

Acts of John: A group of apocryphal tales surrounding the exploits and encounters of John, the son of Zebedee, during his missionary work in Asia Minor.

Acts of Paul and Thecla: A tale of Paul and his female convert Thecla, who reneges on her vows to marry and instead adopts an ascetic lifestyle, leading to her condemnation to death by the state authorities but her miraculous deliverance by God.

Acts of Thomas: A group of apocryphal tales surrounding the exploits and ascetic preaching of Thomas, allegedly the twin brother of Jesus, during his missionary work in Asia Minor.

adoptionism: The view that Jesus was not divine but was a flesh-and-blood human being who had been adopted by God to be his son at his baptism.

aeons: Divine beings who make up the *Pleroma* in gnostic religions.

Apocalypse of Peter: A pseudepigraphic work in the name of Simon Peter that narrates the blessings of the saved and the torments of the damned in the afterlife, based on what appears to be a tour of the two regions conducted by Jesus.

Apocalypticism: A worldview held by many ancient Jews and Christians maintaining that the present age is controlled by forces of evil, but that these will be destroyed at the end of time, when God intervenes in history to bring in his kingdom, an event thought to be imminent.

apocrypha: Literally, "hidden books." Used to refer to books that are of the same "kind" as those of Scripture (such as gospels, epistles, and so on) but that were not included in the canon.

apostle: From a Greek word meaning "one who is sent." In early Christianity, the term designated special emissaries of the faith who were special representatives of Christ.

apostolic fathers: Group of early proto-orthodox church writers whose works were composed soon after the books of the New Testament, including Ignatius, Clement, Polycarp, and Barnabas.

autograph: The original manuscript of a document, from a Greek word that means "the writing itself."

canon: From a Greek word that literally means "ruler" or "straight edge." The term is used to designate a recognized collection of texts; the New Testament canon is, thus, the collection of books that Christians have traditionally accepted as authoritative.

Carpocratians: A group of second-century Gnostics known to us, in part, through the writings of Clement of Alexandria; they were thought to engage in wild, licentious activities as part of their religious practices.

church fathers: Christian authors of the early centuries, normally seen as significant for the development of orthodox theology.

Codex Sinaiticus: Important fourth-century manuscript of the Bible.

Council of Nicea: The first major council of Christian bishops, called by the Emperor Constantine in A.D. 325, in which major doctrinal issues of the church were resolved, resulting in a creed that ultimately formed the basis of the Nicene Creed.

diatesseron: Literally means "through the four." Used as a technical term to refer to a harmonization of the four New Testament gospels into one long narrative, created by a second-century author named Tatian.

Didymus Judas Thomas: The alleged author of the Coptic Gospel of Thomas, whose exploits are narrated in the Acts of Thomas; in these traditions, he is said to be the (twin) brother of Jesus.

docetism: The view that Jesus was not a human being but only "appeared" to be, from a Greek word that means "to seem" or "to appear."

Ebionites: A group of second-century adoptionists who maintained Jewish practices and Jewish forms of worship.

festal letter: Annual letter written to establish the date of the Easter feast.

gematria: Ancient Jewish practice of interpreting words by determining the numerical values of their letters.

Gnosticism: A group of ancient religions, which were closely related to Christianity, that maintained that sparks of a divine being had become entrapped in the present evil world and could escape only by acquiring the appropriate secret *gnosis* (Greek for "knowledge") of who they were and of how they could escape. This gnosis was generally thought to have been brought by an emissary descended from the divine realm.

Gospel of Peter: A gospel mentioned by Eusebius as containing a docetic Christology, a fragment of which was discovered in a monk's tomb in 1886. The fragment contains an alternative account of Jesus' trial, crucifixion, and resurrection, notable for its anti-Jewish emphases and its legendary qualities (including a tale of Jesus actually emerging from his tomb on Easter morning).

Gospel of the Ebionites: A gospel used by the Ebionites that appears to have been a conflation of stories found in Matthew, Mark, and Luke and originally composed in Greek.

Gospel of the Nazareans: A gospel used by the Ebionites that appears to have been very much like our Gospel of Matthew, minus the first two chapters, and possibly written in Hebrew (or Aramaic).

Gospel of Thomas: The most famous document of the Nag Hammadi library; it contains 114 sayings of Jesus, many of them similar to the sayings of the New Testament, others of them quite different in that they appear to presuppose a gnostic understanding of the world.

Gospel of Truth: A gnostic document from the Nag Hammadi library and thought by many scholars to have been written by Valentinus, a prominent Christian Gnostic of the second century (founder of the Valentinian Gnostics), which celebrates the joy of salvation provided by the liberating knowledge brought by Christ.

heresiologist: An opponent of heresy; one who engages in literary polemics against heretical groups.

heresy: Any worldview or set of beliefs deemed by those in power to be deviant, from a Greek word that means "choice" (because "heretics" have "chosen" to deviate from the "truth"; see **orthodoxy**).

heterodoxy: Literally "another belief," used as a synonym for "heresy."

Infancy Gospel of Thomas: Early Infancy Gospel (first half of second century?) that narrates the miraculous and occasionally mischievous activities of the boy Jesus between the ages of five and twelve.

Infancy Gospels: Gospels that narrate events surrounding the birth and early life of Jesus.

manuscript: Any handwritten copy of a literary text.

Marcionites: Followers of Marcion, the second-century Christian scholar and evangelist, later labeled a heretic for his docetic Christology and his belief in two Gods, the harsh legalistic God of the Jews and the merciful loving God of Jesus—views that he claimed to have found in the writings of Paul.

muratorian canon: A fragmentary list of the books that its anonymous author believed belonged in the New Testament Scriptures; named after the eighteenth-century scholar who discovered the manuscript, L.A. Muratori.

Nag Hammadi: Village in Upper (South) Egypt, near the place where a collection of gnostic writings, including the Gospel of Thomas, was discovered in 1945.

orthodoxy: Literally, "right opinion"; a term used to designate a worldview or set of beliefs acknowledged to be true by the majority of those in power. For its opposite, see **heresy**.

paleography: The study of ancient handwriting, used to date manuscripts.

patristic writings: Writings of the orthodox church "fathers" (Latin: *patres*), starting with the period after the New Testament.

pleroma: Literally, the "fullness," used in gnostic sources to refer to the divine realm.

Proto-Gospel of James: An account allegedly written by James, the brother of Jesus, of the miraculous events surrounding the birth and early life of Mary, who is chosen as the special vessel to bear the Son of God.

Proto-orthodox Christianity: A form of Christianity endorsed by some Christians of the second and third centuries (including the apostolic fathers), which promoted doctrines that were declared "orthodox" by the victorious Christian party in the fourth and later centuries, in opposition to such groups as the Ebionites, the Marcionites, and the Gnostics.

pseudepigrapha: Literally, "false writings," commonly used of ancient non-canonical Jewish and Christian literary texts, many of which were written pseudonymously.

pseudonymity: The practice of writing under a "false name," evident in a large number of pagan, Jewish, and Christian writings from antiquity.

Regula Fidei: Literally, "the rule of faith." Used as a technical term to refer to the proto-orthodox doctrines that were understood to lie at the heart of Christian theology.

Secret Gospel of Mark: Allegedly, a second edition of Mark's gospel known to the spiritually elite of Alexandria, quoted in a letter of Clement of Alexandria to an otherwise unknown Theodore, which was discovered in 1958 in the library of the monastery of Mar Saba, southeast of Jerusalem, by Morton Smith.

Separationist Christology: Understanding of Christ typical among Gnostics, which maintained that there was a difference between the man Jesus and the divine Christ.

serapion: Second-century bishop of Antioch known from the *Ecclesiastical History of Eusebius* for his initial acceptance, then ultimate rejection (on theological grounds) of the Gospel of Peter being used in the village of Rhossus under his jurisdiction.

Synoptic Gospels: The Gospels of Matthew, Mark, and Luke, which tell many of the same stories, sometimes in the same words, so that they can be placed side by side "to be seen together" (the literal meaning of *synoptic*).

textual criticism: An academic discipline that attempts to establish the original wording of a text on the basis of its surviving manuscripts.

theodicies: Literally, "the righteousness of God." The term is used to refer to any explanation of how evil and suffering can exist in the world if God is both all-powerful and loving.

Biographical Notes

Athanasius: Athanasius was a highly influential and controversial bishop of Alexandria throughout the middle half of the fourth century. Born around 300 A.D., he was active in the large and powerful Alexandrian church already as a young man, appointed as deacon to the then bishop Alexander. He served as secretary at the important Council of Nicea in 325 A.D., which attempted to resolve critical issues concerning the nature of Christ as fully divine, of the same substance as God the father, and co-eternal with the father. As Bishop of Alexandria from 328–375, Athanasius was a staunch defender of this Nicene understanding of Christ and a key player in the development of the orthodox doctrine of the trinity, in which there were three distinct persons (Father, Son, and Spirit) who were nonetheless one God, all of the same substance. This defense created enormous difficulties for Athanasius in the face of powerful opposition, to which he himself reacted with a show of force (even violence). He was sent into exile on several occasions during his bishopric, spending nearly sixteen years away from Alexandria while trying to serve as its bishop. Author of numerous surviving works, Athanasius is most significant for this course for his role in determining which books should be accepted in his churches as sacred Scripture. In 367 A.D., in his thirty-ninth annual "Festal letter," which like all the others, set the date for the celebration of Easter and included pastoral instruction, he indicated that the twenty-seven books that we now have in the New Testament, and only those twenty-seven, should be regarded as canonical. This decree helped define the shape of the canon for all time and helped lead to the declaration of other books—gnostic gospels and the like—as heretical.

Barnabas: We are not well informed about the historical Barnabas. He is mentioned both by the apostle Paul (Gal. 2:13; 1 Cor. 9:6) and the Book of Acts (Acts 9:27; 11:22–26) as one of Paul's traveling companions, and it appears that he was originally a Hellenistic Jew who converted to faith in Christ, then became, like Paul, a traveling missionary who spread the faith. The Book of Acts goes so far as to consider him one of the "apostles" (Acts 14:4, 14). The Epistle of Barnabas discussed in this course is attributed to him, but modern scholars are reasonably sure that he could not have written it. The book appears to have been written some time around 130 or 135

A.D., some sixty years or so after the historical Barnabas would have died. The book was attributed to him, then, by Christians who wanted to advance its authoritative claims as being rooted in the views of one of the most important figures from the early years of Christianity.

Walter Bauer: Walter Bauer was an influential German theological scholar, whose scholarly works have made a permanent impact on the field of early Christian studies. Born in 1877, he had university positions at Marburg, Breslau, and finally, Göttingen, where he spent the majority of his long career. He died in 1960. Bauer is probably best known for a Greek lexicon (dictionary) of the New Testament and other early Christian writings, which he edited and which, after further revision, is still the standard work in the field and is called by his name. For this course, he is most important for his classic book, *Orthodoxy and Heresy in Earliest Christianity*, in which he set out to dismantle the classical Eusebian understanding of the relationship of orthodoxy and heresy. Looking at an enormous range of ancient sources and subjecting them to careful and minute analysis, sometimes with inquisitorial zeal, Bauer maintained that orthodoxy was *not* always the oldest and largest form of Christianity, but that what later came to be called heresy was, in many regions of Christendom, the oldest form of the faith and that, in many places, it was difficult to draw hard lines between what was heretical and what was orthodox. In his view, what later came to be crystallized into orthodoxy was the form of Christianity prominent in the early years in Rome; because of its administrative skill and material wealth, the Roman church was able to cast its influence onto other churches of the Mediterranean, until eventually, its understanding of the faith became universal. Once this version of Christianity became dominant, its representatives (such as Eusebius) rewrote the history of the disputes, contending that their perspective had been dominant from the very beginning.

Clement of Alexandria: Clement is a shadowy figure from the early days of the Alexandrian church. Born probably around 150 A.D., possibly in Athens, he appears to have come to Alexandria, Egypt, to pursue his theological training with leading Christian thinkers of his day. Tradition indicates that while there, he became the head of the catechetical school (which provided rudimentary training in the faith for Christian converts) but that he fled Alexandria in 202 A.D. during a persecution there. Clement is the author of several surviving works, including an important *Apology for Christianity,* a book on Christian living and manners, and a book called the *Miscellanies,* which sketches out some of his most important philosophical and theological views. For this course, Clement is most important for a letter that he allegedly wrote—if authentic, it is the only surviving letter from his hand—in which he mentions the existence of a secret gospel produced by Mark and used by the spiritually elite Christians of Alexandria, a gospel that had been stolen by the nefarious gnostic group called the Carpocratians and falsified to their own ends.

Epiphanius: Epiphanius was the bishop of Salamis (on Cyprus) in the second half of the fourth century (315–403 A.D.). Known as a rigorous supporter of monasticism, he is most famous for his virulent attacks on anything that struck him as heretical. His most well preserved work is called the *Panarion,* which means "medicine chest." In it, he intends to provide the orthodox antidote for the bites of the serpents of heresy. The book contains detailed accounts (some of them fabricated) and refutations of eighty different heresies that Epiphanius had come across during his ardent search for falsehood in the church (twenty of the heresies are actually pre-Christian sets of false teaching). For some of the lesser known gnostic groups, Epiphanius is our principle source of information; unfortunately, given his lack of intellectual restraint, many of his claims appear to be unreliable.

Eusebius: Eusebius of Caesarea is one of the most important figures in the history of the early church. Born around 260 A.D., he was trained by some of the leading Christian scholars of his day and was to become the first author to produce a full history of Christianity up to his own day, in a book called the *Ecclesiastical* [or Church] *History.* Eusebius was quite active in the politics of the church and empire. Ordained bishop of the large and important church of Caesarea in 315, he was active at the Council of Nicea and the theological disputes in its aftermath, originally opposing but later accepting the creedal statements about Christ that were to become orthodox. He died around 340 A.D. Eusebius was a prolific writer, but it was his *Ecclesiastical History* in particular that made a huge impact on subsequent generations—down to our own day. This chronological sketch of early Christianity provides us with the majority of our information about the spread of Christianity throughout the Roman world, the persecution of the early Christians, the conflicts between what Eusebius considered to be orthodoxy and heresies, the development of church offices and structures, and so on. Of particular value in this ten-volume work is Eusebius's frequent citation, often lengthy, of his actual sources; through his account, we have access to the writings of his Christian predecessors that otherwise have been lost to history. Thus, even though Eusebius puts his own slant on the history that he tells, it is possible to use the sources that he cites to gain significant insight into the conflicts and developments that transpired in the Christian church of the first three centuries, up to his own day.

Hippolytus: Hippolytus was a controversial figure in the Roman church in the early third century, most well known today for his ten-volume work against heresies (of which volumes 2 and 3 are still lost). Born around 170 A.D., Hippolytus became a prominent figure in the church in Rome, often taking strong stands against movements within the church that he considered heretical. He is the first known "anti-pope," that is, one who allowed himself to be elected as the true pope on the grounds that the reigning pope (in this case, a man named Callistus; pope from 217–222) was, in fact, a heretic and had no right to claim the papal office. Probably because of his schismatic activities (and partly because he wrote in Greek, rather than Latin), Hippolytus was largely forgotten in the Western church until modern times, when some of his writings were discovered. The most important writing is called the *Refutation of All Heresies*, which explains the various heresies of the Christian church and tries to show how each of them is rooted not in the Christian revelation but in secular (and, therefore, erroneous) philosophical traditions. Despite the bias against the views he attacks, Hippolytus's work is still considered a valuable source of information on alternative forms of Christianity of the second and early third centuries.

Ignatius: Ignatius is one of the most interesting figures from the early second century. We know little of his life, except that he was bishop of the major church in Antioch, Syria; was arrested for Christian activities; and was sent to Rome under armed guard to face execution by being thrown to the wild beasts in the Roman arena. En route to his martyrdom, Ignatius wrote seven surviving letters to churches that had sent representatives to greet him. In these letters, he warns against false teachers, urges the churches to strive for unity, stresses the need for the churches to adhere to the teachings and policies of the one bishop residing over each of them, and emphasizes that he is eager to face his violent death so that he might be a true disciple of Christ. One of the letters that he wrote was to the bishop of the city of Smyrna, Polycarp, who may have been the one who collected the other letters together. Within a couple of centuries, other Christian authors forged other letters allegedly by Ignatius; throughout the Middle Ages, these forgeries were circulated with the authentic letters and were not recognized for what they were until scholars undertook an assiduous examination of them in the seventeenth century.

Irenaeus: Irenaeus was an important theologian and heresiologist of the late second century. Born probably around 130 A.D., he may have been raised in the city of Smyrna and educated, eventually, at Rome. He ended up in the Christian church of Lyon, Gaul (modern-day France), where he was made bishop around 178 A.D. He died around the year 200 A.D.

Irenaeus is our best patristic source for the gnostic sects of the second century. His most well known book is a five-volume attack on heresy, which he entitled *Refutation and Overthrow of What Is Falsely Called Gnosis*, frequently called simply *Against Heresies*. In it, he gives considerable detail concerning various heretical groups (not simply Gnostics) and, based on his understanding of Scripture and using a full panoply of rhetorical ploys and stratagems, refutes them one by one. This book was used as a source for many of the later heresiologists, including Tertullian and Epiphanius.

Justin Martyr: Justin was an important figure in the church of Rome in the mid-second century. Born of pagan parents (c. 100 A.D.), evidently in Samaria, he undertook secular philosophical training before converting to Christianity when he was about thirty. He began to teach the philosophical superiority of Christianity to secular learning, first in Ephesus, then in Rome, where he established a kind of Christian philosophical school in mid-century.

Justin is the first prominent Christian *apologist*, that is, one who defended the Christian faith against the charges of its cultured (pagan) despisers and strove to show its intellectual and moral superiority to anything that the pagan (or Jewish) world could offer. Three of his major works survive, usually known as his *First Apology* (a defense of Christianity addressed to the Emperor Antoninus Pius and his sons, including Marcus Aurelius, around 155 A.D.), his *Second Apology* (addressed to the Roman senate around 160 A.D.), and his *Dialogue with Trypho*. This last is an account of his conversion and subsequent debate with a (possibly fictitious) Jewish rabbi, Trypho, over the superiority of Christianity to Judaism, based largely on an exposition of key passages in the Old Testament. Justin's defense of Christianity led to political opposition; he was martyred on charges of being a Christian around 165 C.E.

Marcion: Marcion was one of the most infamous "heretics" of the second century. Tradition indicates that he was born and raised in Sinope, on the southern shore of the Black Sea, where as a young man, he acquired considerable wealth as a shipping merchant. His father was allegedly the bishop of the Christian church there, who excommunicated his son for his false teachings. In 139 A.D., Marcion went to Rome, where he spent five years developing his theological views, before presenting them to a specially called council of the church leaders. Rather than accepting Marcion's understanding of the gospel, however, the church expelled him for false teaching. Marcion then journeyed into Asia Minor, where he proved remarkably successful in converting others to his understanding of the Christian message. "Marcionite" churches were in existence for centuries after his death, around 160 A.D.

Marcion's understanding of the gospel was rooted in his interpretation of the writings of the apostle Paul, whose differentiation between the "law" (of the Old Testament) and the "gospel" (of Christ) Marcion took to an extreme, claiming that the old and new were fundamentally different, so much so that they represented the religions of different Gods. Marcion, in other words, was a *ditheist*, who thought that the Old Testament God—who had created the world, called Israel to be his people, and gave them his law—was a different god from the God of Jesus, who came into the world in the "appearance" of human flesh (because he was not actually part of the material world of the creator-God) to save people from the just but wrathful God of the Jews. Marcion's views were based on his canon of Scripture, the first canon known to be formally advanced by a Christian. Marcion's canon did not, obviously, contain anything from the Old Testament, but comprised a form of the Gospel of Luke and ten of Paul's letters (all those in the present New Testament except 1 and 2 Timothy and Titus).

Melito of Sardis: Little is known of the life of Melito, apart from the facts that he was bishop of the city of Sardis near the end of the second century (died around 190 A.D.); that at some point in his life, he made a pilgrimage to the Christian sites of the holy land; and that he was a staunch advocate of proto-orthodox Christianity. The one literary work of his to survive, discovered in the twentieth century, is a homily apparently delivered at an Easter celebration, in which Melito explicates the Old Testament account of the Passover in a way that shows that the Passover lamb represents Christ. In Melito's view, because Christ has fulfilled the foreshadowings and predictions of the Jewish Scriptures, the laws of the Jews are no longer in force. The old has passed away with the appearance of the new. In the course of this highly rhetorical exposition, Melito takes the occasion to lambaste the people of Israel for rejecting their own messiah, and his language at times is vitriolic in its anti-Judaic claims. This sermon represents the first known instance of a Christian charging the Jewish people with *deicide*, the murder of God.

Origen: Origen was the most brilliant and prolific Christian author of the first three centuries. A lengthy account of his life is provided by Eusebius in Book 6 of his *Ecclesiastical History*. Born in 185 A.D. in Alexandria, Egypt, of Christian parents, Origen was trained by some of the leading scholars of his day. Tradition claims that after a severe persecution in Alexandria in 202 A.D., in which his father was martyred, the highly precocious Origen was appointed to be head of the "catechetical school," which trained Christian converts in the rudiments of the faith. But he periodically came into conflict with the bishop of the Alexandrian church, named Demetrius, and eventually (230 A.D.) left Alexandria to settle in Caesarea, where he devoted himself to teaching, research, and writing. He was imprisoned during the persecution of the Roman Emperor Decius in 250 A.D. and died two years later as a result of prolonged torture. Origen's literary output was immense, aided by a literary patron, Ambrose, who provided him with extensive secretarial help (stenographers, copyists, and so on). He is thought to have produced nearly 2,000 volumes, including biblical commentaries, volumes of homilies, theological treatises, polemical tractates (against heresies), apologies, and practical and pastoral works. Most of his works are lost, but those that survive still fill many volumes. As a theologian, Origen developed many ideas that later became highly debated in disputes over the trinity, the person of Christ, and the nature of the soul. As a biblical scholar, he developed and refined methods of interpretation, including the extensive use of figurative modes of exegesis that proved highly influential in interpretive methods used down through the Middle Ages.

Ptolemy: Ptolemy was a second-century gnostic Christian from Italy. Almost nothing is known of his life, even though his teachings proved notorious among the proto-orthodox heresiologists, such as Irenaeus. He was a disciple of Valentinus and developed Valentinian teaching in distinctive ways. The only work to survive from his hand, the Letter to Flora, represents an understanding of the Old Testament that differs in some significant ways from that of his proto-orthodox opponents. He believes that the God who inspired parts of the Old Testament cannot be the one true God, because some laws, such as the *lex talionis*—an eye for an eye, a tooth for a tooth—are harsh and not worthy of the ultimate divinity, whereas other laws had to be "fulfilled" by Christ and, thus, were not in themselves perfect. The letter is, however, irenic in tone and, in many ways, reflects widespread understandings of the Old Testament among Christians (that it anticipates Christ, for example, who brought it to completion).

Morton Smith: Morton Smith (1915–1991), professor of ancient history at Columbia University, was a controversial but highly erudite scholar of antiquity. Author of numerous books and articles, he is most important for this course for his remarkable discovery made while cataloguing the manuscripts and books of the library of the monastery of Mar Saba, in the wilderness southwest of Jerusalem. There, in the blank pages in the back of a seventeenth-century edition of the letters of Ignatius, Smith found copied a portion of a letter allegedly written by Clement of Alexandria, the late second-century church father, in which he discusses and partially quotes a "second" edition of the Gospel of Mark that was not in general circulation but that was available to the spiritually elite Christians of his home city of Alexandria, Egypt. This so-called Secret Gospel of Mark, Clement claims, had been illicitly obtained by a heretical group of Gnostics, the Carpocratians, and falsified in view of their libertine doctrines. Clement goes on to quote two portions of the secret gospel, one of which appears to have homoerotic overtones. Smith maintains that this secret gospel represents clues about how to understand the historical Jesus himself, who, he says, practiced a baptismal rite that involved a mystical experience in which the person being baptized would experience a physical union with Jesus himself. Smith spent fifteen years working to authenticate and analyze this letter of Clement and published the results of his research in two books, an impressively learned account for scholars (*Clement of Alexandria and a Secret Gospel of Mark*) and a fascinating popular account for general audiences (*The Secret Gospel of Mark*). Scholars continue to study and speculate about this letter, in particular about whether it may represent a forgery; if so, what may have motivated it and, if not, how should we evaluate its significance for understanding the historical Jesus and the history of early Christianity.

Tertullian: Tertullian, from Carthage (North Africa), was one of the most influential authors of early Christianity. Much of his life is shrouded in obscurity, but it appears that he was born into a relatively affluent family of pagans, around 160 A.D. and received extensive training in (pagan) literature and rhetoric. He converted to Christianity some time in his mid-thirties and became an outspoken, even vitriolic, proponent of the Christian faith, writing numerous works defending the faith against its cultured despisers (apologies), scathing criticisms of heretics and their beliefs, and severe tractates concerning Christian morality. At some point in his life, he joined a group of schismatics known to history as the Montanists (named after their founder, Montanus), an ethically rigorous, ascetic group that anticipated the imminent end of the world as we know it. For this course, Tertullian is most important for his anti-heretical writings. A bitter opponent of both Gnostics and Marcionites, he is one of our best sources of information concerning what these groups, especially the latter, believed. His five-volume attack on Marcion, for example, still survives and is our principal means of access to Marcion's life and teaching.

Thecla: It is difficult to know whether Thecla was a historical person or a legendary figure. The earliest references to her are in the Apocryphal Acts of Paul, which provide a highly fictionalized account of her conversion, based on the ascetic preaching of the apostle Paul, and her subsequent escapades, as she travels, sometimes in Paul's company, on Christian mission. In these accounts, she twice escapes execution ordered on the grounds of her refusal to participate in the social life of her pagan world, for example, when her fiancé, whom she spurns to devote herself to the gospel, hands her over to the authorities on charges of being a Christian. Thecla became venerated as a sacred virgin in Christian tradition, and tales of her life were in wide circulation throughout the Middle Ages

Valentinus: Valentinus was probably the best known gnostic Christian of the second century. Born in Egypt, he was educated in Alexandria before coming to Rome around 136 A.D. Valentinus was a rhetorically powerful and charismatic person, who developed his theological views in light of Platonic and other philosophical traditions dominant in the world at the time. Tradition indicates that he wanted to receive a high office in the church of Rome (aspiring to be its bishop), but that he was spurned by the church leadership and broke off from it to start churches of disciples who accepted his gnosticized understanding of the faith. Valentinian Gnosticism developed in a variety of ways among his followers after his death and became one of the primary targets for attack by heresiologists, such as Irenaeus and Tertullian. We have few writings that survive from Valentinus himself, but many scholars think that the Gospel of Truth discovered at Nag Hammadi may derive directly from him. If it does, then it shows Valentinus at his best, rhetorically effective and filled with joy at the thought of the salvation that had been graciously given by the true God.

Bibliography

Attridge, Harold W. "Thomas, Acts of," *Anchor Bible Dictionary*, vol. VI, pp. 531–534. New York: Doubleday Books, 1992. A brief but insightful discussion of the major historical and interpretive issues relating to the Acts of Thomas.

Bauer, Walter. *Orthodoxy and Heresy in Earliest Christianity*. Trans. by Robert Kraft et. al., ed. by Robert Kraft and Gerhard Krodel. Philadelphia: Fortress, 1971. One of the most important books of the twentieth century on the history of early Christianity. Bauer argues against the classical understanding of orthodoxy and heresy, by maintaining that what was later called heresy was, in many regions of early Christendom, the oldest and largest form of Christian belief.

Blackman, E. C. *Marcion and His Influence*. London: S.P.C.K., 1948. A clear and useful study of the life and teachings of the second-century philosopher-theologian Marcion and of the impact he made on early Christianity.

Bremmer, Jan N., ed. *The Apocryphal Acts of John*. Kampen: Pharos, 1995. A collection of significant essays dealing with major issues in the interpretation and critical understanding of the Acts of John.

———, ed. *The Apocryphal Acts of Paul and Thecla*. Kampen: Pharos, 1996. A collection of significant essays dealing with major issues in the interpretation and critical understanding of the Acts of Paul and Thecla.

Brown, Raymond. *The Birth of the Messiah*. Garden City, NY: Doubleday, 1977. A full and invaluable commentary on the "infancy narratives" of Matthew and Luke (Matthew chs. 1–2 and Luke chs. 1–2).

———. *The Death of the Messiah*. 2 vols. New York: Doubleday, 1994. A full and invaluable commentary on the Passion narratives of the gospels.

Cameron, Ron. "Thomas, Gospel of," *Anchor Bible Dictionary*, vol. VI, pp. 535–540. New York: Doubleday Books, 1992. A brief but insightful discussion of the major historical and interpretive issues relating to the Gospel of Thomas.

Chadwick, Henry. *The Early Church*. Rev. ed. New York: Penguin, 1993. A useful introductory overview of the history of early Christianity, by one of the world's eminent church historians. Ideal for beginning students.

Chesnut, Glenn F. *The First Christian Histories: Eusebius, Socrates, Sozomen, Theodoret, and Evagrius.* 2nd rev. ed. Macon, GA: Mercer, 1986. An important study of the character (and biases) of the earliest historians of Christianity, our sources for the majority of our information about the early church.

Clabeaux, John. "Marcion," *Anchor Bible Dictionary*, vol. IV, pp. 514–521. New York: Doubleday Books, 1992. A brief but insightful discussion of the major historical and interpretive issues relating to the Acts of Thomas.

Crossan, John Dominic. *The Cross That Spoke: The Origins of the Passion Narrative.* San Francisco: Harper and Row, 1988. A learned but highly controversial study of the Gospel of Peter, which claims that its principal source of information was a gospel text that preceded the gospels of the New Testament. For more advanced students.

———. *Four Other Gospels.* Minneapolis: Winston Press, 1985. An intriguing discussion of four of the major early Christian gospels that did not make it into the canon of Scripture, including the Gospels of Peter and Thomas.

Cullman, Oscar. "Infancy Gospels," in Edgar Hennecke and William Schneemelcher, eds., *New Testament Apocrypha: Gospels and Related Writings*, pp. 414–469. Philadelphia: Westminster/John Knox Press, 1991. A brief but insightful discussion of the major historical and interpretive issues relating to the non-canonical Infancy Gospels.

Dart, John, Ray Rigert, and John Dominic Crossan. *Unearthing the Lost Words of Jesus: The Discovery and Text of the Gospel of Thomas.* Berkeley, CA: Ulysses Press, 1998. A brief but valuable discussion of the discovery of the Gospel of Thomas, accompanied by a translation of Thomas with succinct commentary. Excellent for beginning students.

Davies, Stephen. *The Revolt of the Widows: The Social World of the Apocryphal Acts.* Carbondale, IL: Southern Illinois University Press, 1980. An intriguing discussion of the Apocryphal Acts that tries to understand them in light of the context of women's concerns in early Christianity.

Ehrman, Bart D. *After the New Testament: A Reader in Early Christianity.* New York: Oxford, 1999. A collection of some of the most important early Christian writings from the second and third centuries, in quality English translations. It includes most of the apocryphal accounts discussed in this course. Ideal for beginning students.

————. *The New Testament and Other Early Christian Writings: A Reader*. New York: Oxford, 1998. This is a collection of all the writings by the early Christians from within the first century after Jesus' death (that is, material written before A.D. 130), both canonical and non-canonical. It includes several of the texts discussed in this course. Ideal for beginning students.

————. *The Orthodox Corruption of Scripture: The Effect of Early Christological Controversies on the Text of the New Testament*. New York: Oxford University Press, 1993. A study of the ways scribes were influenced by doctrinal disputes in the early church and of how they modified their texts of the New Testament to make them conform more closely with their own theological views. It is best suited for more advanced students.

Elliott, J. K. *The Apocryphal New Testament: A Collection of Apocryphal Christian Literature in an English Translation*. Oxford: Clarendon, 1993. An excellent one-volume collection of non-canonical gospels, acts, epistles, and apocalypses, in a readable English translation with brief introductions.

Epp, Eldon Jay. "Textual Criticism, New Testament," *Anchor Bible Dictionary*, vol. VI, pp. 412–435. New York: Doubleday Books, 1992. A succinct but detailed discussion of the major issues involved in reconstructing the original text of the New Testament from the surviving manuscripts.

Frend, W. F. C. *The Rise of Christianity*. Philadelphia: Fortress, 1984. A full introductory discussion of the major issues involved with the history of the first six centuries of Christianity.

Froehlich, Karlfried. *Biblical Interpretation in the Early Church*. Philadelphia: Fortress, 1984. A useful discussion of the methods of interpretation prevalent in early Christianity, especially in view of their roots in other interpretive practices of the ancient world.

Gager, John. *The Origins of Anti-Semitism: Attitudes toward Judaism in Pagan and Christian Antiquity*. New York: Oxford, 1983. A seminal study of anti-Jewish attitudes and activities in the Roman world and especially in early Christianity.

Gamble, Harry. "Canon: New Testament," *Anchor Bible Dictionary*, vol. I, pp. 852–861. New York: Doubleday Books, 1992. A brief but insightful discussion of the major historical issues relating to the formation of the New Testament canon.

————. *The New Testament Canon: Its Making and Meaning*. Philadelphia: Fortress, 1985. A clearly written and informative overview of the formation of the canon that shows how, why, and when Christians chose the present twenty-seven books to include in their sacred Scriptures of the New Testament.

Grant, Robert M. *Jesus after the Gospels: The Christ of the Second Century*. Louisville: Westminster/John Knox, 1990. An intriguing discussion of different understandings of Christology in the decades after the New Testament was written, among a variety of early Christian groups.

————, and David Tracy. *A Short History of the Interpretation of the Bible*. 2nd ed. Philadelphia: Fortress, 1983. A survey of the methods used to interpret the Bible from the earliest of times onward.

Hennecke, Edgar, and Wilhelm Schneemelcher, eds. *New Testament Apocrypha*. 2 vols. Trans. by A. J. B. Higgins et. al., ed. by R. McL. Wilson. Philadelphia: Westminster Press, 1991. English translations of all the early non-canonical writings preserved from Christian antiquity, with detailed scholarly introductions; an indispensable resource for advanced students.

Himmelfarb, Martha. *Tours of Hell: An Apocryphal Form in Jewish and Christian Literature*. Philadelphia: University of Pennsylvania Press, 1983. A scholarly discussion of the ancient apocalypses in which a person is taken on a tour of the places of the damned.

Klijn, A. F. J. *Jewish Christian Gospel Tradition*. Leiden: E. J. Brill, 1992. An authoritative discussion of the Jewish Christian Gospels of the Ebionites, Nazareans, and Hebrews, including English translations of the remains of these texts.

Layton, Bentley. *The Gnostic Scriptures: A New Translation with Annotations*. Garden City: Doubleday, 1987. An invaluable translation of important gnostic documents, including those discovered at Nag Hammadi and those quoted by the church fathers, with a useful introductory sketch of Gnosticism.

Maurer, Christian, and Wilhelm Schneemelcher. "The Gospel of Peter," in Edgar Hennecke and Wilhelm Schneemelcher, eds., *New Testament Apocrypha: Gospels and Related Writings*. Philadelphia: Westminster/John Knox Press, 1991. A brief but insightful discussion of the major historical and interpretive issues relating to the Gospel of Peter.

McDonald, Dennis. *The Legend and the Apostle: The Battle for Paul in Story and Canon*. Philadelphia: Westminster, 1983. An intriguing discussion of the controversies over Paul and his legacy in early Christianity among various early Christian groups; of particular importance for the study of the Apocryphal Acts.

Metzger, Bruce. *The Canon of the New Testament*. Oxford: Clarendon, 1987. The most thorough and informative account of the formation of the New Testament canon, by one of the world's eminent scholars of early Christianity.

————. "Literary Forgeries and Canonical Pseudepigrapha," *Journal of Biblical Literature* 91 (1972): 3–24. A fascinating discussion of the motivations and methods of early Christians who produced literary forgeries, including many of the pseudepigraphical works discussed in this course.

————. *The Text of the New Testament: Its Transmission, Corruption, and Restoration*. 3rd ed. New York: Oxford, 1991. The best available introduction to the art and science of textual criticism, which seeks to establish the original text of the New Testament based on the surviving manuscripts.

Mirecki, Paul. "Peter, Gospel of," *Anchor Bible Dictionary*, vol. V, pp. 278–281. New York: Doubleday Books, 1992. A brief but insightful discussion of the major historical and interpretive issues relating to the Gospel of Peter.

————. "Thomas, Infancy Gospel of," *Anchor Bible Dictionary*, vol. VI, 540–544. New York: Doubleday Books, 1992. A brief but insightful discussion of the major historical and interpretive issues relating to the Infancy Gospel of Thomas.

Noll, Mark. *A History of Christianity in the United States and Canada*. Grand Rapids: Eerdmans, 1992. A good overview of the diversity of Christianity in the modern American context, important for this course insofar as it provides a point of comparison with the diverse expressions of Christianity in the ancient world.

Norris, Richard. *The Christological Controversy*. Philadelphia: Fortress, 1983. A useful presentation of some of the major texts from antiquity involving the controversies over the nature and person of Christ.

Pagels, Elaine. *The Gnostic Gospels*. New York: Random House, 1976. This is an enormously popular and provocative account of the views of some of the early Gnostics in relation to emerging Christian orthodoxy.

Parker, David. *The Living Text of the Gospels*. Cambridge: Cambridge University Press, 1998. This is perhaps the best introduction to New Testament textual criticism for beginners, in which the author argues that the modifications made by the Christian scribes who copied the text show that they did not see it as a dead object but as a living tradition.

Pearson, Birger. "Nag Hammadi Codices," *Anchor Bible Dictionary*, vol. IV, pp. 984–993. New York: Doubleday Books, 1992. A brief and informative discussion of the discovery, contents, and significance of the gnostic writings discovered near Nag Hammadi, Egypt.

Pelikan, Jeroslav. *The Christian Tradition*, vol. 1. Chicago: University Press, 1971. An authoritative discussion of the theology of early Christians in the first centuries of the church.

Robinson, James M. "The Discovery of the Nag Hammadi Codices," *Biblical Archaeology* 42 (1979): 2–24. A fascinating account of how the Nag Hammadi library was discovered, by the American scholar who tracked down the principal parties concerned many years later.

———, ed. *The Nag Hammadi Library in English*. 3rd ed. New York: Harper & Row, 1988. A convenient English translation of the documents discovered at Nag Hammadi, with brief introductions.

Rudolph, Kurt. *Gnosis: The Nature and History of Gnosticism*. Trans. by R. McL. Wilson. San Francisco: Harper & Row, 1987. The best book-length introduction to ancient Gnosticism.

———. "Gnosticism," *Anchor Bible Dictionary*, vol. II, pp. 1033–1040. New York: Doubleday Books, 1992. A brief but insightful discussion of the major historical and interpretive issues relating to early Christian Gnosticism, by an eminent expert in the field.

Ruether, Rosemary. *Faith and Fratricide: The Theological Roots of Anti-Semitism*. New York: Seabury, 1974. A controversial discussion of the early Christian attitudes toward Jews and Judaism, which maintains that anti-Semitism is the necessary corollary of Christian belief in Jesus as the messiah.

Rusch, William G. *The Trinitarian Controversy*. Philadelphia: Fortress, 1980. A presentation of key texts in the ancient controversies involved with the doctrine of the trinity.

Schoeps, H. J. *Jewish Christianity: Factional Disputes in the Church*. Trans. by Douglas R. A. Hare. Philadelphia: Fortress, 1969. A standard study of the nature of Jewish Christianity in the early church and the controversies that it engendered.

Simon, Marcel. *Verus Israel: A Study of the Relations between Christians and Jews in the Roman Empire (135–425)*. Trans. by H. McKeating. New York: Oxford, 1986. A standard study of Jewish-Christian relations in the early centuries of the church.

Smith, Morton. *Clement of Alexandria and a Secret Gospel of Mark*. Cambridge, MA: Harvard University Press, 1973. An erudite account of the Secret Gospel of Mark, based on more than a decade of research into its character and importance by its discoverer. For advanced students.

———. *The Secret Gospel of Mark*. New York: Harper and Row, 1973. A fascinating account written for a popular audience of the author's discovery of the Secret Gospel of Mark and of his investigation into its significance for understanding Jesus and this history of earliest Christianity.

Treat, Jay. "Barnabas, Epistle of," *Anchor Bible Dictionary*, vol. I, pp. 611–614. New York: Doubleday Books, 1992. A brief but insightful discussion of the major historical and interpretive issues relating to the Epistle of Barnabas.

Uro, Risto, ed. *Thomas at the Crossroads: Essays on the Gospel of Thomas*. Edinburgh: T&T Clark, 1998. A group of important essays on the interpretation and significance of the Coptic Gospel of Thomas.

Valantasis, Richard. *The Gospel of Thomas*. New York: Routledge, 1997. A scholarly discussion of and commentary on the Gospel of Thomas that tries to understand it *apart* from the assumption that it represents a gnostic understanding of Christ.

Vallée, Gérard. *A Study in Anti-Gnostic Polemics*. Waterloo, Ontario: Wilfred Laurier University, 1981. A useful analysis of the views, perspectives, and biases of the early orthodox opponents of heresy, Irenaeus, Hippolytus, and Epiphanius.

von Campenhausen, H. *The Formation of the Christian Bible*. Trans. by J. A. Baker. Philadelphia: Fortress, 1972. An important and erudite study of the formation of the New Testament canon, for more advanced students.

von Harnack, Adolf. *Marcion: The Gospel of the Alien God*. Trans. by John E. Steely and Lyle D. Bierma. Durham, NC: Labyrinth Press, 1990. The classic study of the life and teachings of the second-century philosopher-theologian Marcion.

Vorster, Willem S. "James, Protevangelium of," *Anchor Bible Dictionary*, vol. III, pp. 629–633. New York: Doubleday Books, 1992. A brief but insightful discussion of the major historical and interpretive issues relating to the Proto-Gospel of James.

Williams, Michael. *Rediscovering Gnosticism*. Princeton: Princeton University Press, 1996. A valuable contribution to the scholarly discussions concerning early gnostic religions, which maintains that the category of "Gnosticism" is in fact not useful for understanding them. For more advanced students.

Williamson, G. A. *Eusebius: The History of the Church from Christ to Constantine*. Rev. and ed. by Andrew Louth. London: Penguin, 1989. A handy and accessible English translation of Eusebius's classic work, the *Church History*.

Wisse, Frederick. "The Nag Hammadi Library and the Heresiologists," *Vigiliae Christianae* 25 (1971): 205–223. An insightful discussion of the accuracy of the proto-orthodox heresiologists' accounts of Gnosticism in light of the primary sources now available from the Nag Hammadi library.

Notes